PACIFIC STEAM NAVIGATION CO.

Ian Collard

AMBERLEY

Reina Del Pacifico.

Reina Del Mar.

ABBREVIATIONS

AB	Able Seaman
bhp	break horsepower
cyl	cylinder
dwt	deadweight
hp	horse power
ihp	inverted horsepower
LS	Leading Seaman
nhp	nominal horsepower
RNR	Royal Naval Reserve
RNVR	Royal Naval Volunteer Reserve
rpm	revolutions per minute
shp	shaft horse power
TEU	Twenty-foot Equivalent Units

ACKNOWLEDGEMENTS

I would like to thank the Merseyside branch of the World Ship Society for the use of many images from their photographic collection.

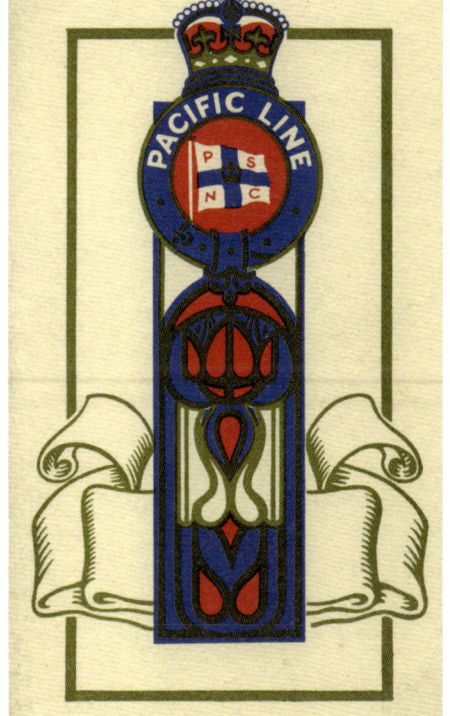

Front cover of a 1934 cruise log of the *Orduna*. An Eisteddfod was held on board and the log is in both English and Welsh.

4 PACIFIC STEAM NAVIGATION CO.

Above: A paddle steamer-trip on the River Dart, passing the *Oroya* and the *Oropesa*.

Left: William Wheelwright.

THE PACIFIC STEAM NAVIGATION COMPANY

The Pacific Steam Navigation Company was founded on 6 September 1838, when the first directors met to discuss a prospectus to be adopted in the name of the company, to be incorporated by Royal Charter. The establishment of a line of steamships for carrying on the large and growing trade which was known to exist on the west coast of South America, was an idea demanding extensive and varied knowledge, a large amount of practical skill, rare administrative talent and the command of extensive resources to bring together all those needed to carry out a commercial undertaking.

William Wheelwright was born on 18 March 1798 at Newbury Port in Massachusetts, USA, and was the son of a Lincolnshire master mariner. He was educated at Phillips Academy, Andover, Massachusetts, and went to sea in 1814 as a cabin boy on a ship owned by his family. He served his apprenticeship on sailing brigs and was given his first command in 1817, when he was nineteen years of age.

In 1823 his ship the *Rising Empire*, which was owned by William Bartlett, was wrecked off the mouth of the River Plate and William obtained a job as a seaman on a vessel sailing from Buenos Aires to Valparaiso. When he arrived at Guayaquil in Ecuador he established a ship broking firm and also became a chandler and the United States Consul in the town.

Five years later, he married Martha Bell at Newbury Port and they travelled to Guayaquil via Panama where he found his business in trouble with debts of nearly $100,000. They decided to move to Valparaiso where he purchased the schooner *Fourth of July*, and used her in the coastal trade. As the road network was poor in Chile most of the trade was carried by sea but ships were regularly delayed by the lack of suitable wind to propel them.

On 5 August 1835 William Wheelwright was granted the exclusive rights to steam navigation by the Chilean Government and requested that he start his steamer service within two years. The following year, merchants in Peru also took an interest in steamships and the British Consul General set up a meeting to look at Wheelwright's ideas. A further meeting was held on 8 November 1836 in Santiago, also chaired by the British Consul General to investigate setting up a company to raise capital to build the steamships. Wheelwright returned to America but was unsuccessful and crossed the Atlantic to attempt to raise the capital in Britain.

As there had been little movement forward by 1837, the two-year clause was deleted and Wheelwright was given more time to establish the project. The Chilean and British Governments were anxious for the trade between the countries to increase and both were impressed by Wheelwright. Lord Abinger's son, the Honourable Peter Scarlett, was advocating a railway to connect the Atlantic terminal with a Pacific port and Baron Friedrich von Humboldt proposed building a ship canal across the Isthmus. Wheelwright was associated with undertakings such as the building of a lighthouse, the construction of gas and water works, and the formation of a brick works. He also prospected for coal, saltpetre, borax and lime. The fact that he discovered the wealth of raw materials in the area showed there was a need for a shipping service to and from Chile.

The Pacific Steam Navigation Company was established on 27 September 1838 at Bucklesbury in London, with a share capital of £250,000 of 5,000 shares of £50 each, with 1,000 reserved for investors in South America. George Brown became the first chairman of the company, as well as a founding director of the Royal Mail Steam Packet Company and Wheelwright proposed operating a service with three iron hulled steamers of around 700 tonnes with a fourth vessel in reserve.

Wheelwright and his friends were fortunate in having so much support from the governments of the South American states concerned, and on 31 August 1839, the company placed orders for two steamers with Thomas Wilson & Company of Liverpool. The order was cancelled and later reinstated by Wheelwright. However, Thomas Wilson decided not to build the ships and the order was given to Curling & Young of London later that year. Despite Wheelwright's protests, wooden, not iron-hull ships were built. In January the following year the Royal Charter was granted and George Peacock was appointed as the company's first captain. Wheelwright became the Chief Superintendent on a salary of £1,400 per

A young Captain George Peacock.

PACIFIC STEAM NAVIGATION CO. 7

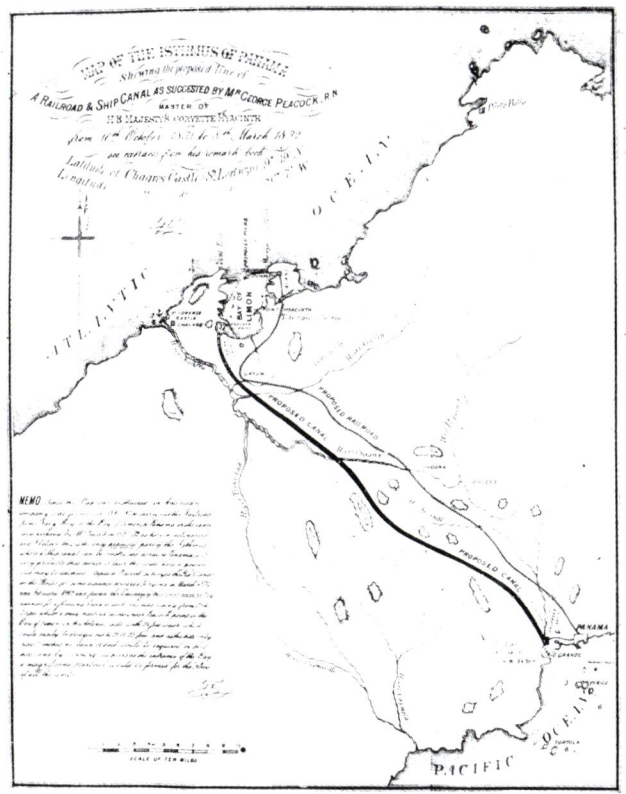

Left: Captain George Peacock's chart.

Above: Charter of 1840.

year and Peacock given the position of Second Superintendent, with responsibility for the operation of the two vessels.

Captain George Peacock was born on 9 June 1805, and was the son of a shipmaster who owned vessels engaged in the Mediterranean trade. He grew up in Exmouth and when sailing in the Mediterranean as a mate, he observed the Archimedes screw for raising water in Egypt and invented a rudimentary screw propeller and adapted the design into his father's vessel *Fanny*. He joined the London firm, Henry Maudslay & Co., Engineers and obtained his master's ticket in 1828. He joined the Navy and became an engineer on the paddle-steamer HMS *Echo* and later patented a method of salving wrecks and making fresh water from salt. He helped to survey parts of Canada and some Central American ports, and during a period of leave without pay, he surveyed a route across Panama and his work was used by the American engineer at the end of the century when the Panama Canal was built. As master in the Pacific Steam Navigation he was the first to travel by a steam paddle vessel around Cape Horn and he also looked at a design for the Corinth Canal in Greece. He discovered guano, a coal substitute in South America and won a prize at a world trade fair for a refuge buoy. In 1843 he carried out a survey of the River Exe and helped to found the Starcross Yacht Club.

Peacock's life was filled with outstanding achievements and he was awarded a medal by the Colombian Government to mark 'his services in solving the Interoceanic Canal question'. Although he had surveyed the Isthmus in 1835 it was not until 1882 that the work on the canal was started, yet his services were not overlooked and he was created a Knight of the Order of the Saviour by King George of Greece. He had, on completion of the survey in 1835, been invited to dine at the Palace and was then given a richly embossed gold snuff-box. He was also awarded a medal from the Royal Humane Society for life saving.

The wooden sailing ship *Elizabeth* was bought by the company in 1840 but the crew refused to sail her and she was replaced by the *Portsea*, which sailed with coal to Valparaiso and was hulked. The coal hulks *Cecilia* and *Jasper* were also positioned at Valparaiso. *Peru* and *Chile* were launched in April 1840, by Curling, Young & Company. They were 700-ton wooden paddle ships, built at a cost of £17 5s per ton. *Chile* sailed from Falmouth on 27 June with passengers and about 200 tonnes of cargo. *Peru* followed on 10 July calling at Plymouth to embark late mails and additional passengers, meeting in the Straits of Magellan. Wheelwright was keen to establish the coastal trade in South America and on arrival, he asked the Government of Ecuador for permission to operate the ships in the coastal waters of that country. Both ships arrived at Valparaiso on 16 October after a voyage of fifty-two days and the *Peru* sailed on her first voyage between Valparaiso and Callao in Peru on 25 October.

However, there were occasions in the first two years of service when the ships were laid up because of the lack of coal to be shipped. In 1843, William Wheelwright was recalled to the London office and was dismissed after being accused of bad management. He appealed and was reinstated as Joint Managing Director and several of his opponents on the board, except George Brown were then dismissed. Soon after this, the head office was moved to Liverpool, as the main shareholders of the company were from that city. William Just of the Aberdeen & London Steam Ship Company was appointed as Joint Managing Director, when Wheelwright returned to look after the South American side of the business. He was then responsible for cargo operations in Columbia, Ecuador, Peru, Panama and Chile and out of a capital of £94,000, £72,000 had been lost.

The *Ecuador* was introduced in 1846 and was based at Callao to extend the Valparaiso service via Guayaquil to Panama. This enabled cargo to be carried on the Royal Mail Line's service from Southampton to Colon and shipped overland to Valparaiso in forty days against the four months it took if shipped via Cape Horn. The *New Granada* sailed on her maiden voyage in August 1846, from Liverpool to Madeira, Rio de Janeiro, Valparaiso and Callao to join *Ecuador* on the Callao, Guayaquil and Panama service. The hulk *Cecilia* was lost at Valparaiso in 1847 and replaced by *Queen of the Ocean*.

The third unit of the Chile class, *Bolivia*, left Liverpool on her maiden voyage, under Captain Brown, on 23 October 1849 and on arrival at Valparaiso she was placed on the service to Antofagasta & Callao route. A dividend of 10 per cent was declared at the board meeting in Liverpool in 1850 and four new ships were ordered from Robert Napier at Govan, the following year. In 1851, *Santiago* and *Lima* were delivered and *Quito* and *Bogota*, in 1852. *Ecuador* was wrecked at Coquimbo and *Peru* was declared a total loss in 1852, when the company was awarded the British Government mail contract.

In 1852 John Elder went into partnership with Charles Randolph as Randolph & Elder. They secured the patent on 24 January 1853 for the vertical direct-acting compound engine. This consisted of a high-pressure cylinder and a low-pressure cylinder, moving in opposite directions to drive two diametrically opposite crankshafts. The compound engine reduced coal consumption by 30 per cent and this was first installed in the *Brandon*. On 15 March 1856 they took out a patent for an improved compound engine, which saved space and was described as compound inverted. The yard of James Napier & Hoey was acquired in 1858 and when Chares Randolph retired ten years later, the firm was known as John Elder & Company, becoming Fairfield Shipbuilding & Engineering Company Limited in 1885. The *Inca* was delivered in 1856, being the first ship to be fitted with the compound inverted engine, followed by the *Valparaiso*.

La Perlita sailed on her maiden voyage from Liverpool on 17 June 1853 under Captain Maugham and was lost without trace. *Osprey* was acquired from the City of Cork Steam Ship Company and was also lost on her delivery voyage to Callao the same year. *Quito* was lost on a reef near Huasco in August 1853, as was the hulk *Hope*. The Panama Railway across the Isthmus was completed in 1854, which opened up the route to the west coast of South America.

Panama was built by John Reid & Company at Glasgow as a replacement for *La Perlita* and was lost when she struck a rock and sank near Point Tamar on her maiden voyage. *Prince of Wales* was built by W. Simons & Company in 1854 and was purchased by the company in 1858 to replace *Valdivia*. However, she was wrecked off Chile the following year.

The company carried letters on its ships and they issued special stamps for use on this mail. The design of the stamps consisted of a two-masted schooner in a central oval surrounded by an engine turned oval. In the corners of the stamps the letters PSNC were shown. In 1857 the Peruvian government decided to issue postal stamps and as a trial they borrowed a supply of stamps from the Pacific Steam Navigation Company. The stamps were placed on sale in the towns of Lima, Chorrillos and Callao on 1 December 1857 and immediately became very popular. Four months later, the PSNC stamps were replaced by an issue bearing the Arms of the Republic. The original one and two *reales* stamps were replaced in 1858, when the one *dinero*, one *peseta* and half-*peseta* stamps were introduced. Facsimiles of two of the original stamps were issued in Peru in 1958 for ten and fifteen *centavos*, in commemoration of the country's postal services.

Santiago was sold in 1857 and *Cloda* was purchased from Irish owners the following year. *Prince of Wales* was wrecked off the coast of Chile in 1859 and was replaced by *Anne*. In 1850 the company had acquired the island of El Morro in Panama Bay for use as a workshop and store. The island which was developed by the company over the following years contained a good water supply, provided by a spring to several storage

PSNC stamps.

tanks, from which it was conducted by a pipe line to a small reservoir and filter tank. It was then fed to the ships, houses and workshops by gravity. The buildings comprised of managers' and labourers' quarters, kitchens, storehouses and a laundry. At one time hundreds of men were employed and housed on El Morro and the local doctor, a company employee, lived in a vine-embowered cottage.

An interesting feature of the port was the fact that vessels were left high and dry by the tide and available for repair when the water went down. Tobago was the terminal for the vessels and a twice-monthly service ran between Valparaiso and Tobago, connecting with the Royal Mail Line steamers at Colon, passengers being conveyed to and from Tobago by the tender *Morro*. Much of the land was given to the growing of pineapples and other fruits, allowing fresh fruit to be included on menus of vessels calling at the island. A number of sea captains, crew and employees of the Pacific Steam Navigation Company were buried at the English graveyard at the top of El Morro Island. The graveyard soon became overgrown and many people were unaware of it until Mr H. Leslie Bowes, C.B.E., Chairman and Managing Director of the Pacific Steam Navigation Company and Royal Mail Lines, discovered it on a visit to Panama over a hundred years since it was acquired by the company. Mr Bowes gave instructions that the cemetery be cleared of jungle and kept that way in the future.

To get to the cemetery, one must climb a long path and a series of stone steps. The view is very beautiful and the epitaphs interesting. One is, 'Erected to the memory of Charles William Walker sometime commander of the Pacific Steam Navigation Company, Mail Steamship *Callao*. After a short illness departed this life on this island on the 16th day of August, 1859. Age 39 years.' The monument was erected by his brother officers as a mark of their respect and esteem'. Another grave is marked, 'Sacred to the memory of James McVicar, Carpenter, who departed this life on the 9th day of January, 1866. Age 25.' This stone was also erected by his shipmates.

In 1865 an American sea captain named Pim wrote the following account of the hazard of landing from ships in Panama Bay, 'The Bay of Panama cannot by any perversion of the term be called a port, it is simply an open roadstead and at certain times not particularly safe. The steamers are obliged to anchor miles from the shore; passengers, goods and supplies have to be transhipped in small steamers and lighters; this can only be done at certain times of the tide, for the rise and fall is great and the water very shallow near the shore. In bad weather there is considerable uncertainty and danger, and sometimes disembarkation is delayed a considerable time'.

In 1860, *San Carlos*, *Guayaquil* and *Peruano* were delivered and the company built its first steel ship, the passenger tender *Morro* for service at Panama. *Morro* was of 132 gross tons, constructed at Glasgow and was propelled by paddles. She was 119 feet long and her engines had 50 hp. The company also purchased the wooden paddle-steamer *Peruano*, which had been built at New York. Her engines developed 250 hp. The iron paddle-steamer *Talca* was added to the fleet, while the wooden ships *Constitution* and *Lord Hungerford* were bought for service as hulks but *Lord Hungerford* foundered en-route.

Peru was ordered from John Reid & Company and left the Mersey on her maiden voyage on 1 January 1862. *Lima* was wrecked off Layerto on 11 July 1863 and *Chile* was launched at Glasgow at a cost of £53,650. *Quito* was designed by Thomas Smith and built by Randolph & Elder at Glasgow in 1864. However, she was only a member of the company's fleet for a year as she was sold in 1865.

Right above: Prince of Wales 1858 advert.

Right below: PSNC Works, Tobago, West Indies, 1864.

FOR MADEIRA, RIO DE JANEIRO, AND VALPARAISO.

To Sail on WEDNESDAY, the 28th JULY next,

The Pacific Steam Navigation Company's Royal Mail Iron Steam-ship
PRINCE OF WALES,
Of 700 tons, and 200 horse-power;
W. H. Ellis, Commander.

This vessel has excellent accommodation for Passengers. For terms of passage or freight of treasure (no other description of cargo will be taken), apply at the Company's office, No. 27, James-street, Liverpool; or in London to Messrs. Griffiths, Tate, and Fisher, White Hart-court.

26th June, 1858.   WILLIAM TAGGART, Secretary.

N.B.—Passengers for the undermentioned Ports will have an opportunity of leaving Valparaiso by the contract mail packets of the Company on the 1st or 16th of each month, namely, Coquimbo, Huasco, Caldera (Copiapo), Cobija, Iquique, Arica, Islay, Pisco, Callao, Huacho, Casma, Huanchaco, Lambayeque, Payta, Guayaquil, and Panama.

William Wheelwright Chile Award.

Anne was soon too small for the fleet and was disposed of in 1864 and the following year the Charter was amended to include the establishment of steamer services between the west coast of South America and the River Plate, including the Falkland Islands and such 'other ports or places in North and South America, and other foreign ports as the said company shall deem expedient'.

In 1865 *Cloda* was lost off Huacho and *Quito* was sold. *Pacific*, *Santiago*, *Limena* and the American paddle-steamer style *Favorita* joined the fleet. The last steamer of the Pacific-class, *Panama* was delivered in 1866 and *Colon* was purchased to replace *Cloda* and *Supe*, *Arica* and *Quito* joined the fleet. Following a disagreement with Panama Railroad Company over the division of rates in 1867, the company agreed to commence a monthly service from Liverpool to Valparaiso via the Straits of Magellan. The Panama Railroad was opened in 1854 and passengers and cargo were booked through from Europe to Colon, across the Isthmus. An order was placed for five screw steamers for the new route and the capital of the company was increased to £2,000,000.

Prior to the delivery of the new ships, *Pacific* left Valparaiso, on 13 May 1868 for Liverpool with 170 passengers and a sailing every six weeks was inaugurated. The route was via Bordeaux, Lisbon, Cape Verde Islands, Rio de Janeiro, Montevideo, Punta Arenas and Valparaiso. *Pacific* made the passage in forty-three days with a full cargo load including £65,000 in gold and silver. Later in 1868, *Calera* joined the fleet, and the iron-screw steamer *Magellan*, the first of the four sister-ships, left Liverpool in March the following year. *Magellan* and her three sisters, *Patagonia*, *Araucania* and *Cordillera* carried 145 first, 75 second and 300 third class passengers in addition to 2,550 tonnes of cargo.

Cargo operations on the Mersey were transferred from Liverpool to Birkenhead where new offices and workshops were built and the company was known locally as the 'Birkenhead Navy'. On 23 January 1869 the paddle-steamer *Santiago* struck an uncharted rock in the Straits of Magellan and sank with a loss of two lives. The two-year-old *Arica* also grounded and was lost. The *John Elder*, which was named after the inventor of the compound engine, was delivered to the company in 1869. She was a three-masted screw steamer and was later lengthened and her tonnage increased.

The company had decided to extend the Liverpool to Valparaiso service northwards to Callao via Arica and Mollendo and the sailings were increased to three per month. The additional calls at French and other Continental ports were successful and brought an increase in cargo. A further building programme was discussed and secondhand tonnage was purchased to maintain the services in the short term. *Atacama*, *Coquimbo*, *Valdivia* and *Eten* were built. *Arequipa* was brought into service and the *Guayaquil* was sold.

In 1869 when the Union Pacific Railroad was built, the Panama Railroad lost its California trade, but retained its trade with South and Central America, which was exclusively retained by the ships of the Pacific Steam

Navigation Company. This business was also lost to the railroad when, following a dispute, the PSNC had to give up its shops and dockyards on the Island of Tabago, in the Bay of Panama and route its ships by way of the Straits of Magellan.

In 1870 orders were placed for eleven vessels, aggregating 25,019 tonnes and valued at £630,044. It was the largest shipbuilding order ever placed by one company within a year. *Chimborazo*, *Cuzco*, *Garonne*, *Lusitania* and *Aconcagua* were delivered and *Coquimbo*, *Santiago*, *Truxillo*, *Huacho*, *Iquique* and *Taboguilla* joined the fleet. The Liverpool to Valparaiso service was extended northwards to Arica, Mollendo and Callao in 1870 and sailings were increased to three a month. The offices of the Pacific Steam Navigation were moved to James Street in Liverpool after a brief move to premises in Castle Street.

On 20 February 1871 *Valparaiso* was wrecked at Lagartiga Island. Her third officer, Mr E. Joste recorded the incident in his diary:

> After a fortnight and pockets empty, I was fortunate in getting appointed third officer of the paddle wheel steamer Valparaiso of the PSNC. Made a few voyages to Tocopilla when steamer was placed on the mail run to Port Montt, making two trips a month. On the third trip, when on the way from Port Montt to Ancud, the vessel was steered too near the west side of Lagartija Island. She struck a rocky point and was very soon filled up and sank close to the shore.
>
> In those days there was no communication by wire south of Valdivia. So the second officer was sent in one of the lifeboats with a few passengers we had on board, to Port Montt from which place he had to ride to Valdivia, more or less 150 miles, to get in touch by wire to Valparaiso. Captain Craig went to Port Montt, leaving the Chief Officer and myself in charge of the wreck. We rigged up three tents on the beach, one for the officers, one for the engineers and the other for the crew.
>
> It was 8.30 when the steamer went down, a fine morning and near the beach, so there was no danger to life and all hands were landed before steamer finally settled on the bottom. Personally I enjoyed the three weeks stay on the island, which supplied us with about 20 gallons of fresh water daily. I employed myself getting stores from the fore hold of the vessel which was fairly accessible at low tide. Got cases of candles, soap and butter and occasionally made a dive for the bar and managed to get some liquors, but these I kept in my sea chest in the tent as the chief was not to be trusted. I also dived for and saved a considerable amount of silverware, which the stewards had hastily taken out of the dining room and placed on deck. At low water a good feed of oysters could be enjoyed.
>
> After a stay of about three weeks we were delighted to see the steamer Peru heave in sight, and this steamer took us back to Valparaiso, from whence I was sent to Callao, where I had to appear before the manager, Mr George Petrie, and to give a resume of the occurrence. Evidently I was not deemed guilty for the disaster, as I was appointed second officer to the Callao, and to run to Port Montt. The Callao was relieved by the Peru, and on March 26, or exactly one year after I joined the Callao, I was appointed chief officer of the Peru.

Favorita was destroyed by fire in Callao Bay and *Bogota* struck a reef on Tarada Point although her hull was saved and she was used as a coal hulk. In December 1871, *Lusitania* shed her propeller after leaving Valparaiso and a caisson was fitted on her stern to enable a new propeller to be installed.

Orders were made for thirteen ships in 1871 totalling 39,780 tons, valued at £1,174,401 and by 1873 the company owned thirty-one steamers in the coastal trade and nineteen larger vessels on the direct service, making it the largest shipping company in the world. The following year, the fleet had increased to fifty-seven ships of 127,700 tons. In 1872 a mail subsidy of £10,000 per annum, was granted to the weekly service to Callao and this was later increased. The White Star Line entered the service as a competitor when *Republic* sailed for Valparaiso and Callao and *Tacoma* was lost on her maiden voyage near Montevideo.

The Chilean Government recognised the lack of an adequate merchant marine, as the country needed ships to take advantage of the central valley, which developed dramatically after the completion of the railroad from north to south, from Santiago to Conception. The government attempted to encourage the development of the merchant fleet by offering tax concessions and subsidies. However, Chilean entrepreneurs invested their capital in mines, railroads, agricultural land and other properties. It soon became apparent to the government that the merchant marine would be developed by foreign-owned vessels and investors. However, the Chilean Steamship Line (Compañia Sud-Americana de Vapores) was formed in 1872 with a subsidy from the Chilean Government. This allowed the company's ships to be used by the government during the War of the Pacific, from 1879–1882.

Sorata left Liverpool on a new weekly service on 8 January 1873 carrying mails under a new contract and *Magellan* negotiated the Smyth's Channel the same year. William Wheelwright died in London on 26 September, aged seventy-five and his body was carried across the Atlantic to be buried in Newbury Port in Massachusetts. On 12 February 1877, a statue was unveiled to the memory of William Wheelwright in the Plaza Aduana in Valparaiso, which was witnessed by over 5,000 people. A salute was fired and the bands played the 'Hymn to Wheelwright', which had been specially composed by Professor Yanfranco.

Ryde Line and the Compagnie Générale Transatlantique joined the White Star Line operating services from Europe to South America. Ryde Line was awarded a Belgian Government contract for a four-ship service between Antwerp, Montevideo, Buenos Aires and Valparaiso, with their steamers

PSNC Memorial in Callao, 1866.

Leopold II and *Santiago*. However, the service was not a success and was closed after a few voyages were completed.

Around 1874 the fleet numbered fifty-seven steamers, of a total of 127,700 tons. However, the weekly service from Liverpool brought a loss of £70,000 in 1873–74 and the company had also entered into expensive charter commitments to maintain this service. The White Star Line withdrew their services in 1874 and it was decided to reduce the frequency of the company's services to fortnightly, with the introduction of a one-knot speed reduction to save coal.

The company found that they had eleven large steamers that were surplus to requirements and were laid up. It was costing around £6,000 per annum for each ship. *Inca* and *San Carlos* were sold in 1874 and the paddle-steamers *Talca* and *Peruano* were broken up. *Puno* and *Corcovado* were sold to the Royal Mail Steam Packet and *Limena* and *Oroya* were acquired by the Government of Peru. A dry-dock was built in Glasgow, dismantled and shipped to Callao where it was reassembled to be used to overhaul the company's coastal vessels. The dock was 300 feet by 75 feet.

The company was approached by Anderson, Anderson & Company, of London in February 1877, who were interested in chartering ships for the inauguration of a new mail and passenger service from London to Australia. The service was to operate via Cape Town outwards and the Suez Canal homeward under a new company, the Orient Steam Navigation Company.

The Times and other newspapers carried the following advertisement in March 1877.

> Steam to Melbourne and Sydney from London–Orient Line. The undermentioned magnificent full-powered steamships belonging to the Pacific Steam Navigation Company will be despatched punctually for Melbourne and Sydney in accordance with the following arrangements:
>
> SS Lusitania, 3,825 tonnes register, last shipping day for goods Friday 22nd June. Will embark passengers at Gravesend 26th June and Plymouth 28th June.
>
> SS Chimborazo, 3,847 tonnes register, last shipping day 8th August. This steamer will call at Glenelg for Adelaide if required.
>
> SS Cuzco, 3,845 tonnes register. Last shipping day 21st September.
>
> The steamers are of 3,000 horse power effective and are expected to make the passage in 40 days. The accommodation for passengers of all classes is unsurpassed and their appointments throughout are of completest character. Passengers will be embarked by steam tender at Gravesend and Plymouth.

Lusitania sailed from Plymouth on 28 June 1877, arriving at Melbourne on 8 August, after a passage of forty days and six hours. She was followed by the *Chimborazo*, *Cuzco* and *Garonne* maintaining a monthly service until 1880, establishing the Orient Line service to Australia. Anderson, Anderson & Company exercised their option to purchase the vessels, and the Pacific Steam Navigation Company came to an agreement with the Orient Line for a joint service, with the *John Elder* taking the first sailing.

The *Mendoza* was introduced in October 1879 and was the first ever liner to be equipped with electric lighting. She was built by Napier's of Glasgow and had accommodation for 100 first-class passengers. The publication *Engineering* wrote, 'The ladies' boudoir, state-rooms etc., are roomy and elegantly and comfortably furnished, and they are well adapted for a hot climate. The main deck, which is entirely open at the side, is specially fitted up for cattle, or for the holding of markets at the various towns visited, stands being let out to parties travelling with provisions, etc.'

The main Liverpool to the River Plate service was operated by *Magellan*, *Araucania*, *Cordillera* and *Patagonia*, which were fitted with refrigerated space for the carriage of meat from South America. The Birkenhead built vessel *Casma* was introduced in 1878 and *Chala* came from the same yard the following year. Gourlay Brothers of Dundee delivered the *Puchoco* and *Arauco* in 1879 and a sister to the *Mendoza*, the *Pizarro* was built by Napier's at Glasgow the same year.

On 14 February that year, war broke out between Bolivia, Peru and Chile. Peru and Bolivia had signed a defensive alliance in 1873 and an import tax on nitrates was introduced by Bolivia in 1878. Chilean troops occupied the Bolivian nitrate port of Antofagasta and declared war on Peru on 5 April 1879. Chile re-purchased the *Amazonas*, which had been bought by the Pacific Steam Navigation Company in 1874. The war lasted for four years and tended to divide the staff's loyalty at local level as the various offices tended to take sides in the dispute. The company always tended to be neutral in political matters and the Chairman of the company was normally the Honorary Consul for Chile in Liverpool under Chilean governments of either party.

In January 1880, the service to Australia became fortnightly instead of monthly and the *Orient* was brought into service. The Pacific Steam Navigation Company agreed to add six more ships, making ten in all and the *John Elder* took the first sailing for the new line, followed by *Iberia*, *Aconcagua*, *Sorata*, *Liguria* and *Cotopaxi*. A coaling station was introduced at Diego Garcia and the wooden ships *Ronachan* and *Arran* were in service as hulks. *Ronachan* was built at Quebec in 1849 and *Arran* two years later at the same port.

The paddle-steamers *Chile* and *Payta* were sold to the Chilean Government and the *Bogota*, *Callao*, *Pacific*, *Panama* and *Peru* became hulks in various ports along the South American coast. *Bolivia* was thirty years old when it was decided to have her scuttled at sea and *Illimani* was lost when she went aground. The *Talca* was also scuttled at sea and *Guayaquil* was broken up. *Puno*, *Serena*, *Arica*, *Ecuador*, *Osorno* and the tender *Morro* joined the fleet in 1881. The company owned forty-one steamers with a total tonnage of 91,217 tonnes in 1881 and a twenty-one year extension to the original charter was negotiated. Later that year *Supe* and *Santiago* were sold and *Quito* and *Truxillo* were hulked.

The iron screw steamer *Chileo* was built by John Elder at Glasgow for the coastal trade in 1882 and *Santiago* was sold. James G. Robinson succeeded Lawrence R. Bailey as chairman of the company and *Iberia* was converted to a troopship during the Arabi Pasha Egyptian Campaign. *Cordillera* sank in the Straits of Magellan and *Valdivia* was wrecked at Huacho. *Manavi* was built by Robert Napier & Sons at Glasgow in 1885 and *Lusitania* and *Britannia* were taken over by the Admiralty for use as Armed Merchant Cruisers when it was thought that Russia would invade Afghanistan. However, Russia withdrew from the invasion and war was averted.

The company's first straight-stemmed vessel, the four-masted *Orizaba* was completed by the Barrow Shipbuilding Company in 1886 and she was followed by her sister-ship, *Oroya*. Both vessels had accommodation for 126 first-class, 154 second-class and 412 third-class passengers and were the first of a long line of 'O' class ships, that in later years were a regular feature in the company's system of nomenclature. The two ships were placed on the Australian service and were the originators of the custom to name vessels beginning with an 'O'. The two vessels introduced the inbound call at Brindisi, Italy where mail was landed for overland transfer to London, saving six days on the normal service. A system of transferring mail from South America by tender at Milford Haven was also introduced. As gold bullion was shipped on the South American service the company took delivery of their own gold bullion railway vans on the London Midland and Great Western Railways. During this period the Australian service became the most profitable route operated by the company. The war and its aftermath between Chile and Peru was affecting the coastal services in South America and the passenger services from Liverpool were also in decline.

Arequipa was sold and *Valparaiso* was lost at Vigo in 1887. The forth *Quito* was built at Birkenhead by Laird Brothers in 1888 and the following year the *Orotava* and *Oruba* entered service. They were originally designed for the South American service but were diverted to the Australian route. The coastal steamers *Santiago* and *Arequipa* were completed at Barrow in 1889. *Cotopaxi* left Liverpool on 8 April and as she sailed through the Straits of Magellan, approaching Cape Forward, the captain left the bridge giving instructions that he should be contacted if anything was sighted. Three hours later the vessel was struck by the German steamer *Olympia*. Captain Hayes returned to the bridge and ordered that the ship proceed at full speed towards land where she became beached. She had sustained a tear of 12 feet by 6 feet in the hull with several other smaller gashes. The crew and passengers helped to shift the cargo and attempt to right the angle at which the ship was leaning.

Fortunately, there were boiler-plates in her cargo hold and the engineers assisted by some Liverpool boiler-makers among the passengers were able to fix the plates over the holes in the hull. Temporary repairs were completed on 15 April and while steaming through the marked channel at 13 knots, she struck an uncharted rock and sank within ten minutes. The boats were lowered and all 202 people on board were saved and later landed on Wellington Island. Two days later, when they attempted to row to the mainland, they were picked up by the German steamer *Setos*.

In 1888 the 'Orient Line Guide' was published covering, 'chapters for travellers by sea and by land'. The guide included the eleven steamers operated by the line, which were the *Austral, Chimborazo, Cuzco, Garonne, Iberia, Liguria, Lusitania, Orient, Ormuz, Orizaba* and *Oroya*. It consisted

Cotopaxi (I).

of 360 pages and its content included engravings and cabin plans of most of the fleet and interiors, illustrations of cities, monuments and natural features en-route to Australia, charts of the Thames, Channel and maps comprising almost a complete atlas. It also covered 'medical aspects of the voyage' and described the voyage chapter by chapter, featuring the ports of call with an explanation of the names of the ships comprising the fleet.

Mr Robert Rankin, partner in the well-known ship owning firm of Rankin, Gilmour & Company, was appointed Chairman of the Pacific Steam Navigation in 1890. It was also during that year that triple-expansion engines were fitted to the *Araucania* and *Patagonia* and eventually the *Iberia* and *Liguria* were similarly treated. *Colombia, Santa Rosa* and *Magellan* were sold in 1890.

The *Santa Rosa* was sold to be used on the local coastal trade and the Dundee shipbuilding company, Gourlay Brothers & Company, delivered the steam tug *Assistance* in 1891. The *John Elder* and *Chile* were wrecked

STEAMSHIP LINE.

The Pacific Steam Navigation Co.

INCORPORATED BY ROYAL CHARTER, 1840. . . . .

MAIL AND PASSENGER SERVICES.

LONDON and AUSTRALIA (in Orient-Pacific Line), calling at Plymouth, Gibraltar, Marseilles, Naples, Port Said, Suez, Colombo, Fremantle, Adelaide, Melbourne and Sydney.

LIVERPOOL and BRAZIL, RIVER PLATE and VALPARAISO, calling at La Pallice (Rochelle), Corunna, Carril, Vigo, Leixoes (Oporto), Lisbon, St. Vincent (Cape de Verdes), Pernambuco, Bahia, Rio de Janeiro, Monte Video (for Buenos Ayres), Stanley (Falkland Islands), Punta Arenas (Straits of Magellan), Coronel and Talcahuano.

VALPARAISO and SAN FRANCISCO (California), calling at all the principal ports of **Chile, Peru, Ecuador, Colombia, Central America** and **Mexico**; also from **Valparaiso** to **Port Montt**, calling at intermediate ports.

CARGO SERVICE.

From GLASGOW and LIVERPOOL.—Fast Cargo Steamers are regularly despatched from Glasgow and Liverpool, delivering cargo direct at Rio de Janeiro, Punta Arenas (Straits of Magellan), Corral, Coronel, Talcahuano, Valparaiso, and at all the principal ports of **Chile** and **Peru**.

Passengers are booked through to all ports and for the round voyage from Liverpool to the Pacific *viâ* the Andes or *viâ* the Straits of Magellan, and back *viâ* Panama or San Francisco.

Return Tickets are issued at reduced rates from Liverpool to the Continental Ports at which the Steamers of the LIVERPOOL and VALPARAISO LINE call, also Tickets to Paris, *viâ* La Pallice (Rochelle), and for Tours in the South of France, the Pyrenees, &c.

Handbook of Fares and all information as to Tours, through Bookings, Freights, &c., may be obtained, and plans of cabins inspected, on application to the Company's Agents in—

Belfast—THOMSON & CO., 25, Victoria Street	Plymouth—W. LEAMAN & CO., 2, Millbay Road
Bradford—ROBERT JOHNSTON, 45, Brook Street	Birmingham—REYNOLD ROGERS, 27, Cambridge Street
Dundee—DAVID BRUCE & CO., 31, Albert Square	London—ANDERSON, ANDERSON & CO., 5, Fenchurch Avenue, E.C.
Glasgow—JAMES DUNN & SONS, 107, St. Vincent Street	West End Office—16, Cockspur Street, S.W.
Manchester—A. W. WILSON, 67, Piccadilly	

Or at the HEAD OFFICES OF THE COMPANY, 31, James Street, LIVERPOOL.

ORIENT STEAM NAVIGATION COMPANY.

PACIFIC STEAM NAVIGATION COMPANY.

MAIL FLAG.

FLAGS OF AUSTRALASIAN COLONIES.

NEW SOUTH WALES.

VICTORIA.

WEST AUSTRALIA.

NEW ZEALAND.

QUEENSLAND.

SOUTH AUSTRALIA.

TASMANIA.

Above: Destruction following the Valparaiso Earthquake of 1871.

Opposite left: PSNC advertisement.

Opposite right: Flags of Australasian colonies.

the following year and by 1893 there were signs that the world economy was improving and export cargo out of Liverpool showed an increase. Consequently, the Board agreed to order their first cargo vessels to operate alongside the passenger fleet. The name *Magellan* was given to the new cargo vessel and she was the company's first ship built and provided with an engine by Harland & Wolff at Belfast and many other ships followed over the years from the Belfast yard. *Inca, Sarmiento, Antisana, Orellana* and *Orcana* followed her into service.

The four-masted steamers, *Orellana* and *Orcana* were built for the Australian service along with the new passenger ship *Orissa. Patagonia* was wrecked seven miles north of Tome, at Lingueral, on 1 October 1895, on a voyage from Liverpool to Valparaiso. All thirty-nine people on board were saved. An important change took place in 1895 with the alteration of the French port of call from Paulliac (Bordeaux) to La Rochelle-Pallice. The pattern of trade between the two continents was changing dramatically at this time and the company ordered more cargo vessels to supplement the passenger fleet.

On 15 January 1895, William Just, the Managing Director from 1843–1875, died aged eighty-three while still serving as a director of the company. He had been Managing Director for twenty years and after that, a director and had been in attendance at the company's offices a few days prior to his death. It was reported at the time that it was under Just's capable management that the Company reached its premier position among the British steamship concerns of the nineteenth century.

The vessels *Chimborazo* and *Acongagua* were disposed of in 1895 and the Laird's-built *Britannia* grounded while leaving Rio de Janeiro on 4 September that year. She was sold to South American interests, salvaged and repaired. Caird's built and engined the twin-screw steamers *Chile* and *Peru* while the smaller *Chiriqui* was delivered by Wigham Richardson on the Tyne.

The largest cargo vessel in the fleet, *Corcovado,* was launched on 25 July 1896 by C. S. Hunter (Limited) of Newcastle. She was 405 feet long, with a 47-foot beam and was fitted with seven water-tight bulkheads and a cellular double-bottom divided longitudinally into ten compartments. The triple-expansion engines were built by the Wallsend Slipway & Engineering Company Limited and she had three large boilers working at 190 lbs per square inch. *Corcovado* ran trials on 16 September that year, reaching a speed of 12.98 knots and 12.58 overall. A tender named *Perlita* was also built for the company that year at Birkenhead. She was 62 feet long, screw propelled with an engine of 10 hp.

The following year, *Sorata*, the sister-ship to *Corcavado*, was delivered by Swan Hunter and *Oravia* was built by Wigham Richardson and the *Taboga* in 1898. The twin-screw passenger liner *Ortona* came from Vickers, Sons & Maxim in 1899 and *Orissa*, *Oropesa* and *Oravia* were built by Harland & Wolff at Belfast. They were claimed to be the first ocean going mail ships fitted with twin-screws. *Colombia* and *Guatemala* were built and engined by Caird & Company of Greenock for the Valparaiso-Callao route as the steamers were the preferred way to travel because of the lack of adequate roads away from the major ports. At the end of the century the Orient Line was suffering from an economic depression in Australia and the name was changed to the Orient Pacific Line reflecting the close collaboration between the two companies. *Galicia* was sold to the Canadian Steam Navigation Company of Liverpool for further service. *Casma*, *Osorno* and *Arauco* were also sold for further trading.

During 1898 Robert Rankin died after guiding the affairs of the company for eight years and he was succeeded by Sir Edward Percy Bates, a well-known Liverpool ship-owner. A reduction in trade on the company's routes led to the sale of the new *Potosi*. She had been designed and built for the Valparaiso service and was sold to Russia soon after delivery. Early in 1901 the coaster *Toboga* was seized for war purposes by the Colombian Government – the company appealed to the British Government who despatched a gunboat to the scene immediately. The officer in charge of the gunboat soon obtained a suitable apology from the Columbian authorities.

The *Galicia* was altered to cater for the general cargo trades and the new collier *Talca* was wrecked on Puchoco Point on 12 July 1901 with a full cargo of coal. The tender *Perico* was built and engined by J. Jones & Sons at Birkenhead to replace the *Morro* at Panama. *Talca* was replaced by the purchase of the German owned steamer *Rupanco* from Ferdinand Prehn, of Kiel and was later re-engined by Ross & Duncan of Glasgow.

Above: *Oropesa* (I) 1895.

Below: *Orissa* (I) 1895.

Top left: *Liguria* (I), saloon.

Top right: Hulk *Mendoza*.

Below left: Quartermaster Cullen on the bridge of *Mexico*.

Below right: *Iberia*.

PACIFIC STEAM NAVIGATION CO.

The four twin-screw liners *Panama*, *Victoria*, *Mexico* and *California* were built in 1902. *Panama* and *Victoria* came from the yard of Fairfield on the Clyde, *Mexico* and *California* were built by Caird & Company of Glasgow. Panama was 401 feet long, with a 52.3 beam, having side hatches for loading from lighters. Her bridge was well forward to assist in navigation in coastal waters and a lower deck for livestock ran the whole length of the vessel. Cabins opened directly onto the long promenade and shade decks.

On 5 December 1902, the Pacific Steam Navigation Company obtained an extension of its privileges of incorporation for twenty-one years. The crown in the house flag was changed from the Royal Crown to St Edward's Crown. The fleet at that time comprised of forty-seven vessels with a total of 162,813 tons. The tug *Gallito* was built by J. Shearer & Son Limited of Glasgow and *Orita* also joined the fleet the following year. However, on 2 June 1903, *Arequipa* sank off Valparaiso with a loss of over eighty lives. *Iberia* was sold and *Liguria* broken up. *Orcana* was requisitioned as a hospital ship and *Orissa*, *Orotava*, *Ortona* and *Victoria* were converted to troopships during the Boer War campaign.

Mendoza and some other vessels were hulked in the period 1890–1904 to replace older hulks. The Mersey loading berth was transferred from Birkenhead to No. 3 Alexandra Dock in 1904 and the company closed the Birkenhead works and the Duke's Dock depot. The Pacific Steam Navigation Company had been operating offices and workshops in Birkenhead for over thirty years and it was probably during that period of the company's history that it became known as the 'Birkenhead Navy'. The offices and workshops had provided a considerable amount of employment in Birkenhead and there was deep regret when they found it necessary to move to the Liverpool side of the Mersey.

On a voyage to Fremantle, the *Orizaba* ran aground off the Australian coast on 17 February 1905, and was eventually sold as a wreck for £3,750.

Above: Ortona.

Below: Victoria.

Right: Pacific Line advertisement, 1900.

Above: Postcard from *Ortona*.

Below: Postcard from *Victoria*.

PACIFIC LINE
OF
ROYAL MAIL STEAMERS.

Fortnightly Sailings
(under Contract with His Majesty's Government)
between
LIVERPOOL and FRANCE, SPAIN, PORTUGAL,
ST. VINCENT (Cape de Verdes),
BRAZIL, RIVER PLATE, FALKLAND ISLANDS,
AND
WEST COAST OF SOUTH AMERICA.

Also (as part of the ORIENT-PACIFIC LINE)
between
LONDON and AUSTRALIA,
calling en route at
GIBRALTAR, MARSEILLES, NAPLES,
PORT SAID, ISMALIA, SUEZ, and COLOMBO.

THE PACIFIC STEAM NAVIGATION COMPANY
(Incorporated by Royal Charter 1840.)

Manchester Office: **ST. MARGARET'S CHAMBERS**, Piccadilly.
Agents in London: **ANDERSON, ANDERSON & CO.**,
5 & 7 Fenchurch Avenue, E.C., and 16 Cockspur Street, Charing Cross, S.W.

HEAD OFFICES OF THE COMPANY:
31 JAMES STREET, LIVERPOOL.

Later that year, it was decided to sell the company's interests in the Australian service, together with *Ortona, Orotava, Oroya* and *Oruba*, to the Royal Mail Steam Packet Company. The four ships were painted with yellow funnels for this service. However, the Royal Mail ownership was short-lived as they withdrew in 1907 and *Oroya* was sold for scrap, the *Orotava* and *Oruba* were transferred to the West Indies service and the *Ortona* was converted to a cruise ship and renamed *Arcadian*.

Orellana and *Orcana* were purchased by the Hamburg America Line in 1905 and a new *Potosi* was delivered to the company by W. Pickersgill & Son of Sunderland. Sir James Laing & Son Limited, also of Sunderland, delivered *Bogota, Duendes, Esmeraldas* and *Flamenco* to the company during 1906 and *Oransa, Ortega* and *Oriana* came into service. The Oceanic Steam Navigation Company vessel *Gaelic* was purchased in 1905 and renamed *Callao* pending the arrival of *Quillota* but only survived with the company until 1907, when she was broken up at Briton Ferry.

Six twin-screw steamers were delivered during 1907, *Huanchaco, Junin, Quillota* and *Quilpue*. *Kenuta* and *Lima* came from the yard of John Brown & Company Limited on the Clyde and the Harrison liner vessel *Explorer* was purchased and *Pizarro* became the last vessel used as a hulk.

On 31 January 1906 an earthquake with a magnitude of 8.8, occurred off the coast of Ecuador near Esmeraldas, producing a five-metre local tsunami that destroyed forty-nine properties and killed over 500 people. Later that year on 17 August, an earthquake of 8.2 magnitude in Chile did considerable damage to buildings and the infrastructure in Valparaiso, where much of the city was destroyed. It was felt from Tacna, Peru to Puerto Montt. Records list the death toll as over 20,000 people.

In 1908, Dr Nicholas Senn wrote, 'The terrible earthquake has had no affect whatever in checking the business interests of Valparaiso or the commercial importance of its port. Business is being conducted on as large a scale as before the earthquake, and the mercantile fleet in the

Orcoma.

open harbour is as large as it was at any time before the disaster. The people have become accustomed to the little shocks and trembling of the earth, and go about their business as unconcernedly as though the foundations of the city had never been disturbed. There is always a certain fascination about danger zones, and repetitions of the same phenomena or occurrences create a sense of security and a contempt for danger. The city has now, as before the earthquake, about 150,000 inhabitants'.

The chairman of the Pacific Steam Navigation, Mr Arthur W. Bibby, giving evidence to a Royal Commission on shipping in 1908 said that the PSNC had suffered considerable delays that year, mainly because of the earthquake and also because of congestion and poor facilities at the South American ports. He said that it was difficult to maintain regular scheduled sailings and consequently the company had suffered considerable losses on chartered tonnage.

Orcoma sailed from Liverpool on her maiden voyage on 27 August 1908. She was built on the Clyde by W. Beardmore & Company Limited and was nicknamed 'the electric ship'. She was fitted with electric devices including laundry equipment, dishwashers, potato peelers, knife cleaning machines, plate and glass washers, ovens and electric lifts. The newspapers described her as a 'floating hotel' and she was probably one of the first luxury liners in design and fittings. *Orcoma* was built with accommodation for 1,140 passengers, including 550 in first-class. On a voyage organised by Thomas Cook & Son she carried the first conducted tour in the British South American travel trade on a four-month itinerary by steamer, train and coach at a cost of £300 per person. *Tobago*, was sold in 1909 and *Sarmiento* and *Antisana* the following year. *Lima* was lost off the coast of South America.

FIRST-CLASS SMOKE ROOM

FIRST-CLASS LOUNGE

Above, right: Interiors of *Orduna*.

Above: Crew of *Orbita*.

Left: *Orbita*.

Above: Panama.

Right: Sarmiento.

In 1910 the proprietary holdings in the Pacific Steam Navigation was taken over by the Royal Mail Steam Packet Company with Thomas Rome remaining as chairman of PSNC. The funnels were repainted buff and the new company commenced a rationalisation exercise looking at the size and composition of the two fleets. The Royal Mail Steam Packet was strong in the Caribbean services and routes to Brazil and Argentina. The Argentine to Chile railway was completed in 1910, which also contributed to further losses in trade to the Pacific Steam Navigation Company's coastal routes. Royal Mail started to issue debenture stock to raise money for new building and was payable out of revenue. This capital came mainly from existing shareholders and created a small but powerful group of Directors. It was decided to dispose of *Sarmiento* and *Antisana*. *Lima* was wrecked in the Straits of Magellan and *Chiriqui* sank after an explosion.

The tug and water-tender *Ponderoso* was completed by H. & C. Grayson Limited at Garston on the Mersey in 1911 and sailed to South America under her own power. On 12 November the following year, *Oravia* was making one of the occasional calls at the Falkland Islands and went aground. She was abandoned several days later. The PSNC funnel colour was changed from black to yellow in 1912, with the Pacific ships retaining their distinctive green boot topping.

The company's first triple-screw steamer, *Andes*, was built and engined by Harland & Wolff at Belfast in 1913. She sailed on her maiden voyage on 26 September from Liverpool to Valparaiso and was then transferred to Royal Mail's Southampton to River Plate service. Harland & Wolff also delivered *Orduna* and *Orbita* in 1914. *Orduna* was chartered by the Cunard Line for their Liverpool to New York service during the First World War. *Orbita* was requisitioned by the Admiralty, and entered service in 1915 as an auxiliary cruiser and later became a troop carrier. *Panama* served as a hospital ship during the War and was used to repatriate German prisoners of war in 1918 and wounded troops from the Eastern Mediterranean the following year. *Panama* became the Admiralty's permanent hospital ship *Maine* in 1920.

On 12 July 1914 *Ortega* was berthed at Rio de Janeiro and was informed by the commander of a British cruiser, which was also at anchor that there was a possibility of war with Germany. *Ortega* proceeded to Montevideo where, on 2 August, Captain Kinnier was told that the United Kingdom was at war by the British Consul. He handed in the names of all Royal Naval Reserve men in his crew. There were five German merchant vessels at Montevideo who were afraid to put to sea because of the presence of the British cruiser. Captain Kinnier agreed to carry some German passengers to other South American ports on his voyage and had guards placed over the engine room and steering gear.

One of *Ortega*'s stewards was a Frenchman, a member of the French Army's First Reserve. He applied for his discharge and left at Punta Arenas and transferred to the steamer *Ville du Havre*, along with other French reservists. At Talcahuano, *Ortega* was informed of the presence of a German warship in the vicinity and the German and Austrian passengers on board were landed at Valparaiso. From there, the ship headed north and a suspicious vessel was sighted, some twenty-five miles NNW of Angamos Point and *Ortega* eventually anchored in Mejillones Bay overnight. At Mollendo on 26 August the wireless operator overheard a message that he thought was being transmitted by a German battleship but the captain decided to put to sea and they reached Callao safely.

Ortega arrived at Valparaiso on 12 September and discovered that a German steamer which was at anchor had been heard communicating with a German ship at sea. Three hundred French reservists were taken on board *Ortega* and coal was loaded at Coronel where they berthed next to the German Kosmos Line vessels, *Luxor* and *Nitokris*, which were seeking coal 'to supply the firm's other steamers in various ports'. On the evening of 14 September the German sailors were heard singing patriotic songs very loudly. The French reservists on board *Ortega* reacted by joining together to sing 'La Marseillaise' at suitable intervals during the night.

Ortega sailed on 16 September and three days later at sea Third Officer Armstrong observed a cargo steamer steering towards them. He could also make out a warship following at full speed and the radio officer could hear them communicating with each other in German. Captain Kinnier altered his course steering for Cape George and the German cruiser opened fire, signalling for the *Ortega* to stop. However, the Chief Engineer of *Ortega* managed to get up a more powerful head of steam and the liner was making 18 knots in style.

When *Ortega* was two miles south of Cape George, the cruiser fired twice more but neither shot touched the ship and when she entered the Nelson Strait, within the three mile limit, the cruiser stopped, turned around and began to steam northwards. The Nelson Strait was 100 miles long and mostly uncharted and no steamer drawing 26 feet had ever considered taking that course. Captain Kinnier decided that he would attempt to take the vessel through the Strait as he suspected that the German cruiser was waiting for him to turn around and put to sea.

Third Officer Armstrong, with four sailors and the Boson's mate manned a boat and rowing ahead they took soundings which were signalled back to the ship by semaphore. At night the blackout was observed and a rota of watches was observed by the officers and crew. *Ortega* attempted to communicate by radio to the shore stations at Punta Arenas, finally getting a message from the British Consul that news had been received by them that *Ortega* had been sunk with all hands.

At first light on the morning of 20 September she left her anchorage and crept along, foot by foot. A passenger observed that, 'The passage through those wild fiords impressed itself very vividly on the minds of those who saw it. The scenery was superb. It was a truly magnificent sight to see the sun rise majestically behind the high mountain of snow, with the black water of the Strait at their base, for sheer mountains rose precipitately on either side of us, mountains of rock and snow. It was fairyland. Frozen waterfalls here and there, and then a little rock peeping up, the danger they must avoid. Not a vestige of human life was to be seen. It was the fullest form of desolate grandeur. So it continued as the crew worked, willingly, doggedly, patiently, hour by hour.'

After two days *Ortega* finally reached Isthmus Bay. 'Never has the *Ortega* lain at anchor in such wild and wonderful surroundings. For all the world she appeared to be in an inland lake, surrounded by mountains of snow which rose up abruptly from the water's edge. Beautiful glaciers here and there, a blue sky overhead, the waters of the bay a sheet of glass, and eagles soaring overhead.'

It was so rare for a steamer to reach this point that several boards were fixed to trees recording the names of previous visitors. Armstrong organised for a board to be made and painted the feat of the *Ortega* and he, and a few passengers, rowed away and secured it to a firmly established tree. As they proceeded through the Smyth's Channel they saw the wreck of the *Hazel Branch* and the remains of another steamer that was slowing breaking up. On reaching the Straits of Magellan they were met by the Chilean battleship *Almirante Lynch*, which had been sent 'to search for the survivors of the *Ortega*, reported to have been sunk'. *Ortega* departed from Punta Arenas at 1.30 p.m. on 22 September, just three days and three hours after the *Dresden* had first sighted her.

At 4.30 a.m. on 25 September the crew of *Ortega* were startled to hear a gun fired and two powerful searchlights turned onto them. When the turned they discovered that it was HMS *Glasgow*. They lowered a boat and a lieutenant was speeding towards them in true navy style. *Ortega* then proceeded to Rio de Janeiro and was met by the British Consul O'Sullivan-Beare who reported the tale to the Foreign Office in London. *Ortega* came across the Russian barque *Favell* before they reached the Cape Verde

Islands. She signalled to the *Ortega* asking for her correct latitude and longitude and for information to set her chronometers. She had been at sea for months and had no idea that her country was at war and the Baltic was closed to them. At Las Palmas, in the River Tagus at Oporto and other ports, the crew witnessed scores of interned German steamers which had been captured by the British Navy. At La Rochelle-Pallice the French reservists departed and every Englishman on board sang 'La Marseillaise' as they left the ship. They were saluted by the battleship *Gloire* in the Bay of Biscay and *Ortega* reached Liverpool without anyone there knowing what she had achieved.

The French Minister of Foreign Affairs, later requested the British Ambassador in Paris to present Captain Kinnier with a gold watch embossed with the national arms. The presentation was at Liverpool Town Hall and Monsieur R. Boeufre, the French Consul said that 'on behalf of his Government, he desired to express admiration for the pluck and skilful seamanship of Captain Kinnier. The Lord Mayor of Liverpool also added a tribute and the Admiralty, in a letter to the Pacific Steam Navigation Company said, 'My Lords desire to place on record their appreciation of the courageous conduct of the master, Captain Douglas R. Kinnier, in throwing off his pursuer by successfully navigating the uncharted and dangerous passage of Nelson's Strait'.

The Liverpool and London War Risks' Association voted one hundred guineas to Captain Kinnier and a number of children subscribed for a large Union Jack, which was handed over to the Captain at a function on board the *Ortega*, on the morning she started her next voyage to South America. The Government conferred the D.S.C. Order upon Captain Kinnier at Buckingham Palace, 'when the King and he talked just as one sailor man would to another'.

The Panama Canal was opened on 15 August 1914. The Canal is forty-eight miles long, joining the Pacific and Atlantic Oceans. It was built between 1904 and 1914 and was one of the largest and most difficult engineering projects ever undertaken at the time. It enabled ships to trade with the Pacific coast ports of South America without having to travel the long and dangerous route around the Straits of Magellan. The major manufacturing sectors of the United States were now as close to Valparaiso as Rio de Janeiro. It reduced the sailing time for a ship travelling from San Francisco to New York by a half. The Canal was controlled by the United States until 1977, when the Torrijos-Carter Treaty enabled a transition to Panama. From 1979 to 1999 the Canal was under joint United States-Panamanian administration and from 31 December 1999 authority was granted to the Panama Canal Authority, which was an agency of the Panamanian Government. The opening of the Canal enabled American companies to compete with their European counterparts and the balance of trade with South America was changed forever.

In February 1916 *Flamenco* was captured by the German raider *Moewe* and sank, 310 miles north-east from Pernambuco and her sister-ship *Esmeraldas*, was captured and destroyed by *Moewe* on 10 March 1917. *Oropesa* was requisitioned by the Admiralty, becoming an Armed Merchant Cruiser and sank a U-boat off Skerryvore, Scotland in March, 1915. She was transferred to the French Navy but retained her British crew and renamed *Champagne*. On 15 October 1917 she was torpedoed in the Irish Sea and sank. Fifty-six persons lost their life. *Bogota* was sunk by a submarine in 1916 and *California* was also lost in October, the following year, after a submarine attack. *Oronsa* was torpedoed off Bardsey Island on 28 April 1918 and she sank with a loss of three lives.

Magellan was torpedoed on 25 July 1918 and sank fifty-three miles, north-east of Cape Serrat and *Galicia* was mined and sank off Falmouth in May 1917. *Orissa* sank in June 1918 when she was torpedoed by a German submarine. *Mexico* was torpedoed on 23 March 1917 in the English Channel, but managed to reach port and was repaired to resume service.

PACIFIC STEAM NAVIGATION CO. 31

The ships, *Darro* and *Ortega* (I) in Brocklebank Dock, Liverpool.

Social Hall, *Essequibo*.

Jamaica was purchased by the company from the Royal Mail Line in 1914 and *Acajutla* and *Salvador* were bought from the Salvador Railway Company in 1915 to operate a feeder service to Panama.

During the First World War the company's ships gave excellent service but enemy action took its toll, eight ships, totalling 42,427 tonnes, were lost. Lieutenant Commander Buckley, RNR was a cadet on the Pacific Steam Navigation Company vessel *Oriana* when she was involved in helping to rescue survivors following a collision between *Otranto* and HMS *Kashmir* on 6 October 1918.

An 'eye witness' account of the tragic loss of HAMC *Ortranto* on the west coast of the Mull of Kintyre October, 1913, by Lieutenant Commander Buckley, RNR Ex Chief Officer PSNC.

Before describing the disaster which overtook this fine ship I must record the events leading thereto.

Having served for just on two years in the Mediterranean Theatre of the war I was transferred to the Western Ocean-Trooping, I was sorry to leave H.M.T.2608 'HUANCHACO' she had been a faithful lady with a very happy ships company under the Command of Captain Chittenden. However, 'Orders were Orders' and I left Marseille on the famous Blue Sky Rapide for Paris and the Coast, duly arriving in the UK at Southport, my home town, for a spot of leave.

On reporting for duty I was appointed Junior Officer to 'ORIANA', one of the crack Wail Boats in peace time of the Pacific Steam Navigation Company. This vessel, lying at Govan Docks on the Clyde, was now H.M.T. 'ORIANA' camouflaged and stripped of anything inflammable, her Tween Decks were gutted and converted for troop carrying to the specifications of the American Naval & Military Authorities.

'GUIANA's' Senior Officers I will touch lightly on for the moment, but you will read later about these great men. In Command, Captain Daniel, a completely dedicated man of the sea. Second in Command, Chief Officer Benson, like his Commander a great seaman, and a great leader of men. Both these persons inspired enormous confidence. Senior Third Officer McWhinney, a TRUE Sailor man this. Purser Nuni'e, Chief Steward Swift, and a grand team of brave Engineers, whose names alas I cannot remember, completed the senior personnel of the vessel.

We duly left the berth, came down river, and anchored off the Tail of the Bank, It was raining like hell. A miserable Saturday afternoon if ever there was one. I was detailed to proceed by launch to Greenock Pier, phone Marine Department Liverpool, (Captain Pooley), requesting an additional six Able Seamen and four Fireman be brought to the vessel, which would be in Jersey 9 a.m. next morning, Sunday.

Accordingly, our requirements reached us by Tug the following morning. At this stage one must remember all movement was by Admiralty. The vessel's peace time owners only knew where she was when she turned up in some Port.

As soon as we had these men signed on we left the river in the company of other crack Liners for New York. We made straight across for Kinsale thence the FASTNET, five ships abreast in three lines steaming nicely in somewhat overcast and drizzly conditions with a slight sea and moderate westerly swell.

Dead on Noon Monday, some twenty four hours after leaving the Jersey, the First Blow struck. The 'MESSANABIE', on our immediate Starboard side, took two torpedoes from a U Boat. The first caught her under the Bridge and the second in her Engine Room. She disappeared from the surface within twenty minutes. The rest of the convoy scattered and we found our way to New York.

Shortly after berthing at Hoboken I was called to the Commander's Cabin and appointed Troop Officer of the vessel, working directly under Chief Officer Benson - for me a great challenge. I was given a small office and a staff of one

Assistant Purser - augmented after embarkation by American Troop personnel. Watching the interests of the American Government was a Lieutenant Petty, a grand Officer, with whom we worked happily throughout.

We had to see all meals served, arrange additional Look-outs, attend all sick cases and visit all decks. In fact, keep records of everything connected with the vessel and her entire hour by hour daily life.

Embarkation day arrived. We carried two thousand, five hundred Officers and men and as each man came over the top of the gangway, he dropped into a large mail bag his letter showing on the back his name and rank. As soon as the vessel's arrival was notified from the United Kingdom to Hoboken most of these letters were despatched to homes all over America. The exceptions were the letters of those men who had died on passage. The checking of such lists and the passing of same under the signature of the vessel's Doctor and the Military Doctors attending at time of death were, as it turned out, a sadly exacting and exhausting business.

We formed convoy off Nantucket Light some thirty two of Britain's finest Liners, sailing in eight lines, four abreast 'ORTRANTO', the Commodore vessel, in the front line on 'ORIANA's' Portside. It is right to mention 'ORTRANTO' was flying the White Ensign, being an Armed Merchant Cruiser, and she had on board the top brass of the divisions of this convoy.

Leaving Nantucket the weather was murky and throughout the East-bound passage worsened daily. Troops became very seasick, indeed. Then an epidemic of influenza struck all vessels and we on 'ORANIA' were burying, nightly, some twenty men of all ranks. Naturally, this was a tremendous blow to the morale of the troops.

Passing Longitude 18 W. with a following howling gale, and indeed the highest seas I had ever seen we failed to rendezvous with our expected Naval escort which was nowhere to be seen. In fact, it wasn't sighted until two hours before the tragedy happened.

At 9.30 a.m. on the fatal Sunday morning, 'ORIANA' sounded two blasts on her siren. Turning to Port at her speed and in those seas meant <u>big trouble!</u> Officer of the watch McWhinney had spotted what turned out to be land in the murk dead ahead and he lost not *a* second with his order to the Helmsman. The Front Line turned likewise to Port. Alas, 'KASHMIRE's' steering jammed and she turned to Starboard ramming 'OTRANTO' amidships and even before she could founder the doomed vessel was being pounded to pieces by the lashing, following gale and heavy seas on the rocks on the West Coast of the Mull of Kintyre. Throughout the following week the local people on the Mull hauled up the cliff face no less than 700 bodies and gave them a decent burial.

On 'ORIANA' how Captain Daniel, his Navigating Officers, his Engineers and Firemen got 'ORIANA' out of the enormously wide and deep trough and the pounding seas I will never know – but they did and eventually we made the North Channel and the calm of the East Coast of Northern Ireland.

Stock was taken of damage to 'ORIANA' Not one Life Boat was left. All had been swept away within minutes with all life rafts. The Boat deck was a complete shambles. Wire reels just torn like pieces of paper from their housings, ventilators gone. The lower decks were a shambles, bodies, men, water everywhere.

We got the Galleys going and served soup all round and later, scratch meals. 'ORIANA' limped alongside the Liverpool Landing stage at 10 a.m. the following morning – a sorry sight. Twelve ambulances were waiting with a team of Doctors and Nurses. The dead were removed, then the chronic sick and later the remaining troops disembarked. Lieutenant Petty and I proceeded to the American Authorities with our reports and lists of the dead.

It was the end of a sad voyage. I pay great tribute to all 'ORIANA's' ships company and all United States Personnel and a special mention to all the ships and Army Doctors who had one hell of an East-bound crossing.

Above left: Oropesa.

Above right: Laguna.

Left: Lobos.

Above left: *Oroya* leaving Liverpool.

Above right: *Oroya*, Panama Canal.

Right: *Loreto*.

Lieutenant Commander Buckley later served as officer in the company's ships, becoming a Chief Officer, and served in the Royal Naval Reserve during the Second World War.

Orca was delivered by Harland & Wolff in 1918 as a cargo vessel, but was returned to her builders three years later for passenger accommodation to be added. She emerged in 1922, sailing on her maiden voyage from Southampton and Hamburg to New York on 18 December that year. She was transferred to the Royal Mail Line in 1923 and sold to the White Star Line in 1927, becoming the *Calgaric*. *Ballena* and *Bogota* were taken over by the company as war-loss replacements and *Arana*, *Almagro* and *Alvarado* joined the fleet in 1920. The German vessel *Alda* was allocated to the company and was renamed *Magellan*.

The first issue of the PSNC magazine *Sea Breezes* was published in December 1919. It was edited by T. E. Edwardes and was later available for sale to the general public at 2d a copy, becoming the authoritative magazine for all interested in ships and the sea. Edwardes died in 1924 and the magazine continued to be popular with ship-lovers. In June 1937, it passed into the ownership of Charles Birchall & Sons Limited, who also published *The Journal of Commerce*. It ceased to be published in 1939 but reappeared in January 1946 and continues publication to the present day.

Thomas Rome retired as Chairman and was replaced by Sir Owen Phillips, who was later to become Lord Kylsant. The company opened services from New York to Valparaiso and New York to Cartagena and *Callao*, *Ebro* and *Essequibo* were transferred from the Royal Mail Line for these routes. *Oropesa* was completed by Cammell Laird in 1920 and the first motor ship, *La Paz* was completed by Harland & Wolff at Glasgow. The motor ships *Lobos* and *Losada* were also delivered by Harland & Wolff the following year followed by *Laguna* in 1923. *Lautaro* and *Lagarto* were built by Harland & Wolff at Glasgow in 1915 for the Glen Line and were acquired by PSNC in 1923 and 1924 respectively.

Corcovada was sold for scrapping in 1921 and *Orduna*, *Orbita* and *Oropesa* were transferred to the Royal Mail for their new Atlantic service. *Almagro* and *Alvarado* were purchased from MacAndrews & Company. The opening of the Panama Canal had a significant effect on the operations of the company and the fact that Valparaiso had become the terminal port rather than the first port of call.

A special report by the Panama Canal Company in 1921 found that approximately one-third of the total traffic through the canal was British. The report found that most freight carried by British vessels through the canal in 1921 was carried on five main trade routes. A total of 950,000 tonnes was carried on the Europe to Australia and New Zealand route and 747,000 tonnes on the trade between Europe and the west coast of South America. The canal was also used by vessels trading between the United States and Australia and New Zealand, the United States and the Far East and Europe to the west coast of North America. It concluded that the Pacific Steam Navigation Company contributed most to Panama Canal traffic with the company sending 299 vessels through the canal in 1921.

The ninth extension to the Royal Charter was granted on 4 January 1922 as long as 'the company shall think fit', and that the company's name and its Liverpool office should remain. To replace the three vessels moved to the Atlantic service, Royal Mail Line transferred *Miltiades* and *Marathon* to the Pacific Steam Navigation and they were renamed *Orcana* and *Oruba*. The coastal vessels *Sorata* and *Quilpue* were sold for further trading in 1922. The Cabotaje Law was passed by Chile on 22 August 1922, which meant that only Chilean-registered vessels could trade within the countries ports. This had a significant effect on the company's services to that country.

Laguna was delivered in 1923 from Harland & Wolff at Glasgow. *Inca*, *Chile*, *Peru*, *Guatemala*, *Victoria* and *Quillota* were sold bringing to an end the company's coastal passenger services in South America. *Oroya* joined the fleet in 1924 and *Glanade, Glenariffe* and *Glenavy* were purchased from the Glen Line. *Glanade* became *Loreto, Glenafiffe* was renamed *Loriga* and *Glenavy* became *Lagarto*. Another MacAndrew vessel, *Arana*, was purchased and the tug/tender *Temuco* was delivered. In an attempt to stabilise freight and passenger rates the Magellan Conference was established in 1924.

On 7 June 1924, Viscount Pirrie, head of Harland & Wolff, Shipbuilders, died suddenly on the Pacific Steam Navigation Company's vessel *Ebro*, on his way to New York. Viscount and Viscountess Pirrie were touring South America and *Ebro* was sailing between Colon and New York at the time. Lord Pirrie was seventy-seven years of age and had celebrated his birthday at Lima on 31 May. His party had left Southampton by Royal Mail steamer visiting Brazil, Uruguay, Argentina, Chile, Peru and Ecuador looking at opportunities for his shipbuilding company and that of the PSNC, in which he held a considerable stock.

He would often arrange trips to see developments in the industry for himself so he could assess the possibilities for business opportunities for the future. When oil fuel for steamships took over from coal he toured the Mexican oil fields to see how long the supply would last and how the raw material was obtained. He pioneered the placing of accommodation amidships on steamships, instead of aft, using this system on the White Star vessel *Germanic* in 1877.

Lord Pirrie was one of the first Senators elected to the new Parliament in Belfast in 1922, when Northern Ireland was separated from the Irish Free State. He was made a Baron in 1906, a Viscount in 1921 and was created a Knight of St Patrick. He was also a member of the Privy Councils of Ireland and England, Pro-Chancellor of Queen's University, Belfast, Comptroller of the Household of the Lord Lieutenant of Ireland, High Sheriff of the Counties of Antrim and Down, and the first Honorary Freeman of the City of Belfast.

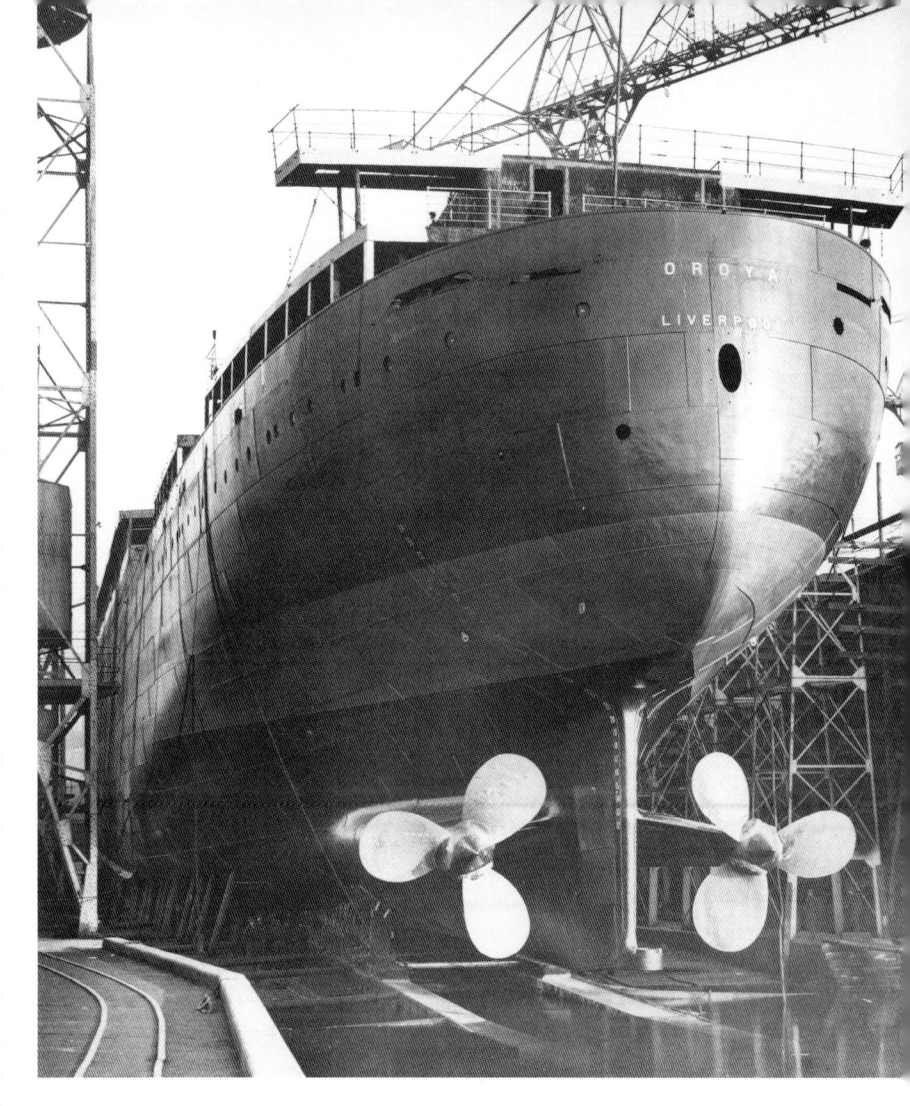

Oroya (III).

Potosi and *Huanchaco* were sold in 1924, *Junin* and *Kenuta* the following year, *Ortega* and *Oriana* were sold for further trading and *Duendes* was purchased by Greek owners in 1927. The following year Peru passed its own 'Cabotaje Law'. After twenty-one years of service, *Jamaica* was sold in 1929 and the following year the three-masted Yeoward steamer *Andorinha* was purchased and renamed *Champerico* to operate on the Falkland Islands service from Montevideo.

The San Francisco *Daily Commercial News* of 21 October 1925, reported that the famous old ship brokerage firm of Fred Holmes & Son, established in Liverpool and San Francisco in 1880, now carried on by James M. Holmes, has printed on its letterheads as a trademark a picture of the steamship *Cordillera*. The late Captain Fred Holmes, founder of the firm was well known throughout the ports of the world as a shipbroker and was generally considered the leader in his profession. He had correspondents in practically every port in the world and held records and files of inestimable value.

However, during the fire in San Francisco of 1906 all these were destroyed and he had to start all over again to accumulate these documents. It was one of his ambitions to obtain a picture of his first steamer, the *Cordillera*, which he brought out new in 1870 on her first trip from Liverpool to Valparaiso. His last wish before he died in December 1924, was that efforts be made to obtain the photograph.

His son James, who took over the business, devoted considerable time and money to the task of locating a photograph and was aided by the officials of the Pacific Steam Navigation Company as well as officers of the company. The picture was later incorporated into the letterheads of the firm of Fred Holmes & Son in memory of the founder of the company.

In 1931, the *Reina del Pacifico* was built by Harland & Wolff at Belfast. She was Britain's highest-powered motor ship with a quadruple-screw

Above: *Oroya* (III) First Class cabin.

Below: *Orbita* (I) lounge.

PROGRAMME
OF
SPORTS AND ENTERTAINMENTS

TO BE HELD ON BOARD

THE PACIFIC STEAM NAVIGATION CO.'S

R.M.S. "ORCOMA"

Sailed from Valparaiso 7th April, 1923.

HON. PRESIDENT:

CAPTAIN A. T. D. PEARSON.

PRESIDENT:

THE RT. HON. COL. SIR R. G. SHARMAN-CRAWFORD.

VICE-PRESIDENTS:

Mr. C. VELARDE.   Mr. J. BARNETT.

Mr. J. DUNCAN.   Mr. G. A. HARVEY.

SPORTS COMMITTEE:

Dr. J. Ramsay Smith (Chairman).

Sra. L. Puelma de Edwards.   Mrs. G. A. Harvey

Mrs. W. Kemp.   Sra. R. Montero de Larrañagea.

Mrs. C. K. Walbaum,   Miss A. L. Chrystal.

Messrs. Coles, Cori, Gazzani, Macrory, Tte. 1º. Nef,

Rivera, Squire, Toovey, Chief Officer,

Purser, Dr. Stott.

SECRETARIES:

Mr. Nicol and Mr. O'Donnell.

TREASURERS:

Tte. 1º. Cuevas and Mr. Walbaum.

---

3. 100 Yards Handicap — Boys
   Handicap de 100 yardas — Niños
4. 100 Yards Handicap — Girls
   Handicap de 100 yardas — Niñas
5. Chalking the Pig's Eye — Girls & Boys
   Colocar el ojo al chancho — Niñas y niños
6. Bun Race — Girls & Boys
   Carrera de galletas — Niñas y niños
7. Egg & Spoon Race — Girls & Boys
   Carrera de huevos con cucharas — Niñas y niños
8. Sack Race — Girls & Boys
   Carrera de sacos — Niñas y niños
9. Three-Legged Race — Girls & Boys
   Carrera de tres piernas — Niñas y niños

BRIDGE COMPETITION.

Particulars will be advised later

A GRAND CONCERT

will be given by the

"ORCOMA" FRAGMENTS

Friday, 27th April, 1923, at 9 p.m.

Viernes 27 de Abril de 1923 a las 9 p.m.

BOOK DINNER,

Friday, 27th April.

FANCY DRESS DINNER & BALL,

Saturday, 28th April, 1923.   Sabado 28 de Abril 1923.

Judges: Jueces:

The Passengers   Los Pasajeros por

by Ballot.   voto secreto.

If possible a Concert will be arranged amongst the Passengers.

PRIZE DISTRIBUTION.

(Reparticion de Premios).

Monday, 30th April at 8.30 p.m.   Lunes 30 de Abril a las 8.30 p.m.

installation designed to give a continuous output of 22,000 shp at 145 rpm. Each of the four engines had twelve cylinders, the installation being of Harland-B and W trunk piston single-acting four-stroke design. The cylinders were of 630 mm bore and the piston stroke was 1,200 mm. She was pressure charged on the Buchi principle, the exhaust gases being taken from the main engines to four turbines coupled to blowers, which supplied air and a delivery pressure of 1.33 kg per square cm to the inlet valve. The exhaust gases were then fed into two Clarkson boilers, which could alternate with oil firing. A third boiler was worked from the exhaust to the auxiliary engines. There were four auxiliary engines also of Harland–B and W design, each with six cylinders and coupled to a 350 kw dynamo.

Above: Loreto, dining room.

Far left: Orcoma (I).

Left: Laguna.

She was designed to carry 253 first, 149 second and 289 third-class passengers and sailed on her maiden voyage on 9 April 1931 from Liverpool to La Rochelle, Vigo, Bermuda, Bahamas, Havana, Jamaica, Panama Canal, Guayaquil, Callao, Antofagasta, and Valparaiso. The voyage took twenty-five-and-a-half days to complete. Her accommodation included a number of suites with dressing room, bathroom and bedroom on 'C' deck and the design of her public rooms was based on the Spanish work of the Moresque and Colonial periods.

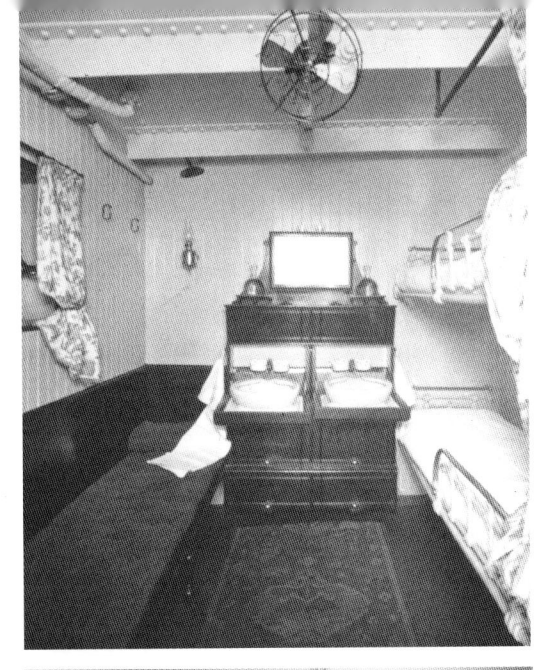

Loreto, two-berth cabin.

Orbita, First Class two-berth cabin.

Oropesa was given an expensive overhaul in 1931 and her speed was increased in order to run alongside the *Reina del Pacifico* but she was then laid up for several years during the Depression. Attempts were made to sell some of the fleet and the line was affected by the collapse of the Royal Mail Line and Lord Kylsant's imprisonment for making false statements in a financial prospectus. However, a special Act of Parliament enabled the PSNC to continue under the control of creditors and several of the creditors were elected to the Board of the company.

The Pacific Steam Navigation Company had been acquired by the Royal Mail Line in 1910 during a period when they had also taken over another twenty companies, including Elder Dempster Line, the Glen and Shire Lines, the Union Castle Line in 1912 and the White Star Line in 1927. In 1928 an application was made to extend the government guarantee on a loan from the Midland Bank. The company was experiencing financial difficulties. It was group policy that each separate line should make a return of 5 per cent on capital, although the bank rate was 3 per cent. Some sectors of the group, such as the White Star Line were under-performing and failed to meet the target and the decision was made to top up the difference out of reserves and by mortgaging their vessels against bank loans.

In 1930 it was announced that the Royal Mail Line had liabilities of £10 million and a government enquiry recommended that the group be placed in the hands of three trustees, appointed by the banks. Lord Kylsant, who controlled the company was arrested and charged with making false statements with regard to the company's accounts for 1926 and 1927, contrary to section eighty-four of the Larceny Act 1861. The company auditor was charged with aiding and abetting and Lord Kylsant was also charged with issuing a document with intent to deceive. The trial took place in 1931 and Kylsant was found guilty of the charge of issuing a document with intent to deceive. Both were found not guilty of the first two charges. Kylsant was sentenced to twelve months in prison and resigned all of his knighthoods and lieutenancies.

Ballena and *Bogata* were sold and *Orita* was broken up. *Magellan*, *Arana*, *Almagro* and *Alvarado* were sold and *Orcoma* was also broken up. It was decided to terminate the New York passenger service in 1934 and *Ebro* and *Essequibo* were sold for further service and *Champerico* was sold to Chilean interests. The passenger trade to Cuba was affected by the Spanish Civil War in 1936 and the following year the Falkland Islands Company cancelled their contract with the company as they had decided to operate their own vessels. In 1938 the Board decided to withdraw *Oroya* from service and the Royal Mail Line became the majority shareholder in the company.

A committee was set up in November 1937 under the chairmanship of Lord Cadman to look at British civil aviation. The report, published on 8 February the following year, made several recommendations including

Below: *Reina Del Pacifico*, Grand Hall.

Pacific Line brochure, 1932.

the formation of the British Overseas Airways Corporation, which took place in June 1939. It noted that there was no British airline flying to South America and felt that this should be rectified as soon as possible. Following the end of the Second World War, the directors of five shipping companies trading with South and Central America decided to look at the possibility of setting up their own airline. These were the Pacific Steam Navigation Company, Royal Mail Line, Lamport & Holt Line, the Booth Steamship Company and the Blue Star Line. Consequently, British Latin American Airlines was formed on 25 January 1944 and its first office was located at Royal Mail Lines and its chairman was John Booth.

"PERU" & "CHILE" · 1840
"QUITO" & "BOGOTA" · 1852
"MAGELLAN" · 1868
"PATAGONIA" · 1868
"BRITANNIA" · 1872
"COLOMBIA" · 1873
"IBERIA" · 1873
"ORIZABA" · 1889
"ORTONA" · 1899

PACIFIC LINE

44   PACIFIC STEAM NAVIGATION CO.

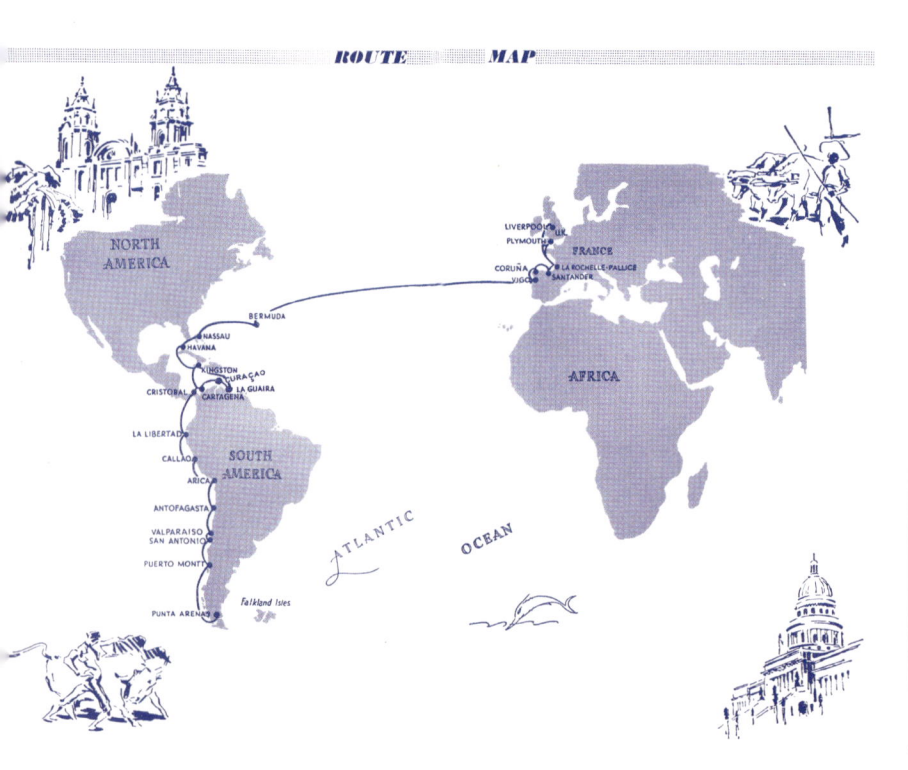

Above: Reina Del Pacifico.

Right: Reina Del Pacifico, bell.

Far left: Reina Del Pacifico, route map.

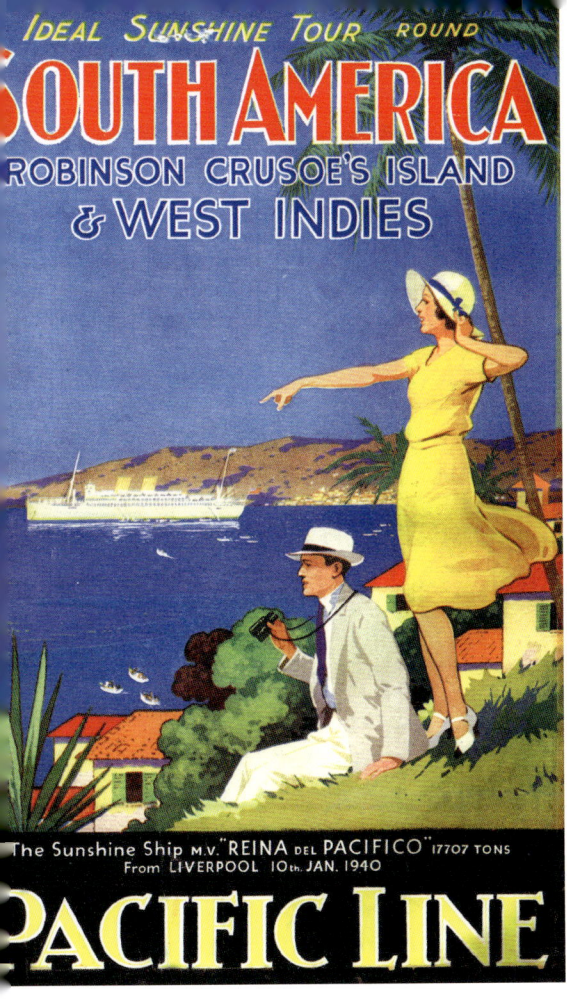

Above: Pacific Line advert for *Reina Del Pacifico*, 1940.

Right: *Reina Del Pacifico*'s itinerary, 1940. Of course, war put paid to this cruise.

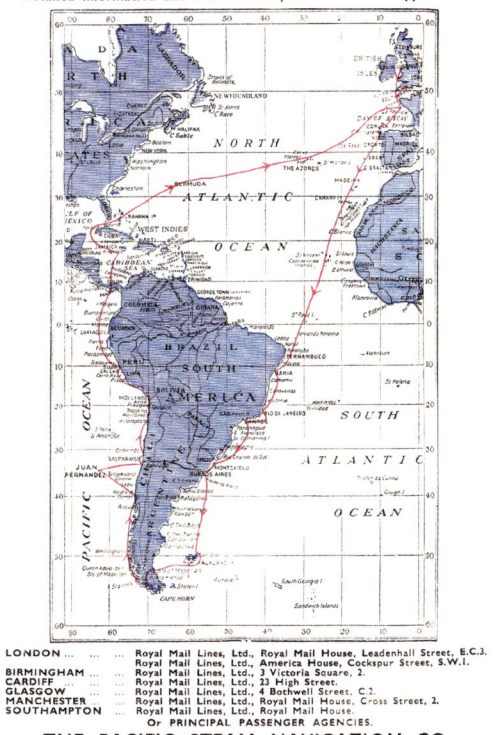

1933. Subject to alteration or cancellation without notice. 1933.

PORTS	Reina del Pacifico	Orduña	Orcoma	Reina del Pacifico	Orduña	Reina del Pacifico
	(Wed.)					
LIVERPOOL	18 Jan.	2 Feb.	9 Mar.	‡13 Apr	11 May	‡22 June
Plymouth	19 ,,	—	—	—	—	—
La Rochelle Pallice	20 ,,	4 Feb.	11 Mar.	15 Apr	13 May	24 June
Santander	21 ,,	5 ,,	12 ,,	16 ,,	14 ,,	25 ,,
Coruña	22 ,,	6 ,,	13 ,,	17 ,,	15 ,,	26 ,,
Vigo	22 ,,	6 ,,	13 ,,	17 ,,	15 ,,	26 ,,
BERMUDA		15 ,,	22 ,,	24 ,,	24 ,,	3 July
HAVANA		19 ,,	26 ,,	27 ,,	28 ,,	6 ,,
CRISTOBAL		22 Feb	29 Mar.	29 April	31 May	8 July
Balboa		23 ,,	30 ,,	30 ,,	1 June	9 ,,
La Libertad (Ecuador)	Outward via Straits of Magellan.	23 ,,	30 ,,	30 ,,	1 ,,	9 ,,
		25 ,,	1 April	2 May	3 ,,	11 ,,
Paita		26 Feb.	2 April	2 May	4 June	11 July
CALLAO		28 ,,	4 ,,	4 ,,	6 ,,	13 ,,
		28 ,,	4 ,,	4 ,,	6 ,,	13 ,,
Mollendo		2 Mar.	6 ,,	6 ,,	8 ,,	15 ,,
Arica		3 ,,	7 ,,	6 ,,	9 ,,	15 ,,
Iquique		3 ,,	7 ,,	7 ,,	9 ,,	16 ,,
Tocopilla		4 ,,	8 ,,	7 ,,	10 ,,	16 ,,
Antofagasta		5 ,,	9 ,,	8 ,,	11 ,,	17 ,,
VALPARAISO	22 Feb.	7 ,,	11 ,,	10 ,,	13 ,,	19 ,,

	(Wed.)	(Tues.)	(Tues.)	(Wed.)	(Tues.)	(Wed.)
VALPARAISO	1 Mar.	14 Mar.	18 April	‡17 May	20 June	‡26 July
Antofagasta	3 ,,	16 ,,	20 ,,	18 ,,	22 ,,	27 ,,
Mejillones	3 ,,	16 ,,	20 ,,	19 ,,	22 ,,	28 ,,
Tocopilla	—	17 ,,	21 ,,	—	23 ,,	—
Iquique	4 Mar.	18 ,,	22 ,,	19 May	24 ,,	28 July
Arica	4 ,,	18 ,,	22 ,,	20 ,,	24 ,,	29 ,,
Mollendo	5 ,,	19 ,,	23 ,,	20 ,,	25 ,,	29 ,,
CALLAO	7 ,,	21 ,,	25 ,,	22 ,,	27 ,,	31 ,,
La Libertad (Ecuador)	—	25 ,,	29 ,,	24 ,,	1 July	2 Aug.
Balboa	11 Mar.	27 Mar.	1 May	26 May	3 July	4 Aug.
CRISTOBAL†	12 ,,	27/8 ,,	1/2 ,,	26 ,,	3/4 ,,	4 ,,
Kingston (Jamaica)	15 Mar.	—	—	—	—	—
HAVANA	18 ,,	1 April	6 May	29 May	8 July	7 Aug.
BERMUDA	—	5 ,,	10 ,,	1 Jun	12 ,,	10 ,,
St. Michael's (Azores)	26 Mar.	—	—	—	—	—
Vigo	29 ,,	13 April	18 May	8 June	20 July	17 Aug.
Coruña	29 ,,	13 ,,	18 ,,	8 ,,	20 ,,	17 ,,
Gijon	—	—	19 ,,	9 ,,	21 ,,	18 ,,
Santander	30 Mar.	14 April	19 ,,	9 ,,	21 ,,	18 ,,
La Rochelle-Pallice	31 ,,	15 ,,	20 ,,	10 ,,	22 ,,	19 ,,
Plymouth	1 April	16 ,,	21 ,,	11 ,,	23 ,,	20 ,,
LIVERPOOL	2 ,,	17 ,,	22 ,,	12 ,,	24 ,,	21 ,,

† Vessels arrive and sail on earlier or later date according to circumstances.

‡ Rapid Voyages: "Reina del Pacifico" { 13th April and 22nd June from Liverpool.
17th May and 26th July from Valparaiso.

☾ "Reina del Pacifico" leaves Valparaiso 23/2/33 for Special Cruise to JUAN FERNANDEZ (ROBINSON CRUSOE'S ISLAND).

The directors were C. C. Barber, S. W. Black, W. H. Davies, L. Dewey and F. H. Lowe and offices were later established at 14 Leadenhall Street, London E.C.3.

A government White Paper published in March 1945 proposed three main British airlines with clearly defined routes. The first was to operate on Commonwealth air routes, the second was to serve the capitals of major cities of Europe and internal British destinations and the third would operate to South America. In 1945 it was decided that the airline would become British South American Airways Limited. It was also announced that it was the government's intention for the three corporations to operate the routes to Commonwealth countries, the United States and the Far East, the Continent and internal United Kingdom routes and routes between the United Kingdom and South America.

Reina del Pacifico was requisitioned as a troopship at the beginning of the Second World War, sailing from the Clyde to Singapore and then bringing the first Canadian troops to Britain. She was then refitted to carry an increased number of troops and on several occasions the enemy claimed to have sunk her. She carried troops to Norway and was there again to evacuate them a few weeks later. Her next employment was in the Middle East where she escaped damage in the Red Sea when she was attacked by Italian aircraft. She was the perfect vessel for these duties as she was able to average over 20 knots for twenty-four hours.

She took troops from Halifax, N.S., to Singapore by the west about route in 1941 and the following year was converted to an assault ship to participate in the French North African and Sicilian landings. At one point she was at Avonmouth during an air attack and escaped serious damage from high explosive and incendiary bombs. She also escaped any damage when bombs fell around her in Walton Bay and later in dock at Liverpool. In 1943 she was attacked by enemy aircraft off Gibraltar but escaped any direct hits. Following the landings in Sicily she took King

Peter of Yugoslavia and his party to Port Said and then sailed to Taranto with troops.

She continued her trooping duties and was part of the last convoy of the war from Gibraltar to the United Kingdom and ended her war service employed on repatriation duties, sailing over 350,000 miles carrying 150,000 men and women of over twenty nationalities. *Reina del Pacifico* returned to her builders at Belfast in January 1947 for a comprehensive overhaul prior to re-entering commercial service again.

By 1939 the fleet of the Pacific Steam Navigation was reduced to only fourteen ships and the Board decided to increase the fleet. However, these plans were put on hold during the years of the Second World War. On 16 January 1941, *Oropesa* was torpedoed by U-96 off Ireland and sank with a loss of 113 lives. *La Paz*, with a cargo of whisky, was attacked and torpedoed by U-109, off the coast of Florida on 1 May the following year. She was beached and later sold to the United States. These were the only war losses of the company during the Second World War.

Orduna was taken over by the Admiralty in 1941 and used as a troopship. Corporal Roy Middleton, 221 Field Coy, Royal Engineers wrote about his voyage from Liverpool to Egypt on her in 1942.

> The company left Liverpool in August on board the RMSP *Orduna*, a decrepit and run-down old liner of the Pacific Steam Navigation Company, formerly on the South America run. This mechanical marvel was shared with, among others, the London Irish Rifles plus their pipe band. We joined up with a large convoy of some 25 ships and destroyer escorts in the Firth of Clyde and set sail, complete with tropical kit and pith helmets and no idea of our destination. Accommodation on board was not luxurious; sixteen men to a mess; that is one table and benches with hooks above to hang sixteen hammocks. Plus, of course, one's kit-bags, etc., which also had to be stored in the area. Meals were collected by Mess orderlies, appointed daily by the NCO i/c Mess (in this case - me), from the galley and dished out at the table. This simple task usually led to strong words and veiled threats, but all was soon forgotten – until the next meal!
>
> There was little to do, apart from life-boat drill, PT, lectures, bingo and sleeping on deck – when we sailed into warmer climes. The first four weeks were spent zig-zagging across the Atlantic until we made landfall at Freetown on the West African coast, where we spent the days sweating in the steamy heat and swearing at the natives trying to sell us their goods from their boats alongside. Two weeks later saw us in Cape Town where the company split up and the sappers went on to Bombay whilst, after two or three days enjoying the hospitality of Cape Towner's, the transport personnel went off to Port Tewfik at the southern end of the Suez Canal. Going ashore at Cape Town was like entering another world – bananas, unseen since 1939, were consumed by the ton, as also were the other foods. A memorable interlude. A further two weeks of sweating it out on the *Orduna* introduced us to the delights of Egypt. We were transported by train to Quassassin to be installed in a very large tented camp in the desert.

On 1 May 1942, *La Paz* was attacked and torpedoed by the German submarine U-109 off Florida. The radio officer, G. V. Monk later reported that after he had transmitted the SOS message one of the Suwanee Fruit Company ships received the distress message and altered course to come to their aid. Two of the lifeboats were lowered on *La Paz* and the remainder of the crew remained on board.

The master thought that there was a distinct possibility of saving the ship and the Suwanee vessel decided that she would take her in tow. When *La Paz* grounded off Cocoa Beach, some twenty-five miles south of Cape Canaveral, the tow stopped. The United States Coast Guard vessel later arrived and the crew of *La Paz* were taken off the vessel and landed at Fort Pierce. The Suwanee ship was owned by William Radford Lovett

SCOUTERS' AND GUIDERS' CRUISE

..TO..

ICELAND, NORWAY, DENMARK and BELGIUM

Commencing from LIVERPOOL
MONDAY, 8th AUGUST, 1938

in the Famous Liner

"ORDUÑA"

R.M.S. "ORDUÑA" (15,507 tons gross register).

Schedule of Accommodation and Fares

THE PACIFIC STEAM NAVIGATION COMPANY

GENERAL NOTES AND REGULATIONS

Conditions. Passengers are accepted under the Conditions and Regulations printed on the Passage Contract, and in accepting the Ticket the passenger agrees to conform to such Conditions and Regulations.

Payment of Fare. A deposit of £5 will secure definite reservation of accommodation, and the balance will be payable not later than *fourteen days* before sailing day.

Passengers cancelling their Booking will be liable to forfeiture of deposit, but no forfeit will be exacted if cancellation is unavoidable and the Company receive timely notice so that accommodation may be re-sold.

Passports will not be required by British passengers making the Round Cruise.

ITINERARY

(Subject to alteration or cancellation with or without notice.)

	ARRIVE			DEPART			Distance (Miles)
LIVERPOOL	..	..	..	Mon. Aug. 8		6 p.m.	—
REYJAVIK (Iceland)	Thur. Aug. 11		8 a.m.	Fri. ,, 12		1 p.m.	923
TRONDHJEM (Norway)	Mon. ,, 15		7 a.m.	Mon. ,, 15		10 p.m.	958
COPENHAGEN (Denmark)	Thurs. ,, 18		8 a.m.	Fri. ,, 19		7 p.m.	749
ANTWERP (Belgium)	Sun. ,, 21		5 p.m.	Mon. ,, 22		7 p.m.	676
DOVER	Tues. ,, 23		7 a.m.	Tues. ,, 23		9 a.m.	136
LIVERPOOL	Thurs. ,, 25		9 a.m.	..	..	..	566

APPLICATIONS FOR ACCOMMODATION
to be sent to :

McGREGOR, GOW & HOLLAND LTD.

20 Billiter Street, London, E.C. 3.

Telegraphic Address : "EASTWARDLY, FEN."   Telephone No. ROYAL 5600.

or

The Pacific Steam Navigation Company

Head Offices : Goree, Water Street, LIVERPOOL, 3

Telegraphic Address : "PACIFIC."   Telephone No. 9150 Bank.

Round Voyages

from LIVERPOOL via France, Spain, BERMUDA, BAHAMAS, HAVANA, JAMAICA, PANAMA CANAL, to Ecuador, PERU and CHILE and back to Liverpool.

Greatly Reduced Fares

TABLE OF DISTANCES.
(Tabla de distancias.)
PANAMA CANAL ROUTE

	Nautical Miles			Nautical Miles	
	Port to Port	From Liverpool		Port to Port	From Liverpool
RPOOL TO OCHELLE-PALLICE	605	605	LA LIBERTAD TO	678	6775
ANDER TO	196	801	PAITA TO	189	6964
NA TO	228	1029	CALLAO TO	515	7479
TO	120	1149	MOLLENDO TO	456	7935
MUDA TO	2698	3847	ARICA TO	132	8067
AU TO	818	4665	IQUIQUE TO	109	8176
ANA TO	381	5046	TOCOPILLA TO	117	8293
OBAL (COLON) TO	1004	6050	ANTOFAGASTA TO	110	8403
OA (PANAMA) TO	47	6097	VALPARAISO	580	8983
			TOTAL MILEAGE		8983

LIST OF PASSENGERS
BOOKED PER
S.S. "OROPESA"
(TWIN SCREW)
SAILING FROM LIVERPOOL
22nd SEPTEMBER, 1938

COMMANDER - - R. E. DUNN, O.B.E.

Chief Engineer: A. W. BARR

Chief Officer: E. F. POTTER

Purser: R. D. CHADWICK

Second Officer: A. LYALL

Assistant Pursers: H. A. G. Jenkins F. R. Shaw R. L. Cartwright

Third Officer: J. Gerety, R.N.R.

Fourth Officer: G. Wallis

Surgeon: A. T. GAILLETON, M.B. Ch.B.

Chief Steward: H. WILLIAMS

The Pacific Steam Navigation Co., Goree, Water Street, Liverpool 3.

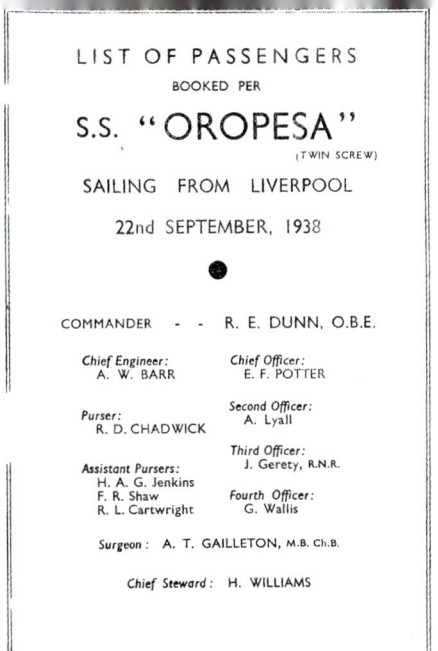

Above: *Oropesa* itinerary, 1938.

Right above: PSCNC centenary advertisement.

Right below: *Orduna* promenade deck.

Above: *Loreta* homeward bound in the Atlantic.

Below: *Lorega* and *Orduna* (I) at Liverpool during the Second World War.

and they placed a $500,000 salvage claim against *La Paz* but this was later withdrawn.

La Paz was later sold at the US Marshall's sale for $10,000 and plans were made to re-float her. After two-and-a-half months, her hull was patched up and as she was being re-floated, she suffered an engine room explosion and sank again. Six months after she was attacked and at a cost of $250,000 she was finally re-floated and towed to Jacksonville. The cargo was later unloaded including $50,000 worth of Black Label Scotch whisky, fine woollens, machinery and plumbing fixtures. The ship was sold to the US War Shipping Administration, and in 1945 to Construction Aggregates of Chicago.

Peter Clowes, who was a writer in the Royal Navy also recalls a voyage on the *Reina Del Pacifico* from Liverpool to Colombo at the end of the war.

At 19.45 on April 15, 1945, we pulled away from the landing stage, being edged into the stream by a couple of tugs, and lay in the middle of the fast flowing Mersey for the night. I joined an informal football match on the after portion of 'E' Deck before going below, queuing with a tin mug for a special ration of grog from the rum boson and slinging my hammock over a lino-topped mess table. There were 'emergency stations' the next morning, each man wearing a blue lifebelt and red safety light, and at 13.00 we steamed down the river with other ships, including several American tankers, before anchoring at New Brighton, for another night.

On April 17 the *Reina del Pacifico* hoisted pennants and steamed out of the Mersey along a line of buoys and past the protruding masts of the cargo ships *Ullapool* and *Tacoma City* which had been sunk by mines earlier in the war. With us was a mixed batch of tankers, cargo steamers, troopships, a destroyer and two frigates, all proceeding in line ahead of the Rock lighthouse abeam and forming two columns when clear of the swept channel. Several more vessels were waiting to join us out to sea.

The *Reina Del Pacifico* formed part of convoy KMF43 which turned to be one of the last escorted convoys to leave the shores of Britain in the Second World War. The destroyers *Escapade* and *Icarus*, the frigates *Loch Katrine* and *Ness*, the sloop *Eme* and the corvette *Oxford Castle* guarded our wings. We steamed at about 13 knots. Morning mist was followed by afternoon sunshine. The escort carrier *Begum*, which had left the Clyde the previous day, joined us. There was a long, steady swell and I swiftly succumbed to a short, sharp bout of sea-sickness. I obtained a couple of tablets from the sick bay and retired early to my swinging hammock.

The fourteen ships being escorted towards the southern Irish coast, then to Gibraltar, were in six columns with a gap of three cables between each ship. The *Reina Del Pacifico* ploughed through calm seas in the fifth column, immediately astern of the *Capetown Castle*, carrying 3,200 men to India. The port or first, column was led by the *Christian Huygens*, followed by the *Lancashire*, carrying 340 troops. Five cables to starboard steamed the liner *Georgic*, with 3,850 troops heading for Malta and Egypt, followed by the *Samaria*, with 3,450 men for Italy and India, with the rescue ship *Straat Soenda* astern. The third column was led by the *Alcantara*, carrying 3,700 troops and airmen to Algeria and Italy with the India bound cargo vessel *Tegelberg* and HMS *Princess Beatrix*, a former Harwich-Hook ferry and veteran of the North Africa landings, astern.

The liner *Orion*, on board which was the convoy commodore, Sir Arthur J. Baxter, led the fourth column, followed by HMS *Begum*, loaded with aircraft and spares for Ceylon. To starboard of the *Reina Del Pacifico* was a column of three, the cargo ships *Ormonde* followed by the *Carthage* and a second rescue ship, the *Clan Chisholm*. On April nineteen several ships in the convoy had a thirty minute exercise for their gun crews, the 40mm Bofors guns on the *Begum* providing the most impressive show. There was some excitement in the early hours of April 22 when the 'River'-class frigate *Ness* dropped a pattern of depth charges at a suspected submarine contact.

The Clyde-based *Escapade* and *Erne* were relieved by two escorts from Gibraltar, *Loch Quoich* and *Evenlode*, on the 20th as the convoy neared the Mediterranean. The corvette *Oxford Castle* also turned north and headed back to Liverpool to refuel. When the Rock of Gibraltar hove in to view, through a giant blanket of haze, most ships in the convoy, and all the escort vessels, steamed into the roadstead. After exchanging signals, Captain J. V. Longford ordered speed to be increased to 15 knots and the *Reina Del Pacifico* headed east, alone, through the Mediterranean.

Sun awnings and canvas air chutes for the engine room were erected. Many of the Navy passengers lolled in the sunshine on 'D' Deck, reading tattered books and magazines from the ship's limited library. We had a medical examination at noon, then washed uniforms with rubbery soap in buckets of sea water and fitted white covers to our caps. I leaned over the bow to watch graceful porpoises keeping pace with the ship which was vibrating considerably as she increased speed.

On April 25 we passed the island of Pantellaria with its high cliffs. There was tombola on 'E' Deck, £15 prize for a full house, but I was unsuccessful. A corvette, name unknown, overtook us during the afternoon and a ship's concert was held in the evening. Captain Longford streamed a smoke float the following morning and gave the RN gunners an hour's practice. The ship zig-zagged to let the Borfors gunners aft have their fair share. Our biggest gun, in the stern, proved to be the most accurate, hitting the target several times at ranges up to two miles. Then rocket-fired crimson parachutes floated in the blue sky as the midships Oerlikon cannons blazed away. Everyone on board was delighted, not least a party of Wrens leaning over the rails on the upper deck.

Later in the week I had to queue for a haircut from a leading stoker in the next mess, but this very painful experience was ameliorated when darkness fell and I clambered onto a lifeboat to watch another concert on the after part of 'E' Deck. Unfortunately, the noise of the overworked ventilation plant made it difficult for many, in the packed audience, who were sitting on lifebelts and perched like monkeys on lifeboats around the deck, to hear what was going on.

There was a commotion on April 27 when fire broke out in the stern galley beneath the Bofors control. Smoke and fumes spread for nearly an hour before members of the crew with fire extinguishers got everything under control. When I went on deck the following day we were steaming slowly past the waterfront of Port Said, taking our place ahead of two other transports in a procession of vessels making their way through the Suez Canal.

Water and fuel boats came alongside when we reached Suez. Egyptian feluccas with high lateen sails arrived to conduct business with fezes, handbags, wallets and belts. Baskets were used to haul the goods to the ship's deck and the lissom, brown merchants, with toes like fingers, climbed their masts to bargain with us. At 6 p.m., however, we weighed anchor and set off down the Red Sea. Black-out restrictions were lifted and everyone was ordered into white tropical rig. I was suddenly appointed mess cook and had to scrub the deck and scrape clean the garbage bins in the sweltering conditions below. There was more laundry work, using sea water, but there were fresh oranges for supper and these made a welcome change from our almost unchanging diet of tinned pilchards.

We were soon in the Arabian Sea and had our first sight of flying fish skimming over the smooth water. There was a film show on 'E' Deck where officers and Wrens danced on the floodlit boat deck. There was another ship's concert on May 7 and at the end we were informed that, to rousing cheers that the end of the war in Europe had just been announced. We sang *Land of Hope and Glory* lustily as the ship sped across the Indian Ocean.

I was scrubbing the mess deck when the *Reina Del Pacifico* passed the breakwaters at the entrance to Colombo harbour at 9 a.m. on May 8, V-E Day. The town of white, red-roofed buildings with a fringe of palm trees behind seemed to be celebrating. The officers, Wrens and Royal Marines disembarked but most of us were confined to the ship and bought pineapples and coconuts from the Sinhalese traders who came alongside in droves. A supply of beer, one bottle per man, was brought on board. As darkness fell at 7.45 Winston Churchill's voice came over the loudspeakers. The *Reina Del Pacifico*'s deep siren joined the shrieks and screams of every other ship in the harbour. Throughout the night searchlights blazed, rockets were fired and flares ignited and the cruiser *Cleopatra* hoisted a mass of fairy lights across her forecastle. I disembarked the following day and went to the Royal Navy's transit camp, HMS *Mayina*, which lay in dense forest a few miles outside Colombo. I never saw *Reina Del Pacifico* again.

Samanco and *Sarmiento* had been delivered to the Pacific Steam Navigation in 1943 during the Second World War. They were built and engined by Harland & Wolff Limited at Belfast. *Santander* and *Salaverry* entered the fleet in 1946 and the smaller vessels *Acajutla* and *Salvador* were sold for further trading, thus ending the transit service through the Panama Canal. *Salinas* was delivered in 1947, *Talca* was purchased and *Lautaro* was sold to the Jenny Steam Ship Company of London. The last of the 'S' class, *Salamanca* was delivered in 1948 and *Lagarto* was sold to be broken up at Troon. Completion of the *Salamanca* marked the end of oil-engined ships as the next additions to the fleet had steam turbine machinery. A comparison of the engine installations in ships of the 'L' and 'S' classes shows how much progress was made in the design and efficiency of the oil engine. The older vessels had single-acting four-stroke machinery and twin-screws. The 'S' class ships has a single-screw installation of double-acting two-stroke design which gave them a service speed of 15 knots compared to the 10 knots of the older vessels.

Salamanca.

Right: Captain Bryant of the *Salamanca*.

Below: *Salamanca*, cabin.

On 11 September 1947, the *Reina Del Pacifico* was undergoing trials, about seven miles noth-east of Copeland Island, after a major refit by Harland & Wolff, when an engine explosion occurred in the main engine room due to overheating of pistons and cylinders. Twenty-eight people lost their lives in the incident including Leonard Septimus Brew, the Victoria Works Manager for Harland & Wolff.

Orbita was sold for scrapping in 1950 and the Board decided to buy two vessels on the stocks from the Clan Line. They were named *Kenuta* and *Flamenco*. Both vessels were built by the Greenock Dockyard Company Limited with a single-screw installation of single reduction

54 PACIFIC STEAM NAVIGATION CO.

s.s. "REINA DEL MAR" - SAILINGS 1961

OUTWARD VOYAGES

IVERPOOL	29th Dec., 1960	LIVERPOOL	17th Mar.		2nd June		11th Aug.		20th Oct.	
A PALLICE	31st ,,	LA PALLICE	19th ,,		4th ,,		13th ,,		22nd ,,	
ANTANDER	1st Jan., 1961	SANTANDER	20th ,,		5th ,,		14th ,,		23rd ,,	
IGO	2nd ,,	VIGO	21st ,,		6th ,,		15th ,,		24th ,,	
AS PALMAS	5th ,,	LA GUAIRA	30th ,,		15th ,,		24th ,,		2nd Nov.	
ARTINIQUE	12th ,,	CURACAO	31st ,,		16th ,,		25th ,,		3rd ,,	
ARBADOS	13th ,,	CARTAGENA	1st April		17th ,,		26th ,,		4th ,,	
RINIDAD	14th ,,	CRISTOBAL	2/3rd ,,		18/19th ,,		27/28th ,,		5/6th ,,	
A GUAIRA	15th ,,	†LA LIBERTAD	5th ,,		21st ,,		30th ,,		8th ,,	
ARTAGENA	17th ,,	CALLAO	7/8th ,,		23/24th ,,		1/2nd Sept.		10/11th ,,	
RISTOBAL	18/19th ,,	ARICA	10th ,,		26th ,,		4th ,,		13th ,,	
A LIBERTAD	21st ,,	ANTOFAGASTA	11th ,,		27th ,,		5th ,,		14th ,,	
ALLAO	23/24th ,,	VALPARAISO	13th ,,		29th ,,		7th ,,		16th ,,	
RICA	26th ,,									
NTOFAGASTA	27th ,,									
ALPARAISO	29th ,,									

HOMEWARD VOYAGES

ALPARAISO	2nd Feb., 1961	VALPARAISO	16th April	2nd July		10th Sept.		19th Nov.	
NTOFAGASTA	4th ,,	ANTOFAGASTA	18th ,,	4th ,,		12th ,,		21st ,,	
RICA	5th ,,	ARICA	19th ,,	5th ,,		13th ,,		22nd ,,	
ALLAO	7th ,,	CALLAO	21st ,,	7th ,,		15th ,,		24th ,,	
A LIBERTAD	9th ,,	†LA LIBERTAD	23rd ,,	9th ,,		17th ,,		26th ,,	
ALBOA	11/12th ,,	BALBOA	25/26th ,,	11/12th ,,		19/20th ,,		28/29th ,,	
ARTAGENA	13th ,,	CARTAGENA	27th ,,	13th ,,		21st ,,		30th ,,	
URACAO	14th ,,	CURACAO	28th ,,	14th ,,		22nd ,,		1st Dec.	
INGSTON	17th ,,	LA GUAIRA	29th ,,	15th ,,		23rd ,,		2nd ,,	
ERMUDA	20th ,,	VIGO	8th May	24th ,,		2nd Oct.		11th ,,	
IGO	27th ,,	SANTANDER	9th ,,	25th ,,		3rd ,,		12th ,,	
ANTANDER	28th ,,	†LA PALLICE	10th ,,	26th ,,		4th ,,		13th ,,	
A PALLICE	1st Mar.	†PLYMOUTH	11th ,,						
LYMOUTH	2nd ,,	LIVERPOOL	12th ,,	28th ,,		6th ,,		15th ,,	
IVERPOOL	3rd ,,								

† No time for transit passengers to go ashore.

AILINGS ARE SUBJECT TO CANCELLATION OR ALTERATION

The Pacific Steam Navigation Company

Pacific Building
James Street
Liverpool 2
Telephone 051 CENtral
Telegrams 'Pacific'

London Agents—Royal Mail Lines Ltd., Royal Mail House, Leadenhall Street, E.C.3

BERMUDA BAHAMAS CUBA COLOMBIA ECUADOR PERU CHI

Cargo is accepted for

BERMUDA	COLOMBIA	PERU	Puerto Chicama	CHILE	San Antonio
Hamilton	Buenaventura	Talara	Salaverry	Arica	Talcahuano
BAHAMAS	ECUADOR	Paita	Samanco	Iquique	Corral
Nassau	Manta	Pimentel	Callao	Tocopilla	Ancud
Freeport	La Libertad	Eten	Pisco	Antofagasta	Puerto Montt
CUBA	Guayaquil	Pacasmayo	Matarani	Chanaral	Castro
Havana			Mollendo	Coquimbo	Puerto Chaca
			Ilo	Valparaiso	Punta Arenas

and other ports by special arrangement

Vessel	Sailing	Accepting cargo for direct delivery at the undermentioned ports. Dates of arrival are indicated in brackets after main ports.
S.S. Pizarro ‡ø	Hull Wed 13 Feb London Thu 21 Feb	Buenaventura (24 Mar), Guayaquil, Callao (1 Apr) Matarani, Arica, Antofagasta, Valparaiso (11 Apr), San Antonio, Talcahuano (with inducement) (with liberty to call at Hamilton, Nassau, Freeport, Santo Domingo, Port-au-Prince, Cristobal)
M.V. Cienfuegos ‡	London Wed 13 Feb Liverpool Fri 22 Feb	Callao (16 Mar), Antofagasta, Valparaiso (25 Mar), San Antonio, Talcahuano (with liberty to call at Santo Domingo)
M.V. Paraguay	Glasgow Tue 26 Feb Liverpool Tue 5 Mar	Hamilton, Nassau, Buenaventura (28 Mar), Guayaquil, Paita, Huacho, Callao (6 Apr), Pisco, Matarani, Arica, Antofagasta, Valparaiso (16 Apr) Talcahuano, Ancud
M.V. Salinas ø	Hull Sat 9 Mar London Thu 14 Mar	Buenaventura (14 Apr), Guayaquil, Callao (22 Apr), Matarani, Arica, Antofagasta, Valparaiso (2 May), San Antonio, Talcahuano (with inducen (with liberty to call at Hamilton, Nassau, Freeport, Santo Domingo, Port-au-Prince, Cristobal)
M.V. Eleuthera ‡	London Wed 6 Mar Antwerp Fri 8 Mar Liverpool Fri 15 Mar	Callao (7 Apr), Valparaiso (16 Apr), San Antonio, Talcahuano, Castro, Pto. Chacabuco, Punta Arenas (23 Apr) (with liberty to call at Santo Dom
S.S. Reina del Mar *	Liverpool Wed 20 Mar La Pallice Fri 22 Mar Santander Sat 23 Mar Vigo Sun 24 Mar	Callao (9 Apr), Antofagasta, Valparaiso (14 Apr) (with liberty to call at Trinidad, LaGuaira, Curacao, Cartagena, Arica, San Antonio
M.V. Ebro ‡ø	Liverpool Sat 23 Mar	Hamilton, Nassau, Buenaventura (14 Apr), Guayaquil, Paita, Callao (22 A Matarani, Arica, Antofagasta, Valparaiso (2 May), San Antonio, Talcahu (with inducement)
M.V. Santander ‡ø	Hull Thu 21 Mar Antwerp Sat 23 Mar London Wed 27 Mar Liverpool Fri 5 Apr	Callao (27 Apr), Valparaiso (6 May), San Antonio, Talcahuano (with liberty to call at Santo Domingo)

‡Refrigerated space available   *First, Cabin & Tourist Class Passengers   øSuperior Accommodation for limited number of Pass
All sailings subject to cancellation or modification
Nothing herein contained shall have effect so as to deprive the Company of any powers, rights, liberties or immunities cor on the Company by any Bill of Lading or Passage Ticket issued by it for any of the above-mentioned voyages, and Sh and Passengers should particularly note the wide liberties permitted to the Company in respect of the route.

Loading berths: Liverpool
North Side
Canada Branch Dock No. 1

Shipping Notes must be initialled
before cargo is sent down to quay

Agents addresses overleaf

Receiving and closing dates on application

5th February 1963   O.F

Above left: Potosi.

Above right: Cuzco.

Right: Pizarro.

Above: Cotopaxi.

Left: Cotopaxi.

Woodside Ferry Terminal, 1954, with *Reina Del Pacifico* behind.

geared turbines manufactured by Parsons Marine Steam Turbine Company Limited. *Orduna*, *Loreto* and *Loriga* were broken up the following year and *Cuzco* joined the fleet. She had been built by Blyth Dry Dock & Shipbuilding Company Limited and was another vessel that the company purchased on the stocks. She had been laid down as *Thurland Castle* for the Lancashire Shipping Company Limited of Liverpool. Her machinery was provided by Parsons and she proved to be one of the most economical ships in the company's fleet.

Lobos, *Laguna* and *Losada* went to the ship breakers in 1952 and the crown at the centre of the house flag reverted from St Edward's to the Royal Crown that year. The following year the company sold the Liberty ship *Talca* to Cia Naveira Aris SA, Puerto Limon of Costa Rica. *Cotopaxi* was delivered by William Denny & Brothers Limited in April 1954 and *Potosi* and *Pizarro* were completed by the Greenock Dockyard Company during 1955. *Cotopaxi*, *Potosi* and *Pizarro* were turbine steamers and had accommodation for twelve passengers in first-class accommodation. Also in 1955, the company took on a bareboat time charter of two modern motor ships, the *Afric* and the *Scycamore* to supplement the 'Island' services to the West Indies and Bermuda. They were renamed *Albemarle* and *Walsingham* and allowed the larger ships to be routed, as and when cargo commitments allowed, direct to the West Coast.

Samanco was sold to Deutsche Dampschiff 'Hansa' in 1956 and renamed *Reichenfels* and the passenger vessel *Reina del Mar* was completed by Harland & Wolff at Belfast. She was built to operate with the *Reina del Pacifico*, with each ship making five round voyages a year, in regular service from the United Kingdom, France and Spain, to Bermuda, the Bahamas, Cuba, Jamaica, Panama, Colombia, Ecuador, Peru and Chile.

Reina del Mar was designed with four complete steel decks, also lower deck forward and aft of machinery space, tunnel deck aft, promenade, boat and navigating bridge decks. Her hull was divided into eleven compartments by ten watertight bulkheads. A double bottom, also divided was fitted fore and aft and arranged for the carriage of fresh water, water ballast, oil fuel and lubricating oil with the fore and aft peaks also arranged for fresh water or water ballast. Deep tanks were arranged immediately forward and aft of the machinery space, the forward tanks to carry oil fuel and the after tanks to carry fresh water. She was fitted with five cargo holds, three forward and two aft of the machinery space with lower 'tween decks at all except No. 5 hold. A special cargo compartment was arranged in No. 3 lower 'tween decks and insulated cargo spaces fitted in No. 4 tunnel and lower 'tween decks.

Her cargo handling equipment consisted of four 10-ton and thirteen 5-ton tubular steel derricks, also ten electric cargo winches. Insulated

Above: *Kenuta* (II) in the Panama Canal.

Below: *Kenuta* (II) unloading a circus at Callao in 1962, following a voyage from Peru to Chile.

Above: *Kenuta* (II) in the Mersey on 21 July 1951.

Below: *Journal of Commerce* advertisement, October 1955.

P. S. N. C.

BERMUDA, BAHAMAS, CUBA, COLOMBIA, ECUADOR, PERU & CHIL

		RECEIVING FROM	SAILI
m.v. TILIA GORTHON —For HAM'TON, NASSAU, HAVANA and SANTIAGO DE CUBA (with option to tranship at Havana)	Liverpool	17 Oct.	28 O
m.v. SALAVERRY — For BUENAV'TURA, LA LIBERTAD, GUAYAQUIL (Puna), LOBITOS, PAITA, CALLAO, M'LENDO, ARICA, TOCOPILLA, ANTOFAGASTA, VALPARAISO, SAN ANTONIO	Liverpool	14 Oct.	1 No
m.v. SAMANCO —For B'VENTURA, GUAYAQUIL (Puna), CALLAO, M'LENDO, ARICA, AN'FAGASTA, V'PARAISO, SAN ANTONIO	London ... ... Antwerp...	on application on application	5 No 7 No
s.s. CUZCO — For B'VENTURA, GU'AQUIL (Puna), CALLAO, MOLLENDO, ARICA, AN'FAGASTA, V'PARAISO, SAN ANTONIO	Liverpool	31 Oct.	18 No
m.v. WALSINGHAM — For BERMUDA, NASSAU, HAVANA and SANTIAGO DE CUBA (with option to tranship at Havana)	Liverpool	31 Oct.	18 No

Liverpool Loading Berth: N.E. No. 1 Canada Dock

THE PACIFIC STEAM NAVIGATION CO.
PACIFIC BUILDING, JAMES STREET, LIVERPOOL, 2

LONDON: McGregor, Gow & Holland, Ltd., 16, St. Helen's Place, E.C.3 GLASGOW: Hould
Bros. & Co. (Glasgow), Ltd., 19, St. Vincent Place.   BIRMINGHAM: Royal Mail Lines, Lt
2, Calthorpe Road, Five Ways.   MANCHESTER: Royal Mail Lines, Ltd., 22, St. Ann's Squa

spaces included thirteen refrigerated chambers, on the lower deck abaft the machinery room, for the carriage of several foodstuffs for ships use; these were fitted with galvanised mild steel perforated shelving, trays and racks for the storage of various cargo. An electric windlass was fitted forward and two electric capstans aft. Her steering gear was electro-hydraulic 2-motor 4-ram type, and each power unit was capable of moving the rudder from hard-a-port in thirty seconds at full speed. She was also fitted with the latest Denny-Brown stabilisers to minimise the rolling in bad weather.

First-class accommodation provided for 207 persons in single and two berth rooms on 'C' and 'D' decks including fourteen special two-berth rooms with all rooms having their own private toilet and bath, hip bath or shower with hot and cold running water. On 'D' deck there were six deluxe cabins each with a private shower, and capable of conversion into a sitting room to form a suite when required. Each of these cabins was decorated in the theme of one of the countries served by the vessel.

Accommodation for the 216 cabin-class passengers was provided in single, two and three berth rooms. The walls in the first and cabin class accommodation were panelled in light coloured wood veneers. The 343 tourist-class passengers were accommodated in single, two, three, four and six-berth rooms on 'A' and 'B' decks. The first-class public rooms consisted of a restaurant seating 218 people, lounge, library, writing room, card room, cocktail bar and smoke room.

Reina del Mar was also fitted with an open air swimming pool with adjacent lido cafe, covered veranda promenade and open promenade, sports deck, veranda abaft sports deck, hairdressing saloons, shop and arcade, money exchange and inquiry office and children's dining saloon, play room, play deck and paddling pool. The bulkhead in the restaurant was panelled in French-figured birch, Australian walnut, burry ash and sycamore. A large mural depicting scenes on the route was at the forward end of the restaurant and the musician's gallery faced the mural. On 'D' deck there was a number of deluxe cabins with twin beds and private bathrooms and fourteen specially decorated cabins on 'D' and 'C' decks. She sailed on her maiden voyage on 3 May 1956 from Liverpool to Valparaiso via the Panama Canal.

In January 1957, Brian Shaw was appointed as a graduate trainee with the Pacific Steam Navigation Company. He began his career in Liverpool and the following year he was appointed as the company's agent on the Pacific coast of South America. By 1960 he had the foresight to see the threat to passenger ships posed by the increase in air travel at the time and recommended that the *Reina del Mar* be redeployed as a cruise ship.

Shaw was appointed as chairman of the Shaw Savill Line in 1973 and was responsible for the development of the consortium of British shipping companies and the transfer of cargo from conventional vessels to the carriage of containers in specially designed vessels and the development of new container facilities at ports. He was appointed chairman of the Furness Withy Group from 1979, chairman of the Council of European and Japanese National Ship Owners' Associations from 1979 to 1984, the president of the General Council of British Shipping from 1985 to 1986 and chairman of the International Chamber of Shipping from 1987 to 1992. He was knighted in 1986 and was admitted as an Elder Brother of Trinity House in 1989, becoming chairman of the Port of London Authority from 1993 to 2000. He died on 5 February 2011.

In 1957 *Albemarle* and *Walsingham* were returned to the Furness Group. On 8 July 1957 *Reina del Pacifico* was leaving Bermuda after being at anchor in Grassy Bay off Hamilton and she went aground in the Outer Channel. The ship took on a list, which fortunately decreased as the tide was rising. The tugs, *Bermudian*, and *Justice* and the US coastguard cutter *Castlerock*, took lines from the ship's stern and attempted to tow the ship from the sandbank. The line attached to the Coastguard cutter

TABLE OF DISTANCES
PANAMA CANAL ROUTE

	NAUTICAL MILES	
	Port to Port	From Liverpool
LIVERPOOL		
CRISTOBAL, C.Z.	5178	5178
BALBOA, C.Z.	47	5225
BUENAVENTURA	359	5584
LA LIBERTAD, EC.	678	6262
GUAYAQUIL	164	6426
PAITA	189	6615
CALLAO	515	7130
MOLLENDO	456	7586
ARICA	132	7718
IQUIQUE	109	7827
TOCOPILLA	117	7944
ANTOFAGASTA	110	8054
VALPARAISO	580	8634

ALL PARTICULARS ON APPLICATION

THE PACIFIC STEAM NAVIGATION CO.

HEAD OFFICE
PACIFIC BUILDING, JAMES ST. LIVERPOOL
Telephone CENtral 9231   Cables "PACIFIC, LIVERPOOL"

Offices
THE ISTHMUS OF PANAMA
CRISTOBAL, C.Z.
REPUBLIC OF PERU
CALLAO   LIMA
REPUBLIC OF CHILE
VALPARAISO   SANTIAGO   ANTOFAGASTA

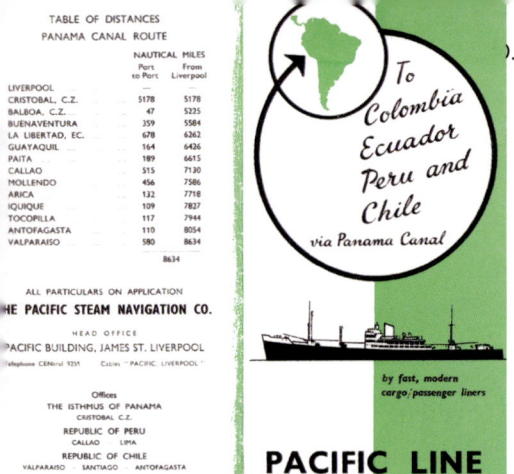

To Colombia Ecuador Peru and Chile via Panama Canal

by fast, modern cargo/passenger liners

PACIFIC LINE

S.S. 'CHILE' 1840

"During the summer of 1840, while the public attention was focussed on the North Atlantic steamship crossing, two small wooden paddle steamers quietly left the Thames on a 10,000 miles' voyage to the West Coast of South America. These pioneer ships established an undertaking which has exercised a remarkable influence in promoting the commercial development of half a continent."

This is an extract from the book "Steam Conquers The Pacific" by Arthur C. Wardle. It is reprinted here to show that for over a century this Company have been leaders in the field of navigation, and are proud to have kept their place in offering the finest of facilities to passengers and the world of commerce, in their transport requirements to and from the West Coast of South America.

Accommodation is provided in each ship for twelve passengers. This limitation ensures a pleasant atmosphere and a happy party spirit for the duration of the voyage. Apart from the 'S' Class vessels, all cabins have private bathrooms with toilet etc., the majority of the "S" vessels having private toilet and shower and in some cases, bath. In all ships there are cabins with inter-communicating doors, which can be had en suite. The public rooms are decorated to meet the most discerning tastes. The service and comfort distinguish the Pacific Line's wish to please its passengers. P.S.N.C. cargo/passenger liners are famous for the commodious deck-space available for recreation. Games, rugs and cushioned deck-chairs are provided without charge. Doctors, State Registered Nurses or Stewardesses are carried as required.

All these vessels are fine modern dual-purpose cargo/passenger liners. All cabins are outside rooms and the passenger accommodation has been carefully designed to appeal to those who require the elegance and comfort of the first class passenger liner combined with the quiet and restfulness of a modern cargo/passenger vessel.

All ships are equipped with the latest navigational devices, including Radar. A modern system of ventilation is installed in the passenger accommodation, and s.s. "Potosi," s.s. "Pizarro" and s.s. "Cotopaxi" are air-conditioned throughout.

PACIFIC LINE MAKE TRAVELLING TIME HOLIDAY TIME

S.S. 'PIZARRO' 1955

Total Round Voyage Fares

"SANTANDER"   **"SALAVERRY"**
(8,549 tons)   (8,544 tons)

"SALINAS"   **"SALAMANCA"**
(8,610 tons)   (8,610 tons)

(a) Berth in cabin for two
    (without private bath
    or shower)   ... £320 0 0

(b) Single berth cabin
    (without private bath
    or shower)   ... £355 0 0

(c) Berth in cabin for two
    (with private bath
    and toilet)   ... £375 0 0

(d) Single berth cabin
    (with private *shower*
    and toilet)   ... £385 0 0

★

"KENUTA"   **"FLAMENCO"**
(8,494 tons)   (8,491 tons)

"CUZCO" (8,038 tons)

(All cabins with private bath and toilet)

(a) Berth in cabin for two... £375 0 0
(b) Single berth cabin   ... £385 0 0

AIR CONDITIONED VESSELS

"PIZARRO"   **"POTOSI"**
(8,564 tons)   (8,564 tons)

"COTOPAXI" (8,559 tons)

(All cabins with private bath and toilet)

(a) Berth in cabin for two... £410
(b) Single berth cabin   ... £420

★

All the rates quoted provide for use of ship as hotel throughout, including during the turn-round in Chilean waters, taxes and any necessary launch and tender charges between ship and shore at ports of call.

Accommodation may only be termed "Secured" upon payment of 20% of passage money.

★

Fast, Modern Cargo/Passenger Liners

PSNC Cargo and Passenger Liners Brochure.

Accommodation Plans

S.S. 'KENUTA', S.S. 'FLAMENCO', S.S. 'COTOPAXI' S.S. 'POTOSI' and S.S. 'PIZARRO'

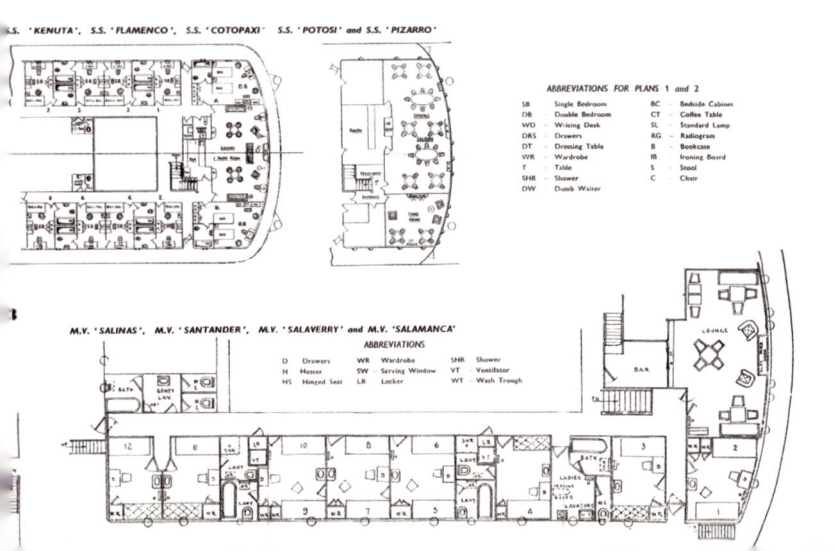

ABBREVIATIONS FOR PLANS 1 and 2

SB	Single Bedroom	BC	Bedside Cabinet
DB	Double Bedroom	CT	Coffee Table
WD	Writing Desk	SL	Standard Lamp
DRS	Drawers	RG	Radiogram
DT	Dressing Table	B	Bookcase
WR	Wardrobe	IB	Ironing Board
T	Table	S	Stool
SHR	Shower	C	Chair
DW	Dumb Waiter		

M.V. 'SALINAS', M.V. 'SANTANDER', M.V. 'SALAVERRY' and M.V. 'SALAMANCA'

ABBREVIATIONS

D	Drawers	WR	Wardrobe	SHR	Shower
H	Hanger	SW	Serving Window	VT	Ventilator
HS	Hinged Seat	LR	Locker	WT	Wash Trough

Left above: Artist's impression of the 'new' *Reina Del Mar*.

Left below: *Reina Del Mar* leaves Liverpool on her maiden voyage on 3 May 1956.

Right above: *Reina Del Mar*.

62 PACIFIC STEAM NAVIGATION CO.

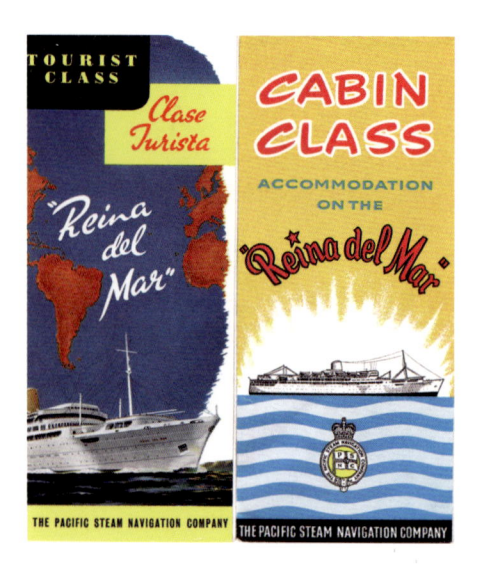

PSNC advertisements.

PACIFIC STEAM NAVIGATION CO. 63

Above: PSNC roundel.

Right: Bon Voyage on *Reina Del Mar*.

Above: Scottish dancing on *Reina Del Mar*.

Below: *Reina Del Mar*, First Class Lounge.

Right above: *Reina Del Mar*, First Class double cabin.

Right below: *Reina Del Mar* in the Panama Canal.

snapped and at low tide the ship was listing at nearly thirty degrees and the attempt was abandoned.

The ferry *Chauncey M. Depew* took passengers to Hamilton over the next few days and another unsuccessful attempt was made to re-float the vessel by lightening its load and removing some cargo from the forward holds onto barges. On the fourth day another attempt was made to re-float the ship. Passengers were taken aboard the *Chauncey M Depew* and the two Bermudian tugs, *Justice* and *Bermudian* attached lines to the ship and the *Topmast* 16, a salvage ship which was working on a wreck nearby, also assisted. The attempt was successful and the *Reina del Pacifico* was towed back to Grassy Bay where her hull was inspected and she was declared seaworthy. The cargo was reloaded back onto the vessel and she left Bermuda six days late for the voyage back to the United Kingdom. Her call at Plymouth was cancelled and she proceeded to Liverpool after calling at Vigo, Corruna and La Pallice.

On the following voyage she developed generator problems in the Irish Sea and was diverted to Milford Haven. After inspection the voyage was cancelled and she proceeded back to Liverpool for repairs. In November, that year she lost her inner starboard propeller at Havana and a replacement was sent out to her on *Salinas*. *Reina del Pacifico* left Liverpool on her last voyage on 27 April the following year and on her return, she was withdrawn from service. She was sold to the British Iron & Steel Corporation and was broken up at Newport. *Sea Breezes* reported that 'People swarmed to see the huge liner *Reina del Pacifico* pass under Newport's famous transporter bridge over the River Usk, on her way to the breaker's yard'.

Above: *Reina Del Mar* at Valparaiso.

Below: *Reina Del Mar* in the Panama Canal.

Cienfuegos, *Eleuthera* and *Somer's Isle* were delivered in 1959 replacing *Albermarle* and *Walsingham* on the Bermuda, Caribbean Ports and Panama service. H. Leslie Bowes was appointed chairman of the company, moving to the same role in the Royal Mail Line the following year. A tanker named after the founder, William Wheelwright, was delivered in 1960 and she was placed on long-term charter to Shell Tankers. The following year another tanker, *George Peacock*, joined the fleet and was placed on charter to British Petroleum. When the United States withdrew diplomatic recognition of the Cuban government on 3 January 1961 economic sanctions were introduced which affected the company's trade with that country.

Below: *Somers Isle*.

Below right: Launch of *William Wheelwright* at Belfast.

Below far right: *William Wheelwright* is handed over to PSNC by Harland & Wolff.

At the beginning of December 1960, Eric Shipton, a well-known Everest explorer arrived in Punta Arenas to lead an expedition, consisting of himself and three other mountaineers across the Patagonian Ice Cap from the Rio Baker Inlet in Chile to Lago Argentino on the Argentine side of the Andean range, a trek of two month's duration. The starting point on the Baker inlet was some 600 miles north of Punta Arenas and sixty miles east of the usual track of steamers proceeding through the Patagonian Channels from this last point to Valparaiso, a most isolated spot. To reach the starting point, Shipton enlisted the help of the Chilean Navy who transported the party in the frigate *Covadonga* and diverted it up the inlet to land him.

However, it was discovered that the *Covadonga* was forced to leave Punta Arenas the day before the Pacific Steam Navigation vessel *Salaverry* was due to arrive. *Salaverry* had on board four cases of Shipton's equipment

PACIFIC STEAM NAVIGATION CO. 67

Left: Captain's dayroom and office on *William Wheelwright*.

Below, below left: Launch of *George Peacock* on 17 March 1961.

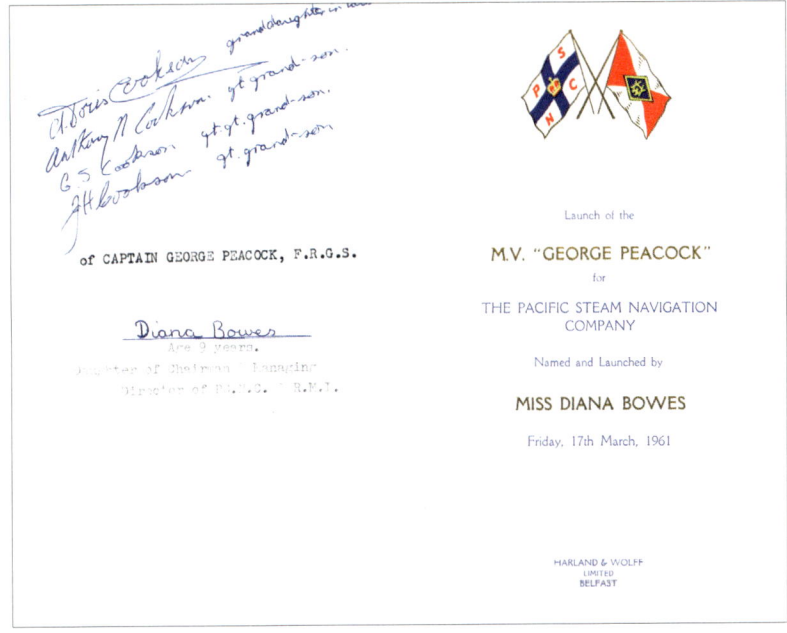

Above: *Salaverry*.

Below: Launch of *Coloso* at Aberdeen.

Right: *William Wheelwright* in Liverpool Docks.

and stores for the expedition, without which it would have been impossible to proceed. The Chilean Navy told Shipton that the sailing could not be delayed and that the next opportunity would be in three month's time, by which time it would be too late, as the expedition could not be completed before winter set in.

The Commander of *Covadonga* offered to rendezvous with *Salaverry* in the Patagonia Channels, subject to approval by the customs authorities and her Captain, R. K. C. Thomas. Thanks to a local amateur radio enthusiast, Captain Thomas was contacted and arranged to anchor in a cove known as Port Eden, where there was a small meteorological station manned by two sergeants from the Chilean Air Force. However, it was discovered that two of the cases were too large to be lowered into a lifeboat and it was agreed to open them and *Salaverry*'s crew made them up into twenty-seven small parcels. The cargo was then transferred to the care of the two sergeants who looked after them until *Covadonga* arrived at the isolated spot. Consequently it was thanks to the Chilean Navy and the Pacific Steam Navigation that the expedition across the Patagonian Ice Cap actually took place.

To celebrate Commonwealth Technical Training Week, from 29 May to 3 June 1961, the Employers Association of the Port of Liverpool agreed with the civic authorities to organise an exhibition on shipping and it was staged at the Market Hall of the Liverpool Cotton Exchange. Amongst those who held stands were the City of Liverpool Education Department, the Shipping Federation, the Mersey Docks & Harbour Board, the training ships *Indefatigable* and *Conway*, the Royal Navy and a number of leading shipping companies, including the Royal Mail Lines and the Pacific Steam Navigation Company. The Company's stand contained details of the principal routes upon which the vessels were engaged, together with photographs of apprentices, boys, etc. undergoing training at sea, and the facilities and accommodation aboard vessels for their work and play. The PSNC stand also included photographs of officers who had risen to positions of responsibility at a comparatively early age.

Mr J. J. Gawne was appointed Managing Director of the Company on 1 April 1963. His career began in the Secretarial Department in 1934 and after experience in the Freight and Accountant's Departments he joined the Royal Army Ordnance Corps on the outbreak of the Second World War. On demobilisation he rejoined the Secretarial Department and became Assistant Secretary in 1947. He was a Fellow of the Chartered Institute of Secretaries from 1952 and became Treasurer of the Liverpool and District Council of the Institute in 1955, and about the same time Chairman of the Education Advisory Committee of the Liverpool Chamber of Commerce. In 1953 he succeeded Mr T. T. Ford as Secretary of the Company. In 1957, Mr Gawne became Assistant Manager whilst continuing as Secretary. In 1959, he moved to London as Manager of Royal Mail Lines. In 1960, on becoming a Director of both companies, he relinquished the PSNC Secretaryship. In October of the same year, he returned to Liverpool, taking charge of the direction of the Company's affairs in the following January after the retirement of Mr A. E. Molyneux. In 1961, Mr Gawne was appointed by the President of Chile as Honorary Consul for that Country in Liverpool.

The death occurred on the 20 May 1963, of Mr Walter Curry Warwick who was, from July 1944 until 30 June 1960, Chairman of Royal Mail Lines and the Pacific Steam Navigation Company. His long and successful career in shipping began in 1896 when, at the age of eighteen, he joined Furness Withy & Company and soon became secretary to Sir Christopher Furness. His first directorship came in 1900 and by 1911 he was managing director of Houlder Brothers, of which company he was Chairman from 1941 to 1961. Mr Warwick joined the Board of Directors of Royal Mail Lines in August 1932, under Lord Essendon whom he succeeded, in 1944, as Chairman of Royal Mail Lines and of The Pacific Steam Navigation Company.

The ordeal of taking a ship through a hurricane was related by the Chief Officer of the *Pizarro* early in 1964. Ray Davies told a reporter from the Royal Gazette in Bermuda that the ship's radio had received a report that Hurricane Flora was moving in a north-easterly direction and Captain G. E. Turner, master of the *Pizarro*, accordingly plotted a westerly course which would take the vessel clear of the Hurricane, known to be the worst in this area for many years. The hurricane had changed its course several times venting her fury on such Islands as Haiti, Cuba and Tobago.

Instead of continuing on a north-easterly course, the hurricane suddenly went due north, as if her target was the *Pizarro* and the winds got worse and worse and were eventually up to 100 miles an hour. Hours later the ship entered the eye of the hurricane and while the winds were calmer the swell was very bad and the ship was buffeted around with waves of between 60 and 70 feet high coming over the funnel. When the vessel came out on the other side of the storm the winds were just as bad and the captain ordered that they turned into the wind and heave to.

Chief Officer Davies said that the ship stood up to the ordeal remarkably well and she rode out the hurricane. However, the twelve passengers were unable to lie down in their bunks and were forced to stand in the alleyways holding on to the rails either side so that they would not be hurt as the ship rolled and pitched. An eighty-two-year-old passenger was strapped down in her bunk to prevent her from falling. It took *Pizarro* over twelve

MEDITERRANEAN CRUISE
BY "REINA DEL MAR" August 1963.

PORT	MILES	ARRIVE	DEPART	HOURS IN PORT
LIVERPOOL	—	—	Saturday 3rd August 4 p.m.	—
LA CORUNA	682	Monday 5th August 8 a.m.	Monday 5th August 4 p.m.	8
NAPLES	1593	Friday 9th August 10 a.m.	Saturday 10th August Midnight	38
VILLEFRANCHE	386	Monday 12th August 6 a.m.	Tuesday 13th August 6 p.m.	36
LISBON	1069	Friday 16th August 8 a.m.	Friday 16th August 8 p.m.	12
LIVERPOOL	1021	Monday 19th August 9 a.m.	—	—

FIRST CLASS FARE TARIFF

Deck	Group	Type of Accommodation	Cabin Numbers	Fare per Adult
B	1	OUTSIDE FOUR-BERTH CABINS	325/8; 355/8	£96
B & C	2	INSIDE THREE-BERTH CABINS	314/6; 370/2 203/5, 206/8; 215/7; 218/20; 228/30; 241/3 268/70; 283/5; 293/5; 296/8; 305/7; 308/10	112
B	3	OUTSIDE THREE-BERTH CABINS	373/5; 329/31; 340/2; 352/4; 367/9	120
B	4	INSIDE TWO-BERTH CABINS	317/8; 319/20; 321/2; 323/4; 332/3; 334/5; 336/7; 338/9; 344/5; 346/7; 348/9; 350/1; 359/60; 361/2; 363/4; 365/6	120
C	5	OUTSIDE TWO-BERTH CABINS	224/5; 279/80; 288/90	128
C	6	INSIDE TWO-BEDDED CABINS	244/5; 246/7; 254/5; 256/7; 264/5; 266/7	128
C	7	OUTSIDE TWO-BEDDED CABINS	201/2; 209/10; 213/4; 222/1/2; 226/7; 231/2; 233/4; 235/6 237/8; 248/9; 252/3; 258/9; 262/3; 273/4; 275/6; 277/8; 281/2; 286/7; 291/2; 299/300; 303/4; 311/2	136
B & C	8	OUTSIDE SINGLE CABINS	343 200; 211; 212; 223; 239; 240; 250; 251 260; 261; 271; 272; 290; 301; 302; 313	144
C	9	OUTSIDE TWO-BEDDED CABINS (With Private Shower and Toilet)	116; 122; 124 111; 119; 121; 127; 129; 135; 143; 145; 151	184
C & D	10	OUTSIDE TWO-BEDDED CABINS (With Private Bath and Toilet)	128; 109; 153 12; 14; 16; 18; 20; 22; 68 11; 15; 17; 19; 21; 23; 25; 69	200
D	11	DE LUXE OUTSIDE TWO-BEDDED CABINS (With Private Bath and Toilet)	52; 54; 56; 58; 60 53; 55; 57; 59; 61	216
C	12	DE LUXE OUTSIDE TWO-BEDDED CABINS (With Private Bath and Toilet)	110; 112; 114; 130; 132; 134; 136; 138; 140 137; 139; 155; 157; 159; 161; 163	232
D	14	SUITES DE LUXE FOR TWO PERSONS OUTSIDE TWO-BEDDED CABIN AND SITTING ROOM (With Private Bath and Toilet)	50; 51	288
C & D	15	INSIDE SINGLE CABINS (With Private Shower and Toilet)	118; 120; 126; 115; 117; 123; 125; 131; 133; 141; 147; 149 28; 30; 36; 38; 64; 29; 31; 37; 39; 65	176
D	16	OUTSIDE SINGLE CABINS (With Private Shower and Toilet)	10; 26; 32; 34; 40; 42; 62 27; 33; 35; 41; 43; 63	192
D	17	OUTSIDE SINGLE CABINS (With Private Hip Bath and Toilet)	66; 9; 67	200
D	18	OUTSIDE SINGLE CABINS (With Private Bath and Toilet)	44; 46; 45; 47	216

THE PACIFIC STEAM NAVIGATION COMPANY

Children are always looking for something new, something exciting, somewhere they feel is their own, somewhere they can be, without being watched by their parents.

Parents want their children to be somewhere safe, with someone who will keep them occupied, happy and contented whilst travelling and the adults can relax and enjoy a restful sea voyage.

We hope this leaflet will show you we make it our business to take good care of the little ones who travel on our Passenger Liner s.s. "REINA DEL MAR." This ship carries specially trained Children's Hostesses as well as Stewardesses exclusively to attend to the wants of our young passengers. A Surgeon and State Registered Nursing Sister are part of the ship's complement.

Reina Del Mar cruise brochure, August 1963.

PACIFIC STEAM NAVIGATION CO.   71

hours to ride Hurricane Flora and the passengers and crew were certainly glad to see Bermuda's shores.

When the decline in passenger numbers were discussed by the Board in 1963 it was decided to charter the *Reina del Mar* to the Travel Savings Association, in which the company had a 25 per cent share. The other partners being British & Commonwealth Shipping Company Limited, Canadian Pacific Steamships Limited and Mr Max Wilson. The chairman of the company told staff that, 'Apart from the sentimental angle, the sale of the ship is a forward step and one which should considerably strengthen the company's financial position. We are relieved of the heavy losses which have been resulting from the ship's voyages and we will not have to provide depreciation for her; these two items alone amount to a very considerable sum. I therefore view the future with equanimity and indeed with enthusiasm, and have no hesitation in stating that there is no need for despondency'. The Union Castle Line took over the management of the liner for the period of this project.

Reina del Mar was sent to her builders at Belfast and structurally rebuilt for her new role as a cruise liner. Her three classes were converted for one-class cruising and her capacity increased from 766 to 1,047 berths by extending the number of beds and adding 135 new staterooms, built in former cargo space. Her restaurant was enlarged and the superstructure was extended forward of the bridge creating a new Coral Lounge with 650 seats. A new cinema was provided forward of the funnel with a viewing area above.

In 1965 the Pacific Steam Navigation and the Royal Mail Line became part of the Furness Withy Group and *Cuzco* was sold to the Ben line that year. *Orcoma* joined the fleet in 1966 and *Flamenco* was sold to Cia de Nav. Abeto S.A. for further trading. *Sarmiento*, *Santander*, *Salaverry* and

Travel Savings Association Cruise by *Reina Del Mar*.

Above: *Somers Isle* in London Docks.

Right: Damage to *Flamenco* (II) in 1963, following a collision.

PACIFIC STEAM NAVIGATION CO.

Royal Mail House,
Leadenhall Street,
London, E.C.3.

2nd October, 1963.

To the Staff of The Pacific Steam
Navigation Company.

"REINA DEL MAR"

The staff at home and abroad, afloat and ashore, will have learned with sorrow of the sale of this ship of which we are all so proud, and that after nearly one hundred years we will no longer have a passenger ship plying between this country and the West Coast of South America, although of course our cargo vessels will continue to cater for some passengers, offering, as you know, very fine accommodation. It was in 1868 that the transatlantic service of the Company was inaugurated, and since that time we have maintained a passenger service without interruption (except during the last war) employing a succession of fine ships, each of which in its turn incorporated the latest developments and reflected great credit on the designers and the builders. They became household words on the West Coast, and many thousands of the present-day inhabitants of the West Coast Republics hold them in special regard because they or their forebears emigrated from Europe in a P.S.N. ship.

I am sure everyone will understand, therefore, that the decision to break this link was not lightly taken, and that every endeavour was made to keep "REINA DEL MAR" in the service for which she was built. Unhappily, and for reasons which I will not repeat as I am sure you are all aware of them,

cont ....

- 2 -

it was found impossible to operate the vessel profitably, and we were forced to face up to hard economics.

The ship, therefore, has been sold to Travel Savings Ltd., and will undergo extensive alterations to convert her into a full-time cruising ship. The Pacific Steam Navigation Company is taking a 25% interest in T.S.L., the other partners being British & Commonwealth Shipping Co. Ltd., Canadian Pacific Steamships Ltd. and Mr. Max Wilson. The Company will therefore continue to have a direct interest in the ship's operation.

Apart from the sentimental angle with which I have already dealt, the sale of the ship is a forward step and one which should considerably strengthen the Company's financial position. We are relieved of the heavy losses which have been resulting from the ship's voyages, and we will not have to provide depreciation for her; these two items alone amount to a very considerable sum. I therefore view the future with equanimity and indeed with enthusiasm, and have no hesitation in stating that there is no need for despondency.

With the whole-hearted co-operation of you all - and we are indeed fortunate to have that co-operation, and grateful for it - the Company will go from strength to strength. Our fleet will be maintained at the highest standard and arrangements will be made to diversify our activities as opportunity presents.

Chairman.

S.S. "COTOPAXI" DRY-DOCK REPORT.

This vessel was inspected in Gladstone Graving Dock at 09.30 hours Thursday, 3rd September, 1964, in company with Mr. Emmett, Assistant to the Superintendent Engineer, Lloyds and Underwriters surveyors.

The condition of the hull plating below the green boot-topping was good with the exception of approximately 14 plates, including the fore part of the keel-plate, which require scaling.

The remainder of the bottom plating had a good body of paint with the possible exception of the fore-end of the vessel where there had been a certain amount of chafing caused by the anchor cables.

It was also noticed that many plates of the vessel's bottom have a fairly thick build-up of paint with consequent roughness of surface.

The stern, frame and rudder were in good condition but the anodes situated at the stern frame will require renewing.

The black top sides and green boot-topping area are in reasonably good condition, with the exception of 10 plates between wind and water on the starboard side, from amidships aft. The opportunity will be taken to scale approximately 24 plates including those on the bottom.

There was a moderate amount of grass on the hull but no shell and the bottom area has been washed and scrubbed. All bare patches on the bottom plating will be sliced, wire brushed and after receiving a coat of wash primer paint and build-up with navy protective paint, a full coat of anti-fouling paint will be applied before leaving the graving dock. All scaled plates will be painted in accordance with our normal practice.

Anchors and cables were lowered to the bottom of the Graving Dock and after examination the anchor lengths placed in locker, as is customary.

Noted and discussed

Above left, right: 1963 *Reina Del Mar* letter from the chairman.

Above far right: *Cotopaxi* (II) dry-dock report, 3 September 1964.

74 PACIFIC STEAM NAVIGATION CO.

Above: Burial at Sea on *Potosi* (IV).

Right: Deck cargo on *Potosi* (IV).

Salamanca were also sold the following year and *Salina* in 1968. They were replaced by three vessels from Shaw Savill & Albion Line, which were renamed *Orita*, *Oropesa* and *Oroya*. The tanker *George Peacock* was disposed of in 1969 when she was sold to V. J. Vardinoyannis of Piraeus and renamed *Georgios V*.

In 1970 the Furness Withy Group consisted of the following shipping companies:
- Furness, Withy & Co. Ltd.
- Shaw, Savill & Albion Line Ltd. (SS&A)
- Royal Mail Line Ltd. (RML)
- Pacific Steam Navigation Company Ltd. (PSNCo)
- Prince Line Ltd/Rio Cape Line Ltd.
- Manchester Liners Ltd.
- Houlder Line Ltd.
- Johnston Warren Line Ltd.
- Bermuda & West Indies Line Ltd.
- Kaye, Son & Co. Ltd. (since 1973)

John Gawne was appointed Chairman of the company in 1970 and *Kenuta*, *Cotopaxi* and *Pizarro* were transferred to the Royal Mail Line. *Eleuthera*, *Somer's Isle* and *Cienfuegos* were sold that year and *Potosi* was sold in 1972. The following year *Reina del Mar* also left the fleet, when she was sold to the Union Castle Line. In June 1974 the Union Castle Line announced that the *Reina del Mar* would be withdrawn from service the following April because of the greatly increased costs of operation. The tremendous increase in the price of oil had played a major part in the

Above: Huskisson Dock loading berth, Liverpool.

Below: Huskisson Dock, Liverpool.

decision as well as crew wages and the cost of maintenance and repairs. She completed her 1974 cruise programme and operated cruises from South Africa to South America in 1975. She was laid up at Southampton and sailed for Kaohsiung to be broken up later that year. *Orbita*, *Orduna* and *Ortega* were delivered to the company in 1972/73 and a three-weekly service was provided from Liverpool.

A new Liverpool Cargo Terminal was opened on 11 April 1972 with a ceremony aboard *Cotopaxi*, which was the first vessel to berth alongside. The terminal was situated at North Sandon and South Huskisson Docks and was formally opened by Mr John Gawne, Chairman of PSNC and Mr John Marshall, General Manager of the Mersey Docks & Harbour Company. It was licensed to the Company to handle the import and export trade between the United Kingdom and West Coast of South America ports. It replaced an older berth at North No. 1 Canada Dock.

The Facility included three deep sea berths with a new shed 1,025 feet long and 100 feet wide, which was built at South Huskisson Dock. The Terminal also included the existing North Sandon Dock Shed, which was 1,066 feet long by 120 feet wide, providing an undercover cargo stacking area of 127,920 square feet. The new berths were designed for the handling of break-bulk, unitised and containerised cargo by the three new cargo vessels, *Orbita*, *Orduna* and *Ortega*, which were under construction by Cammell Laird at Birkenhead.

The construction of this facility was brought about because loading and unloading cargo at the ports was becoming very labour intensive. It was estimated that in the 1950s, dockers could typically handle around 10 to 15 tonnes of cargo an hour and there was also a risk of theft, loss and accident and damage to the men and the cargo. One study in the 1950s found that approximately 60–70 per cent of transporting goods by sea was made up of costs at the ports, and cargo handling alone amounted to 37 per cent of the total cost. It was common, at the time for a cargo vessel

Construction and launch of *Orbita* (II) at the yard of Cammell Laird & Company at Birkenhead.

Above: *Orbita* (II) in the Panama Canal.

Below: Loading a heavy lift at Liverpool onto *Orcoma* (II).

Above: *Orbita* (II), *Ortega* (II) and *Orcoma* (II).

Below: Engine room controls on *Orcoma* (II).

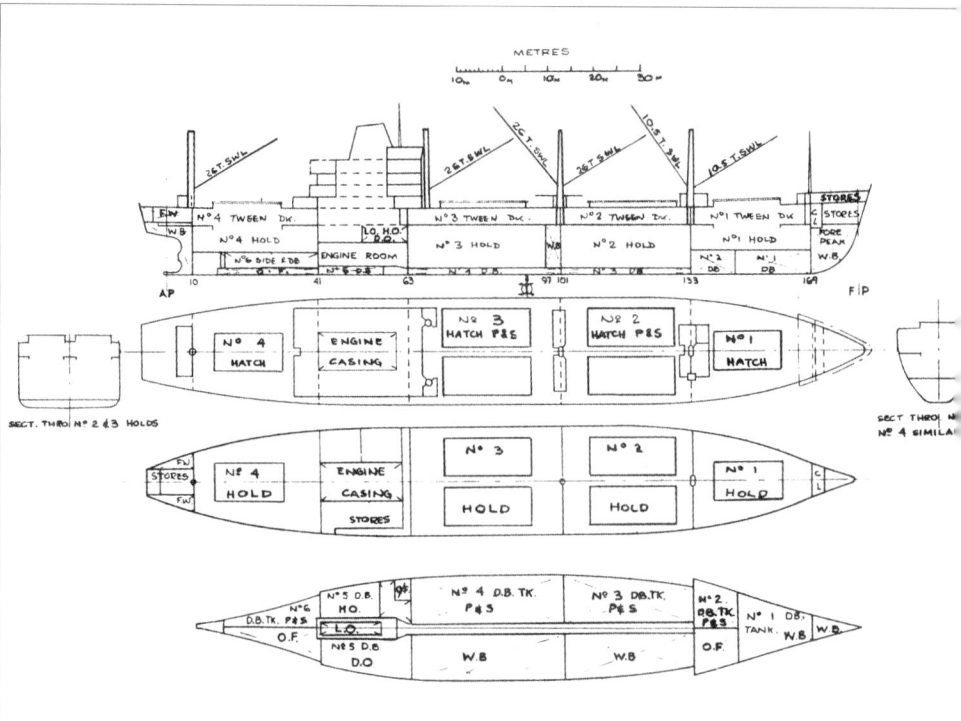

Above: *Orbita* (II).

Left: Bridge on *Orcoma* (II).

to spend as much time in port as it did sailing on a voyage. By 1961 freight costs made up 12 per cent of the value of imports to the United States.

At this time the Company was looking at the developing practice of carrying goods in containers. This had been developed since the Second World War when the United States Military had used 8-foot 6-inch, by 6-foot 3-inch, by 6-foot 10-inch shipping containers and this practice continued into the 1950s. However, the technology had clearly improved but the infrastructure in ships and port facilities did not exist in Liverpool and South American ports at the time.

Containers had been used by railroad companies in the United States for many years. From 1926 to 1947 the Chicago North Shore & Milwaukee Railway transported motor vehicles in flatcars and on its vessels sailing between New York and Cuba. By 1953 the Eastern Illinois and Southern Pacific railroads were embracing this method of transport and ships started carrying goods in containers between Seattle and Alaska in 1951. The *Clifford J. Rogers*, owned by the White Pass & Yukon Line, carried 600 containers between North Vancouver, British Columbia, and Skagway, Alaska, in 1955 and the containers were lifted onto rail vehicles for delivery to the Yukon.

The haulier Malcolm McLean is credited with being 'the father of containerisation' and in the early 1950s he sold his interest in the family business and purchased the Pan Atlantic Steamship Company. He started with four ships and had 5,000 trailers built to his specification. A container port was constructed at Port Elizabeth, New Jersey and on 26 April 1956 his first container ship, the *Ideal X* sailed to Houston with fifty-eight containers on board. He later renamed his company Sea-Land Service Incorporated. In 1969 he sold it to R. J. Reynolds for $160 million and it was bought by CSX Corporation in 1987 and was later sold to Maersk in 1999 for $800 million.

On 31 August 1958, the Matson Line vessel *Hawaiian Merchant* sailed from San Francisco with twenty, 24-foot containers on her deck. Two years later, the *Hawaiian Citizen* became the first vessel in the Pacific to be converted to a container ship and the first to incorporate a large-scale reefer container capacity to the Matson Lines service. The *Hawaiian*

Orduna (II) in the Mersey.

Enterprise and the *Hawaiian Progress* were the first purpose-built container ships to enter service. Port facilities had been provided and in 1959 the world's first A-frame gantry crane was erected in Alameda, California. The Maersk Line ordered its first container vessel in 1973 and the *Adrian Maersk*, with a 1,400 TEU capacity took the line's first sailing. The early containers were standardised to 20 and 40-foot lengths. The

20-foot container was referred to as a Twenty-foot Equivalent Unit (TEU) and this later became the industry standard.

It was against this background that the Pacific Steam Navigation Company embarked on the planning and building of this new facility to handle freight at Liverpool. Some attempts had been made to transport goods in containers to South American ports from the United States but this had proved to be disappointing. The Grace Line commenced a container service to Chile and in 1969 the Port of Valparaiso was handling 3,827 containers and 5,445 the following year. Several South American countries were realising the potential of this means of carrying freight and 'through billing' was introduced with rates covering the transportation of cargo from the inland point to the port, and then through to its eventual destination by sea.

Oropesa and *Oroya* were designed for flexible trading on the liner routes of the General Shipping Division of Furness Withy and incorporated the many different features required for carrying heavy bulk concentrates, grain, general and refrigerated containers, and edible oil. They were able to transit the St Lawrence Seaway into the Great Lakes and were initially placed on the West Coast of South America route. They incorporated five holds and nine hatches, Nos 2, 3, 4, and 5 being double hatches. The main engine, a Scott-Sulzer 6 RND 76 developing 12,000 bhp was situated aft, giving a service speed of 16.25 knots. The engine room was designed to be unmanned at night. Nine sets of electric derrick cranes were fitted, eight at 22 tonnes and one at 100 tonnes serving Nos 3 and 4 hatches which were each 63 feet long. The weather and 'tween deck hatch covers were electro-hydraulic folding, all opening and closing operations controlled by push buttons. The hatch sizes were arranged to suit the stowage of containers and a total of 536 20-foot containers could be carried. Air-conditioned accommodation for forty-one crew was fitted, with each member having a single cabin and

Above: *Andes* (III) in the Panama Canal.

Left: Wheelwright House on Dock Road, Liverpool.

toilet. The ships also had swimming pools fitted as well as gymnasiums and hobbies rooms.

On 26 December 1975, the *William Wheelwright* went aground in ballast off Sinoe, south of Monrovia. She was re-floated on 29 December and towed to Lisbon and was later found to be beyond repair. Her charter was terminated and she was returned to the Pacific Steam Navigation Company but was towed to Santander and broken up the following year. *Coloso* was sold in 1976. In September 1978, the company moved its berth across the Mersey from Huskisson Dock to Vittoria Dock at Birkenhead, which had been vacated by the Ocean Group when they withdrew from cargo services. Consequently, the Pacific Steam Navigation returned to Birkenhead again after a gap of over seventy years when they operated from various berths in the Liverpool dock system.

Orcoma was sold to P. T. Samudera of Indonesia in 1979 and the Compañia Sud Americana de Vapores purchased *Orbita* in 1980. *Ortega* was renamed *Andes* and by 1983 the fleet comprised of *Oroya*, *Oropesa* and *Andes*. The name of the Pacific Steam Navigation Company disappeared into the Furness Withy Group in 1984 and the container ship *Andes* joined Eurosal consortium.

Andes (III) transits the Panama Canal.

Andes was one of seven ships joining the container consortium Eurosal (Europe-South American Line) which was formed by nine members of the European South Pacific and Magellan Conference. The Pacific Steam Navigation Company, Armement Deppe of Belgium, Hapag-Lloyd of West Germany, Johnson Line of Sweden, Nedlloyd of Holland, Marasia of Spain, CSAV of Chile, Linabol of Bolivia and Transnave of Ecuador. Sailings were offered every twenty-four days to and from Britain, Sweden and Northern Spain and every twelve days to and from North Continental ports, serving the main South American ports of Antofagasta in Chile, Callao in Peru, Guayaquil in Ecuador and Buenaventure in Colombia. The smaller South American ports were served by three conventional vessels.

Andes was built by Hyundai Heavy Industries for the Furness Withy Group, which was now owned by the Hong Kong-based Tung Group. She was designed with five holds forward of the superstructure and machinery space and one hold aft. She was fitted with a considerable amount of refrigerated space, utilising 40-foot temperature controlled units suitable for the carriage of bananas and other fruits from Chile and Ecuador. She could carry 1,902 TEUs. The cargo space was designed to carry unitised copper in Nos. 2, 3, 4 and 6 lower holds and dangerous cargo in No. 1 hold.

A large gantry crane, to handle containers and general cargo at some South American ports ran on tracks along the length of the foredeck and had a lifting capacity of 40 tonnes. She was fitted with a Hyundai-built B&W slow speed oil engine, developing 19,390 bhp and giving a service speed of 18.5 knots. Andes was 202 metres long by 32.2 metres wide and had a draft of 12 metres. She carried a crew of twenty-three and all accommodation was air-conditioned. Each crew member had a single cabin with toilet and washing facilities and the vessel also incorporated a swimming pool, sauna, sports/hobbies room, gymnasium and television lounge. She was renamed *GCM Magellan* in 1994, became *Cap Blanco* in 1997, owned by the Andes Shipping Company of the Cayman Islands and was beached at Alang on 28 February 2009 and broken up.

The Liverpool office was closed in 1984 and integrated into the Furness Withy operations in Manchester. In 1990, the Furness Withy Group was acquired by Hamburg Sud, including the Royal Mail Line and the Pacific Steam Navigation Company. The Hamburg Sudamerikanische Dampfschiffahrts-Gesellschaft (Hamburg America Steamship Company or Hamburg South America Line), was established in 1871 by eleven Hamburg-based merchants. They started a monthly service to Brazil and Argentina and by 1914 were operating over fifty ships totalling 325,000 tonnes. The company lost all of its ships in the First World War and continued by chartering vessels.

They operated sea cruises in the 1920s and 1930s with vessels like the *Cap Polonio* and *Cap Arcona* with Dr. August Oetker taking an interest in its affairs in 1939, when they owned fifty-two ships totalling 400,000 tonnes. The second loss of its complete fleet was experienced during the Second World War with some vessels surrendered as part of repatriation payments. Dr. August Oetker's company took over the line in 1955 and the Deutsche Levante Linie was taken over the following year, extending its services into the Mediterranean. The Columbus Line initiated a new container service between North America and Australia and New Zealand in 1971, on a route that had been operating under Hamburg Sud since 1956.

Hamburg Sud also acquired the Swedish Laser Lines, Rotterdam Zuid-America Lijn (RZAL) and Havenlijn in 1990. In 1998 they took over the Brazilian shipping company Alianca and South Seas Steamship. The following year they also acquired South Pacific Container Lines and Transroll's Europe to South America East Coast liner services. In 2000 the Inter-America Services of the American shipping company Crowley American Transport (CAT) were taken over and in 2003 they acquired the Ellerman services to the Mediterranean and to India and Pakistan, also taking over the Kien Hung liner services from Asia to South America in April 2003.

The Columbus Line and Crowley American Transport lines vanished on 1 January 2004, and became Hamburg Sud with the first of six identical 5,552 TEU container ships launched in July 2004. By 2005, the Ellerman name was replaced with Hamburg Sud and the company purchased all the shares of Ybarra y Cia Sudamerica S.A. (Ybarra Sud). The following year they purchased the Australia-New Zealand and Asia and North American services from Fesco, under the name of FANZL Fesco Australian New Zealand Liner Services. The liner operations of Costa Container Lines to the Mediterranean, South America East and North Coast, Central America and the Caribbean were taken over by Hamburg Sud in 2007 and the name Ybarra y Cia Sudamerica S.A. (Ybarra Sud) was replaced by the Hamburg Sud Iberia S.A. Line. In 2008 the FANZL Australia and New Zealand Liner Services company name became Hamburg Sud, as did the Costa Container Lines (CCL), on 1 January 2009.

In 2011 Hamburg Sud operated 148 ships and maintained a global inventory of some 338,000 containers in a wide array of sizes and configurations that were strategically positioned to meet the needs of the customers. The present fleet also includes dry-bulk carriers and tankers. Scheduled liner services for containers make up around 85 per cent of the company's revenue and it also operates in the tramp shipping market and runs its own travel agency service. It is now one of Germany's largest maritime transportation companies and employs 4,700 staff across the globe. The Company operate as the German, Hamburg Sud and Alianca, under the Brazilian flag. The bulk and product tanker services are operated under the names of Rudolf A. Oetker (RAO) and Alianca Bulk (Aliabulk). Columbus Ship management GmbH (CSG) provide technical management and crewing and Columbus Logistics Services GmbH offer ship and cargo management agency services.

Orbita

PSNC-FLEET LIST

Chile (I).

1. *Chile* (I) (1840–1852)
682 grt, 198 x 29 x 18 feet.
Wooden paddle-steamer, simple; two side lever direct acting 2 x 1 cyl. By Miller Ravenhill & Company, London, 8 knots.
Passengers 116. Crew: 64.
Cargo: 200 tons.
Safety boats inverted over paddle boxes and armed with 2 x 2 pounder canon.
Delivered by Curling & Young, Limehouse, London, at a cost of £11,935.

18.4.1840	Launched
24.6.40	Maiden voyage, Gravesend–Falmouth–Rio de Janeiro–Straits of Magellan–Valparaiso. Met *Peru* at Point Famine in the Straits of Magellan, so that both could steam into Valparaiso on 16 October. Capt. Glover.
1841	Struck a reef and returned to Valparaiso for repairs. Returned to service with funnel fore of paddle boxes.
1852	Replaced by *Santiago* and sold at Valparaiso.

2. *Peru* (I) (1840–1852)
690 grt, 198 x 29 x 18 feet.
Wooden paddle-steamer, Simple; two side lever direct acting 2 x 1 cyl. By Miller Ravenhill & Company, London, 8 knots.
Passengers 116. Crew 64.
Safety boats inverted over paddle boxes and armed with 2 x 2 pounder canon.
Delivered by Curling & Young, Limehouse, London at a cost of £11,935.

21.4.1840	Launched
10.7.40	Maiden voyage, Capt. George Peacock, Gravesend–Falmouth–Straits of Magellan–Valparaiso. Met *Chile* at Point Famine, so that they could both sail into Valparaiso together on 16 October.
1852	Stranded and lost.

3. *Bolivia* (I) (1849–1879)

773 grt, 197 x 26 x 15 feet.

Wooden paddle-steamer, Simple; two side lever direct acting 2 x 1 cyl, by Miller Ravenhill & Company, London, 8 knots.

Delivered by Robert Napier, Govan, Glasgow.

Safety boats inverted over paddle boxes and armed with 2 x 2 pounder canon.

Passengers 116. Crew 64.

23.10.1849	Maiden voyage, Capt. Brown, Liverpool–Madeira–Rio de Janeiro–Valparaiso. Then on Valparaiso–Antofagasta–Callao route.
1870	Hulked at Valparaiso and used to store coal.
1879	Towed out to sea and scuttled.

4. *Ecuador* (I) (1845–1850)

323 grt, 271 n, 120.8 x 21.6 x 15 feet.

Iron paddle-steamer, simple; 2 cyl, by builders, 8 knots.

Delivered by Tod & MacGregor, Glasgow.

The company's first iron ship.

10.1845	Launched.
1.1846	Maiden voyage, Capt. N. Glover, Liverpool–Valparaiso–Callao. Then on the coastal service Callao–Guayaquil–Panama, linking Valparaiso with Panama to connect with the Royal Mail Line at Panama, then overland to Valparaiso.
7.1850	Made one Panama City–San Francisco–Panama City voyage.
1851	The company decided that she was too small for the service and was sold to the Panama Mail Steam Ship Corporation of America.
1853	Wrecked at Coquimbo.

5. *New Granada* (I) (1846–1851)

694 grt, 177.5 x 24.7 x 14.7 feet.

Iron paddle-steamer, 2 x 1 cyl, by builders, 8 knots.

Schooner, rigged, no stern galleries.

Delivered by Smith and Rogers, Glasgow.

8. 1846	Maiden voyage, Capt. John Williams, Liverpool–Madeira–Rio de Janerio–Valparaiso–Callao. Then with *Ecuador* on the Callao–Guayaquil–Panama service.
1851	Out of register.

6. *Santiago* (I) (1851–1857)

961 grt, 246.4 x 28.2 x 17 feet.

Iron paddle-steamer, simple; two direct acting; 2 x 1 cyl, 400 hp, by builder, 10 knots.

Two decks.

Delivered by Robert Napier, Govan, Glasgow, at a cost of £140,000 for four ships which were replacements for *Chile, Peru, Ecuador* and *New Granada*.

1851	Maiden voyage, Capt. Hind, Liverpool–Valparaiso.
1857	Sold to the Government of Peru and became a frigate and non-seagoing training ship.

7. *Lima* (I) (1851–1863)
Sister to *Santiago*.
1,461 grt, 249.6 x 29.2 x 17.1 feet.
Iron paddle-steamer, simple; two direct acting; 2 x 1 cyl, 400 hp, by builder, 9¼ knots.
Two decks.
Delivered by Robert Napier, Govan, Glasgow.

2.10.51	Maiden voyage Liverpool-Valparaiso.
1852	Fired on by shore batteries at Guayaquil as she delivered the mail.
1854	Lengthened and engine compounded at Liverpool. New speed 10½ knots on 1 tonne of coal an hour.
11.7.1863	Wrecked off Lagartija Island, Southern Chile.

8. *Quito* (I) (1852–1853)
Sister to *Santiago*.
1,461 grt, 248.8 x 29.2 x 17.1 feet.
Iron paddle-steamer, simple; two direct acting; 2 x 1 cyl, by builder, 10 knots.
Two decks.
Delivered by Robert Napier, Govan, Glasgow.

25.1.1852	Maiden voyage Liverpool–Valparaiso.
8.1853	Lost on a reef twelve miles from Huasco, on a voyage from Panama to Valparaiso.

9. *Bogota* (I) (1852–1878)
Sister to *Santiago*.
1,461 grt, 248.8 x 29.2 x 17.1 feet.
Iron paddle-steamer, simple; two direct acting; 2 x 1 cyl, by builder, 10 knots.
Two decks.
Delivered by Robert Napier, Govan, Glasgow

25.2.1852	Maiden voyage Liverpool–Valparaiso.
1856	Returned to Liverpool for compounding engines.
1871	Struck a reef off Tarada Point, salvaged becoming a hulk.
1878	Scuttled at sea.

10. *La Perlita* (1853–)
140 grt, 106 x 17.5 x 8.6 feet.
Iron paddle-steamer, simple; 2 cyl, by builder, 9 knots
Delivered by Bank Quay Foundry Company, Warrington, for the

Buenaventura (Colombia)–Panama service.

17.6.1853　　Maiden voyage, Capt. Maugham, Liverpool–Buenaventura and disappeared without trace.

11. *Osprey* (1852)
609 grt, 169.7 x 18.6 x 8.9 feet.
Iron paddle-steamer, simple; 2 cyl, by builder, 9 knots.
One deck.

1852　　Built as *Osprey* for the City of Cork Steam Ship Company.
1852　　Purchased by PSNC for Callao–Pisco–Huacho route, and lost on first voyage out to Peru.

12. *Valdivia* (I) (1853–1857)
573 grt, 128.6 x 21.2 x 10.4 feet.
Wooden, single-screw, simple; 2 cyl, by builder, 9 knots.
Delivered 1853 by Caird & Company, Greenock.
The company's first screw steamer but with a wooden hull.

1853　　Delivered from Liverpool to Valparaiso for the coastal services.
1857　　Stranded and lost near Valparaiso.

13. *Panama* (I) (1856–)
Sister to *Valdivia*
270 grt, 128.6 x 21.2 x 10.4 feet.
Wooden, single-screw, simple; 2 cyl by builder, 9 knots.
Delivered by John Reid & Company, Glasgow as a replacement for *La Perlita*.

4.1856　　Maiden voyage from Liverpool, sank near Point Tamar after striking a rock.

14. *Inca* (I) (1856–1874)
290 grt, 130.8 x 20.9 feet.
Iron, compound inverted engine by Randolph & Elder, Glasgow.
Delivered by Caird & Company, Greenock.

1856　　*Inca* and *Valparaiso* were the first ships to be fitted with the compound inverted engine by Robert Napier and Charles Randolph. INCA was delivered to Callao.
1857　　Then on the Callao–Chala mail service
1862　　W. & J. Tyrer & Company introduced a similar INCA on their South American service.
1874　　Sold and renamed *Union*.
11.1874　　Wrecked at Puerto Bueno, Chile.

15. *Valparaiso* (I) (1856–1871)
1,060 grt, 841 n, 234.1 x 29.1 x 14.5 feet.
Iron, paddle-steamer, compound diagonal, 2 x 2 cyl, 320 hp, by John Elder & Company, 13 knots. Passengers: 300.
First steam vessel fitted with the new compound steam engine, invented by John Elder. Consumed 30 per cent less coal. On a voyage from Valparaiso to Panama and back, a distance of 5,166 miles, her coal consumption was only 640 tons, against 1,150 tonnes for the older steamers.
Delivered 1856 by Randolph & Elder, Glasgow.

1856　　Sailed on maiden voyage Liverpool-Valparaiso then on Valparaiso-Chiloe service with nine ports of call. *Callao* and *Valparaiso* were given the name 'Express Steamers'.
20.2.1871　　On a voyage from Calbuco to Ancud she was wrecked on Lagartiga Island, about three miles off the mainland, near Puerto Montt, Chile.
1976　　The wreck was identified and some items were recovered from it.

16. *Callao* (I) (1858–1880)

Sister to *Valparaiso*.
700 grt, 235 x 29 x 14.5 feet.
Iron, paddle-steamer, compound diagonal, 2 x 2 cyl, 320 hp, by John Elder & Company, 13 knots.
Delivered by John Reid & Company, Glasgow.

1858	Maiden voyage Liverpool–Valparaiso and placed on Valparaiso–Pacific services.
1870	Converted to hulk at Valparaiso.

17. *Cloda* (1857–1865)

699 grt, 214.5 x 30.5 x 16.1 feet.
Iron, single-screw, 2 cyl, by John Elder & Company, 9 knots.
One deck.

1857	Delivered by Randolph & Elder as *Cloda* for Irish interests.
1857	Purchased by PSNC for Pacific coastal services.
25.1.1865	Lost off Huacho, Peru. All crew survived.

18. *Prince of Wales* (1858–1859)

700 grt, 195.5 x 26.4 x 17.7 feet.
Iron single-screw, simple horizontal direct acting, 2 cyl, by builder, 10 knots.
Passengers: 75.
Delivered by W. Simons & Company, Whiteinch.

1854	Completed as *Prince of Wales*.
1858	Purchased by PSNC to replace *Valdivia*.
1859	Wrecked off Chile.

19. *Anne* (1859–1864)

344 grt, 153.4 x 22 x 11 feet.
Iron, single-screw, simple, 2 cyl, by Wallsend Slipway & Engineering Company, 9 knots.
Delivered by Chas. Rennoldson, South Shields

1854	Completed as *Anne* for the South American Mining Company, London. Based in Valparaiso for services to Puerto Montt.
1859	Purchased by PSNC, replacing *Prince of Wales*.
1864	Sold.

20. *San Carlos* (1860–1874)

652 grt, 444 n, 199.9 x 30.2 x 18.7 feet.
Iron brig, single-screw, compound, 2 x 2 cyl, 270 hp, by Randolph & Elder, Glasgow, 9 knots.
Delivered at Renfrew. Passengers: 75.

1860	Delivered for Callao–Guayaquil–Panama service.
1874	Sold.

21. *Guayaquil* (1860–1870)

Sisiter of *San Carlos*.
661 grt, 444 n, 208.8 x 30.2 x 18.7 feet.
Iron brig, single-screw compound, 2 x 2 cyl, 270 hp, by builder, 9 knots.
Passengers: 75.
Delivered by Randolph and Elder, Glasgow.

1860	Entered service on the Callao–Guayaquil–Panama route.
1870	Sold to local interests for the Callao–Galapagos Island service.
1880	Broken up at Callao.

22. *Morro* (I) (1860–1881)

132 grt, 119.7 x 20.1 x 7.10 feet.
Steel paddle-steamer, simple, 2 cyl, by builder.
Passengers: 120 (deck). Crew: 16.
The company's first steel ship.

1860 Delivered as a passenger tender at Panama.
1881 Replaced by *Morro*.

23. *Peruano* (1861–1874)
639 grt, 404 n, 181.6 x 29.6 x 11.6 feet.
Wooden paddle-steamer, 250 hp.
One deck.
Built at New York.
1861 Delivered for Guayaquil services.
1874 Sold to Schuber & Company, Guayaquil.
1884 Engine removed as used as a hulk, for warehouse and offices.

24. *Peru* (II) (1861–1881)
1,307 grt, 260.5 x 32.1 x 22.11 feet.
Iron paddle-steamer, compound direct acting, 2 x 2 cyl; 360 hp; by John Elder & Company, 10 knots.
Two decks.
Delivered by John Reid & Company, Glasgow.
1.1.1862 Maiden voyage Liverpool–St Vincent–Rio de Janeiro–Valparaiso. Based at Valparaiso. During the American Civil War the ship was fitted with three canons, with Royal Navy gun crews.
1881 Hulked although records show her as wrecked near Layerto in 1863. However, she was still on Lloyds Register until 1879/80.

25. *Chile* (II) (1863–1883)
Near sister of *Peru* (24)
1,672 grt, 1,174 n, 274.10 x 36.1 x 22.11 feet.
Iron paddle-steamer, compound direct, 2 x 2 cyl; 400 hp; by builder, 10 knots.
Delivered by Randolph & Elder, Glasgow at a cost of £53,650.
1863 Delivered to Valparaiso.
1870 Purchased by the government of Chile, retained name.
1883 Deleted from Lloyds register.

26. *Talca* (I) (1862–1880)
708 grt, 469 n, 194.1 x 30.1 x 16 feet.
Iron paddle-steamer, compound direct acting, 2 x 2 cyl; 260 hp, by builder, 10 knots.
First company vessel to be built with a straight stem opposed to a clipper bow.
Delivered by Randolph & Elder, Glasgow.
1862 Delivered for Chilean coastal services.
1865 When under command of Capt. George Chambers she was taken over by the Ecuadorian President to control a local dispute. However, when she arrived the rebels fled and the ship was allowed to continue her voyage.
1874 Her engines were removed and she became a storage hulk.
1880 Scuttled at sea.

27. *Quito* (II) (1863–1865)
1,388 grt, 1,004 n, 271 x 32.10 x 20.2 feet.
Iron paddle-steamer, compound; 2 x 2 cyl; 320 hp; Steam pressure 25 lb, by builder, 13½ knots.
One deck and shade deck.
Passengers: 125.
Delivered by Randolph & Elder, Glasgow at a cost of £48,750, designed by Thomas Smith as the first of a class of coastal steamers that carried both cabin and deck passengers, including cattle. They normally berthed stern first at ports to enable them to leave safely during strong winds.

| 27.1.1864 | Maiden voyage Liverpool–Valparaiso. |
| 1864 | Sold. |

28. *Payta* (1864–1878)

1,344 grt, 997 n, 263.8 x 38.5 x 14.11 feet.
Iron paddle-steamer, compound; 2 x 2 cyl; 320 hp; Steam pressure 25 lb, by builder,
13½ knots. One deck and shade deck. Passengers: 125.
Delivered by Randolph & Elder, Glasgow.

| 1864 | Delivered to the Pacific coastal services. |
| 1870 | Sold to the Government of Chile. |

29. *Ecuador* (II) (1863–)

500 grt, Iron single-screw steamer, 100 hp. One deck.

| 1863 | Delivered |
| 1866–1873 | Left Lloyds Register, records show she was lost in 1870. |

30. *Pacific* (1865–1870)

1,631 grt, 1,004 n, 267.5 x 40.2 x 17.6 feet.
Iron, paddle-steamer, compound direct, 2 x 2 cyl; 450 hp, by builder, 10 knots.
Two decks.
Passengers: 200.
Delivered by Randolph & Elder, Glasgow.

28.1.1865	Launched.
4.1865	Delivered for Pacific coastal routes.
1868	*Pacific*, *Santiago*, *Limena* and *Panama* were placed on the Trans-South Atlantic route and were the only compound engine paddle-steamers to be employed on a transatlantic service.
1870	Hulked.

31. *Santiago* (II) (1865–1869)

Sister of *Pacific* (30)
1,619 grt, 1,004 n, 267.5 x 40.2 x 17.6 feet.
Iron paddle-steamer, compound direct, 2 x 2 cyl; 450 hp, by builder, 10 knots.
Two decks.
Passengers: 200.
Delivered by Randolph & Elder, Glasgow.

| 27.5.1865 | Launched |
| 9.1865 | Delivered for Pacific services. |

13.3.1869	News of the loss reached England when a telegram was received from Lisbon.
21.3.1869	*La Plata* landed the surviving crew from *Santiago* on the Isle of Wight.

32. *Limena* (1865–1874)
Sister of *Pacific* (30)
1,622 grt, 1,004 n, 267.5 x 40.2 x 17.6 feet.
Iron paddle-steamer, compound direct, 2 x 2 cyl; 450 hp, by builder, 10 knots.
Two decks.
Passengers: 200.
Delivered by Randolph & Elder, Glasgow.

1865	Delivered to Pacific coast services.
1868	Placed on Valparaiso–Liverpool service.
1874	Sold to Peruvian interests
1880	Hulked at Callao.

1868	Placed on the Valparaiso–Liverpool service and carried copper and zinc which was discharged at Bramley-Moore Dock, Liverpool. They were the only compound-engined paddle-steamers on transatlantic service.
13.1.1869	Sailed from Valparaiso with 172 passengers on board.
21.1 1869	Entered the Straits of Magellan and had to anchor off Mercy Harbour because of bad weather. She was carrying 172 passengers from Valparaiso to Liverpool.
23.1.1869	When conditions improved she sailed and was wrecked on an unchartered rock at the outlet of Puerto Misericordia. Two seaman and a young child lost their lives. This was the second loss for the Company in ten days as, on 13 January, the *Arica* had been wrecked and sank off Peru.

33. *Panama* (II) (1866–1870)
Sister of *Pacific* (30)
1,642 grt, 1,241 n, 267.5 x 40.2 x 17.6 feet.
Iron paddle-steamer, compound direct, 2 x 2 cyl; 450 hp, by builder, 10 knots.
Two decks.
Passengers: 200.
Delivered by Randolph & Elder, Glasgow.

1866	Delivered to Pacific coastal services.
1868	Transferred to Valparaiso-Liverpool route.
1869	Replaced by *Magellan* (41) class.
1870	Hulked.

34. *Favotita* (1865–1871)
837 grt, 197.1 x 30.4 x 16.6 feet.
Wooden, copper sheathed paddle-steamer, single direct acting, 2 x 1 cyl; 200 hp, by builder, 9 knots.
Built at New York.

1865	Delivered as PSNC's last wooden vessel. Riverboat style similar to *Peruano* (23).
2.1871	Destroyed by fire in Callao Bay.

35. *Colon* (1866–1872)
1,995 grt, 286.1 x 39 x 27 feet.
Iron, single-screw compound steamer, 2 cyl, by builder, 8 knots.
Two decks.
Delivered by Randolph & Elder, Glasgow in 1861.

1866	Purchased by the company to replace *Cloda* (17).
1872	Sold to Valparaiso interests.

36. *Arica* (I) (1867–1869)
740 grt, 465 n, 204 x 30 x 14.7 feet.
Iron paddle-steamer, compound direct, 2 x 2 cyl; 250 hp, by builder, 10 knots.
One deck.
Delivered by Randolph & Elder, Glasgow.

1867	Delivered to South American coastal services.
13.1.1869	On a voyage from Lambayeque–Callao she stranded off Pacsmayo Point, Peru as she was entering port. It was discovered that the lighthouse was unlit at the time.

37. *Quito* (1867–1882)
Sister of *Arica* (36)
743 grt, 468 n, 204 x 30 x 14.7 feet.
Iron paddle-steamer, compound direct, 2 x 2 cyl; 250 hp, by builder, 10 knots.
One deck.
Delivered by Randolph & Elder, Glasgow.

1867	Delivered to the Pacific coast services.
1882	Hulked as a coal store at Arica.

38. *Supe* (1867–1882)
298 grt, 145.7 x 25.1 x 10.9 feet.
Iron single-screw, compound inverted, 2 cyl; 50 hp, by builder.
One deck.
Delivered by Randolph & Elder, Glasgow.

1867	Entered service.
1882	Sold.

39. *Atlas* (1867–1890)
56 grt, 70.2 x 17.4 x 7.7 feet.
Iron, single-screw tug, simple; 1 cyl; by builder, 9 knots.
Delivered at Paisley.

1867	Delivered to Valparaiso by *Supe*.
1890	Ran ashore at Valparaiso and abandoned.

40. *Caldera* (1870–1879)
1,741 grt, 1,124 n, 282.2 x 34.3 x 25 feet.
Iron, single-screw (4 bladed), inverted 2 cyl, direct acting surface condensing boilers, steam pressure 251 lb, 440 hp, by builder, 10 knots.
Two decks.

Passengers: 99 first-class and 39 steerage.
Cargo: 28, 190 cubic feet.
Delivered by William Denny & Brothers, Dumbarton.

28.6.1868	Launched as *Assam* for P&O, who did not purchase her.
1.1.1870	Compounded, it was Denny's first conversion, two crank, 4 cyl, steam pressure 38 lb, 11 knots.
4.1.1870	Collided with dyke in River Leven, later docked.
8.1870	Sold to PSNC for £37,000.
1876	Sold to J. Laird. New compound engines fitted by Laird's at Birkenhead and lengthened to 335.5 feet.
1879	Sold to Compagnie Generale Transatlantique for Marseilles–New York service.
1883	Major overhaul at Le Havre.
1886	Purchased by F. Stumore & Company, London.
5.1887	Abandoned off Suakin, Sudan.

41. *Magellan* (I) (1868–1893)

2,856 grt, 1,791 n, 359.7 x 41 x 26.1 feet.
Iron single-screw, compound inverted; 2 cyl; 500 hp; by John Elder & Company, Glasgow, 13½ knots.
Three decks.
Passengers: 145 first-class, 75 second-class and 300 third-class.
Cargo 2,550 tons.
Delivered by Randolph & Elder, Glasgow at a cost of £74,550.

30.12.1868	Launched.
13.3.1869	Maiden voyage, Capt. C. H. Sivell, Liverpool-Valparaiso.
29.3.1870	Sailings doubled to twice a month.
1893	Broken up on River Thames.

42. *Patagonia* (1869–1894)

Similar to *Magellan* (41)
2,866 grt, 1,798 n, 353 x 41 x 26.1 feet.
Iron single-screw, compound inverted; 2 cyl; 500 hp; by John Elder & Company, Glasgow, 13½ knots.
Three decks.
Passengers: 145 first-class, 75 second-class and 300 third-class.
Cargo 2,550 tons.
Delivered by Randolph & Elder, Glasgow at a cost of £74,550.

1.3.1869	Launched.
13.5.1869	Maiden voyage Liverpool–Valparaiso.
3.1877	Transferred to River Plate services.
4.5.1880	Chartered to White Star Line for a single voyage from Liverpool to New York.

| 1890 | Triple expansion engines installed; 3 cyl, 258 nhp; two single boilers, six furnaces, by Naval & Construction Company, Barrow, 11 knots. |
| 1.10.1894 | On a voyage from Liverpool to Valparaiso she grounded seven miles north of Tome, at Lingueral. No lives were lost. |

43. *Araucania* (1869–1897)
Similar to *Magellan*.
2,877 grt, 1,807 n, 354.8 x 41 x 26.1 feet.
Iron single-screw, compound inverted; 2 cyl; 500 hp; by John Elder & Company, Glasgow, 13½ knots.
Passengers: 145 first-class, 75 second-class and 300 third-class.
Cargo: 2,550 tons.
Delivered by Randolph & Elder, Glasgow.

29.4.1869	Launched.
13.7.1869	Maiden voyage Liverpool–Valparaiso.
7.1877	Transferred to River Plate services.
1890	Triple expansion engines installed 3 cyl, 258 nhp; two single boilers, six furnaces, by Naval & Construction Company, Barrow, 11 knots.
1897	Purchased by Macbeth & Gray, Liverpool.

44. *Cordillera* (1869–1882)
Similar to *Magellan*.
2,860 grt, 1,791 n, 353.2 x 41 x 26.1 feet.
Iron single-screw, compound inverted; 2 cyl; 500 hp; by John Elder & Company, Glasgow, 13½ knots.
Passengers: 145 first-class, 75 second-class and 300 third-class.
Cargo: 2,550 tons.
Delivered by Randolph & Elder, Glasgow.

26.6.1869	Launched.
13.10.1869	Maiden voyage Liverpool–Valparaiso.
8.1877	Transferred to River Plate services.
20.9.1884	Lost in Straits of Magellan off the rocky shoals that are the projection of San Isidro Point.

45. *John Elder* (1869–1892)
3,832 grt, 2,242 n, 381.10 x 41.7 x 35 feet.
Iron, single-screw, compound inverted; 2 cyl; 550 hp; steam pressure: 63 lb, by builder, 12½ knots.
Three decks, five steam winches.
Passengers: 70 first-class, 100 second-class and 273 third-class. Crew: 104.
Delivered by John Elder & Company, Glasgow.

| 29.8.1869 | Launched and named as a tribute, after the death of John Elder. Originally intended to be named *Sarmiento*. |

13.12.1869	Maiden voyage Birkenhead-Valparaiso. The company's largest ship and prototype for eleven others.
2.2.1872	Rebuilt, becoming 406. 4 feet, with new boilers and a second funnel, at a cost of £17,500.
1877	Transferred to joint Orient-PSNC Australian service. Mizzen mast removed.
19.4.1877	Sailed on Adelaide–Suez Canal–Liverpool route.
3.11.1886	Back on Liverpool–Valparaiso route.
17.1.1892	On a voyage from Valparaiso–Talcuhuanco, with 139 passengers, she was stranded in fog on Cape Carranza Rocks, ran aground and was wrecked. No lives were lost.

46. *Atacama* (1870–1877)
1,821 grt, 1,131 n, 290 x 38.2 x 22.9 feet.
Iron single-screw, compound inverted; 2 cyl; 300 hp; by builder, 11 knots.
Two decks.
Delivered by John Elder & Company, Glasgow.

| 1870 | Delivered as a Chilean coastal vessel. |
| 30.11.1877 | Ran aground and wrecked at the mouth of the Copeapo River, Chile. 100 lives lost. |

47. *Coquimbo* (1870–1901)
Sister to *Atacama* (46)
1,821 grt, 1,131 n, 290.7 x 38.2 x 22.9 feet.
Iron, single-screw, compound inverted; 2 cyl; 300 hp; by builder, 11 knots.
Two decks.
Delivered by John Elder & Company, Glasgow at a cost of £42,495.

| 1870 | Launched and delivered to South American coastal service. |
| 1901 | Hulked. |

48. *Valdivia* (II) (1870–1882)
Sister to *Atacama* (46)
1,162 grt, 1,131 n, 287 x 38.2 x 22.9 feet.
Iron, single-screw, compound inverted; 2 cyl; 300 hp; by builder, 11 knots.
Two decks.
Delivered by John Elder & Company, Glasgow.

| 1870 | Delivered to South American Pacific coastal services. |
| 1884 | Wrecked off Huacho, one life lost. |

49. *Eten* (1871–1877)
Sister to *Atacama* (46)
1,853 grt, 1,159 n, 292 x 38.2 x 22.9 feet.
Iron, single-screw, compound inverted; 2 cyl; 300 hp; by builder, 11 knots.
Two decks.
Delivered by Laird Brothers, Birkenhead.

| 1871 | Delivered for the South American Pacific coastal services. |
| 1877 | Wrecked off Ventura Point, 120 lives lost. |

50. *Arequipa* (1870–1887)
1,065 grt 662 n, 231.9 x 35.2 x 14.8 feet.
Iron, paddle-steamer, compound; 2 x 2 cyl; 300 hp; by builder, 11 knots.
Cargo 775 tons, fuel; 180 tonnes of coal.
Delivered by John Elder & Company, Glasgow.

1870	Ordered as *Casma* and delivered for the South American coastal routes.
1883	Hulked.
1887	Sold.

51. *Huacho* (1870–1914)

329 grt, 249 n, 149.5 x 25.6 x 11.2 feet.
Iron, single-screw, compound inverted; 2 cyl; 50 hp; by J. Jack & Company, Liverpool,
9 knots.
One deck.
Delivered by Thos. Royden & Sons, Liverpool.

6.1870	Delivered for Peruvian coastal service, Callao–Arica–Iquique route.
1882	Sold to the Governor of Ecuador at Guayaquil.
1894	Registered owner; M. J. Kelly, Guayaquil.
1914	Deleted from Lloyds Register.

52. *Iquique* (1871–1877)

Sister to *Huacho*.
323 grt, 245 n, 149.5 x 25.6 x 11.2 feet.
Iron, single-screw, compound inverted; 2 cyl; 50 hp; by J. Jack & Company, Liverpool, 9 knots.
One deck.
Delivered by Thos Royden & Sons, Liverpool at a cost of £9,350.

12.2.1871	Delivered for the Peruvian coastal services based at Callao.
1877	Wrecked.

53. *Chimborazo* (1871–1895)

3,847 grt, 2,443 n, 384 x 41.1 x 35.4 feet.
Iron, single-screw, compound inverted; 2 cyl; 550 hp; Steam pressure 65 lb, by builder, 13 knots.
Three decks, 5 steam winches.
Passengers: 80 first-class, 100 second-class and 270 third-class. Cargo: 2,500 tons.

Delivered by John Elder & Company, Glasgow at a cost of £91,010.
The *Chimborazo* class vessels undertook the voyage to Callao in fifty-six-and-a-half days calling at nine ports. Their average speed was 11.4 knots, with a coal consumption of 47 tonnes a day, over forty-and-a-half days at sea.

21.6.1871	Launched.
13.10.1871	Maiden voyage Liverpool–Valparaiso service.
1877	Chartered to Anderson & Anderson for Orient-Pacific service.
1878	Purchased by Orient Steam Navigation Company, same name.
12.5.1887	Final voyage London–Suez–Sydney.
1889	Cruise ship duties to the Norwegian Fjords.
1895	Sold to P. J. Pitcher, Liverpool and renamed *Cleopatra*. Employed in cruising by the Polytechnic Touring Association.
1895	Owned by the Ocean Cruising and Yachting Company, London.
1897	Broken up at Preston.

PACIFIC STEAM NAVIGATION CO.

54. *Cuzco* (I) (1871–1878)
Sister to *Chimborazo* (53)
3,898 grt, 2,439 n, 384 x 41.1 x 35.4 feet.
Iron, single-screw, compound inverted; 2 cyl; 550 hp; Steam pressure 65 lb, by builder 13 knots.
Three decks, five steam winches. Cargo: 2,500 tons.
Passengers: 80 first-class, 100 second-class and 270 third-class.
Delivered by John Elder & Company, Glasgow at a cost of £90,990.

18.10.1871	Launched.
13.1.1872	Maiden voyage Liverpool–Valparaiso service.
1877	Chartered by Anderson & Anderson for the Orient-Pacific Line service.
29.9.1877	First sailing London–Suez–Adelaide–Sydney. Voyage took forty days and twelve hours to Adelaide, which was a record.
1878	Sold to Orient Steam Navigation Company, retained same name.
1888	Triple-expansion engines fitted; 3 cyl; 615 nhp; steam pressure; 150 lb; three double and one single ended boilers, twenty furnaces; by builder, 15 knots. Taller funnel fitted with fore and aft schooner rig. Derrick gaff on foremast.
1905	Sold and scrapped at Genoa.

55. *Garonne* (1871–1897)
Sister to *Chimborazo* (53)
3,871 grt, 2,468 n, 328.1 x 41.1 x 35.4 feet.
Iron, single-screw, compound inverted; 2 cyl; 550 hp; Steam pressure 65 lb, by builder 13 knots.
Three decks, five steam winches. Cargo: 2,500 tons.
Passengers: 72 first-class, 92 second-class and 265 third-class.
Delivered by John Elder & Company, Glasgow.

4.1871	Launched.
29.6.1871	Maiden voyage Liverpool–Valparaiso.
6.1877	Sold to Orient-Pacific Line.

17.4.1878	First voyage to Australia.		Passengers: 80 first-class, 100 second-class and 270 third-class.
6.7.1889	Final voyage to Australia, then placed on cruising duties.		Delivered by Laird Brothers at Birkenhead at a cost of £91,852.
1897	Sold to V. Porter of Liverpool and immediately resold to F. Waterhouse of Seattle and employed in Alaska.	6.1871	Launched.
		29.9.1871	Maiden voyage Liverpool–Valparaiso. When leaving Valparaiso she lost three of her four propeller blades. A wooden caisson, 24 feet by 26 feet was built on the stern and the water pumped out. The operation was successful.
1899	Troopship duties by United States Government during Spanish-American war.		
1905	Scrapped at Genoa.	2.1877	Chartered to the Orient-Pacific Line for the Australian service.

56. *Lusitania* (1871–1878)
Sister to *Chimborazo* (53)
3,825 grt, 2,494 n, 384 x 41.1 x 35.4 feet.
Iron, single-screw, compound inverted; 2 cyl; 550 hp; Steam pressure 65 lb, by builder 13 knots.
Three decks, five steam winches. Cargo: 2,500 tons.

28.6.1877	Sold by PSNC and made her first voyage for the Orient-Pacific Line; Plymouth–Cape of Good Hope–Melbourne, in forty days six hours. This beat the previous record and her return voyage was via the Suez Canal and took forty-one days.
1878	Owned by Orient Line.
1885	Requisitioned by the Admiralty for six months as an Armed Merchant Cruiser
1886	Triple-expansion engines fitted; 3 cyl; 638 nhp; steam pressure; 150 lb; three double and one single ended boilers, twenty furnaces; by T. Richardson & Sons, Hartlepool, 13 knots.
31.3.1900	Purchased by Elder Dempster's Beaver Line for the Liverpool–St John (New Brunswick) service. However, she was on PSNC service for six months.
2.1901	Returned to Elder Dempster and chartered to the Allan Line.
26.6.1901	Wrecked on Cape Race, no loss of life.

57. *Acongagua* (1872–1895)
Sister to *Chimborazo* (53)
4,105 grt, 2,639 n, 404.9 x 41.5 x 35.4 feet.
Iron, single-screw, compound inverted; 2 cyl; 550 hp; Steam pressure 65 lb, by builder 13 knots.

Three decks, five steam winches.
Passengers: 60 first-class, 90 second-class and 335 third-class. Cargo: 2,500 tons.
Delivered by John Elder & Company, Glasgow, at a cost of £90,970, and the plans were altered during construction when she was lengthened and engine size increased to 600 hp, at a cost of £5,685.

6.6.1872	Launched.
28.9.1872	Maiden voyage Liverpool–Valparaiso.
1878	Stand by vessel for the Orient-Pacific Line.
1880	First sailing to Australia from London via the Cape of Good Hope.
24.10.1883	Transferred back to Liverpool–Valparaiso service.
1895	Purchased by Verdeau et Cie Bordeaux and renamed *Egypte* for their Lavant routes.
1896	Sold and broken up.

58. *Santiago* (III) (1871–1882)
1,451 grt, 979 n, 251.7 x 35.6 x 22.1 feet.
Iron, paddle-steamer, compound direct acting, 2 cyl; 300 hp; by builder, 11 knots.
Two decks.
Delivered by John Elder & Company, Glasgow at a cost of £44,000.

14.10.1871	Delivered for the West coast of South American services.
1882	Sold.

59. *Taboguilla* (1871–1893)
154 grt, 85 n, 115.4 x 21.1 x 7.9 feet.
Iron, single-screw, compound inverted; 2 cyl; 48 hp, by J. Taylor & Company, Birkenhead, 9 knots.
Delivered by Bowdler Chaffer & Company, Liverpool.

1871	Delivered to Callao and operated as a tender, single hold.
1893	Sold.

60. *Sorata* (I) (1872–1895)
4,014 grt, 2,573 n, 401.4 x 42.9 x 34.1 feet.
Iron, single-screw, compound inverted; 2 cyl; 600 hp, by builder, 12½ knots.
Three decks.
Passengers: 80 first-class, 100 second-class and 275 third-class.
Delivered by John Elder & Company, Glasgow, at a cost of £106,725.

2.10.1872	Launched, three months late.
8.1.1873	Maiden voyage on a new weekly service, Liverpool–Bordeaux–Vigo–Lisbon–Rio de Janeiro–Montevideo–Sandy Point–Valparaiso–Callao.
1879	Transferred to Orient Line management.
13.2.1880	First voyage London–Cape Town–Australia.
3.9.1880	Ran aground two miles south of the Cape Jervis Lighthouse on a voyage from London to Sydney, via Port Adelaide and Melbourne.

13.11.1880	Towed back to Port Adelaide by the tug *Albatross*.
4.12.1880	Sailed to Melbourne with *Albatross*.
8.12.1880	Arrived at Melbourne.
29.4.1886	Last Orient Line voyage to Australia. Transferred back to PSNC management
22.9.1886	On Liverpool–Valparaiso service.
1895	Scrapped at Tranmere, Birkenhead.

61. *Corcovado* (I) (1872–1875)

3,805 grt, 2,406 n, 387.6 x 43.1 x 33.11 feet.
Iron, single-screw, compound inverted; 2 cyl; 600 hp, steam pressure 65 lbs, by builder, 13 knots.
Three decks.
Passengers: 60 first-class, 70 second-class and 240 third-class.
Delivered by Laird Brothers, Birkenhead.

9.1872	Designed for Liverpool–South America–service.
19.2.1873	Maiden voyage Liverpool–South America–Valparaiso service.
1875	Sold to Royal Mail Line, renamed *Dom* to replace *Shannon*.
17.1.1876	First Royal Mail Line sailing, Capt. Woolward, Southampton–West Indies.
1889	In a major overhaul her tonnage was altered to 4,050 grt, 3,772 n and Triple expansion; 3 cyl; 678 hp, eight single ended boilers, twenty-four furnaces were installed by Earle's Company of Hull, giving her a speed of 15 knots. Passengers: 245 first and 26 second class.
1901	Broken up.

62. *Puno* (I) (1873–1875)

Sister to *Corcovado* (61)
3,805 grt, 2,406 n, 387.6 x 43.1 x 33.11 feet.
Iron, single-screw, compound inverted; 2 cyl; 600 hp, steam pressure 65 lbs, by builder, 13 knots.
Three decks.

Passengers: 60 first-class, 70 second-class and 240 third-class.
Delivered by Laird Brothers, Birkenhead.

14.5 1873	Maiden voyage Liverpool-South America–Valparaiso service.
1875	Sold to the Royal Mail Line, renamed *Para* to replace *Boyne*.
6.1876	On Southampton–West Indies service.
16.10.1876	On her second voyage there was an explosion in her hold creating a large hole in her saloon and three people lost their lives. The hold was being used to carry bananas in carbon dioxide at low temperatures as an experiment.
1990	She received a major overhaul when her tonnage was increased to 4,028 grt 3,772 n. Triple expansion; 3 cyl; 678 hp, eight single ended boilers, twenty-four furnaces were installed by Day, Summers & Company of Southampton, giving her a speed of 15 knots.
1901	Broken up.

63. *Santa Rosa* (1872–1890)

1,817 grt, 1,139 n, 308 x 38.2 x 20.5 feet.
Iron, single-screw, compound inverted; 2 cyl; 375 hp; by builder, 11 knots.
Two decks and shade deck. The deck beneath the foremast was open space, not a cabin deck.
Passengers: 116.
Delivered by Laird Brothers, Birkenhead.

1872	Delivered for the Valparaiso-Callao-Panama service.
1890	Purchased by the Lota Coal Company and later that year to Cousino Cia Valparaiso, renamed *Luis Cousino* and operated by Compañia Esplotadora de Lota y Coronel.
1902	Broken up.

64. *Colombia* (I) (1873–1890)
Sister to *Santa Rosa* (63)

1,823 grt, 1,137 n, 308 x 38.2 x 20.5 feet.
Iron single-screw, compound inverted; 2 cyl; 375 hp; by builder, 11 knots.
Two decks and shade deck. The deck beneath the foremast was open space, not a cabin deck.
Passengers: 116.
Delivered by Laird Brothers, Birkenhead.

1873	Delivered to the Valparaiso–Callao–Panama service.
1890	Sold and broken up.

65. *Rimac* (1872–1877)

1,805 grt, 1,227 n, 291.9 x 40 x 19.7 feet.
Iron, single-screw, compound inverted; 2 cyl; 340 hp; steam pressure 70 lb, by Fawcett, Preston & Company, Liverpool. 11 knots.
Two decks and awning deck.
Delivered by Evans & Company, Liverpool.

11.1872	Delivered to Vapariaso services.
1877	Purchased by the Valparaiso Steamship Company, Valparaiso. Retained same name.

66. *Ilo* (1872–1882)

1,794 grt, 1,229 n, 289.8 x 38.2 x 21.1 feet.
Iron, single-screw, compound inverted; 2 cyl; 300 hp; by builder, 11 knots.
Two decks.
Delivered by John Elder & Company, Glasgow at a cost of £47,728.

1.1872	Entered service.
1882	Hulked.

67. *Truxillo* (1872–1882)

Built as a replacement for *Santiago* (31).
1,449 grt, 978 n, 251.4 x 35.7 x 22.4 feet.
Iron, paddle-steamer, compound direct; 2 x 2 cyl; 300 hp; by builder, 11 knots.
Two decks, main deck was open across width of vessel.
Passengers: 175.
Delivered by John Elder & Company, Glasgow, at a cost of £44,000.

14.11.1871	Launched.
1.1872	Delivered to Pacific coast services.
1882	Hulked.

68. *Tacora* (1872–)

3,525 grt, 2,279 n, 375.7 x 41.4 x 33 feet.
Iron, single-screw, compound inverted; 2 cyl; 580 hp, steam pressure 65 lb, by builder, 13 knots.
Two decks.
Passengers: 60 first-class, 75 second-class and 300 third-class.
Delivered by John Elder & Company, Glasgow, at a cost of £103,475.

23.5.1872	Launched with engines built for *Acongagua* (57).
4.10.1872	Maiden voyage, Capt. C. M. Stewart, Liverpool–Rio de Janeiro–Valparaiso–Callao. She was competing with the White Star vessel *Republic*, which sailed on 5 Oct.
28.10.1872	Wrecked off Cape Santa Maria near Montevideo. *Tacora* came off the rocks and was beached. Ten passengers and three crew lost their lives.

69. *Galicia* (I) (1873–1898)

Similar to *Tacora* (68)
3,829 grt, 2,449 n, 383.5 x 43 x 33.7 feet.
Iron, single-screw, compound inverted; 2 cyl; 600 hp, steam pressure 65 lb, by builder, 13 knots.
Two decks.
Passengers: 60 first-class, 75 second-class and 300 third-class.
Delivered by Robert Napier & Sons, Glasgow.

14.1.1873	Launched.
23.4.1873	Maiden voyage Liverpool–Valparaiso.
1898	Sold to the Canadian Steam Navigation Company, Liverpool, and renamed *Gaspasia*.
1900	Scrapped at Genoa.

70. *Valparaiso* (II)(1873–1887)

Similar to *Tacora* (68)
3,575 grt, 2,284 n, 379.2 x 41.9 x 33.2 feet.
Iron, single-screw, compound inverted; 2 cyl; 550 hp, steam pressure 66 lb, by builder, 12 knots.
Two decks.
Passengers: 116 first-class, 50 second-class and 800 third-class.
Delivered by John Elder & Company, Glasgow at a cost of £129,850.

30.7.1873	Launched.
8.10.1873	Maiden voyage Birkenhead–Valparaiso.
28.2.1887	Lost at Vigo.

71. *Baja* (1872–)

74 grt, 8 n, 81.2 x 16 x 7.10 feet.
Iron, single-screw tug, compound; 2 cyl; 35 hp, by builder.
One deck.
Delivered by John Elder & Company, Glasgow.

1872	Delivered to Callao.

72. *Iberia* (1873–1903)

4,671 grt, 2,982 n, 433.6 x 45 x 35.1 feet.
Iron, single-screw, compound inverted; 2 cyl; 750 nhp; steam pressure 70 lb; four cylindrical boilers, by builder, 14 knots.
Two decks. Passengers: 100 first-class, 150 second-class, 340 third-class.
Delivered by John Elder & Company, Glasgow at a cost of £151,600.

6.12.1873	Launched, the world's largest ship after *Great Eastern*.
21.10.1874	Maiden voyage. Her construction had been held up by strikes.
12.5.1880	First sailing to Australia for the joint Orient-Pacific Line.
1881	Stand by vessel on the London-Australia service, replacing *Acongagua* (57).
1882	Requisitioned by Government during the Egyptian Arabi Pasha Campaigns for trooping duties. Fitted with refrigeration machinery.
25.1.1883	On the UK–Australia service via Cape Town.
1884	Returned to the Australia route via Suez. Electric lighting installed.
31.1.1890	Left London on her last Australian voyage.
11.6.1890	Transferred to Liverpool–Valparaiso route.
1893	Triple expansion engine fitted; 3 cyl; 600 nhp; four cylindrical boilers, by J. Rollo & Sons, Liverpool, 13 knots.
1895	Positioning voyage to Australia to replace another vessel on the service. The voyage via the Cape of Good Hope took thirty-two days.
1903	Broken up at Genoa.

73. *Liguria* (1874–1903)

Similar to *Iberia* (72)
4,666 grt, 2,980 n, 433.6 x 45 x 35.1 feet.
Iron, single-screw, compound inverted; 2 cyl; 750 hp; steam pressure 70 lb; 4 cylindrical boilers, by builder, 14 knots.
Two decks.
Passengers: 100 first-class, 150 second-class, 340 third-class.
Delivered by John Elder & Company, Glasgow at a cost of £150,350.

9.9.1874	Maiden voyage Birkenhead–Valparaiso.
1880	Transferred to Orient Line management.
12.5.1880	First voyage London–Suez–Melbourne–Sydney.
1882	Fitted with refrigeration machinery.
1882–83	Sailed to Australia via Cape Town.
1884	Electric lighting installed.
9.5.1890	Last Australian voyage.
17.9.1890	On Birkenhead–Valparaiso service.
1893	Triple expansion engine fitted; 3 cyl; 600 nhp; four cylindrical boilers, by J. Rollo & Sons, Liverpool, 15 knots.
7.1895	Left the United Kingdom to relieve a steamer in Australia, via Cape Town and averaged a speed of 14 knots for the voyage.
1903	Broken up at Genoa.

74. *Potosi* (I) (1873–1897)

4,218 grt, 2,704 n, 421.7 x 43.9 x 35.6 feet (lengthened by 25 feet during construction).

Iron, single-screw, compound inverted; 2 cyl; 600 hp; steam pressure 65 lb, by builder, 13 knots.
Two decks.
Passengers: 80 first-class, 110 second-class and 350 third-class.
Delivered by John Elder & Company, Glasgow.

14.5.1873	Launched.
6.8.1873	Maiden voyage Birkenhead–Valparaiso.
1880	Transferred to Orient Line management.
7.7.1880	First voyage to Australia.
26.5.1887	Final voyage to Australia, transferred back to Valparaiso service.
1897	Broken up at Genoa.

75. *Cotopaxi* (I) (1873–1889)

4,022 grt, 2,583 n, 402.2 x 42.9 x 33.9 feet.
Iron, single-screw, compound inverted; 2 cyl; 600 hp; steam pressure 65 lb, by builder, 13 knots. Engine was slightly different for *Potosi* (74).
Two decks.
Passengers: 100 first-class, 140 second-class and 320 third-class.
Delivered by John Elder & Company, Glasgow, at a cost of £105,750.

15.3.1873	Launched
18.6.1873	Maiden voyage Birkenhead–Valparaiso.
1879	Transferred to Orient Line management for Australian service.
14.4.1880	Final voyage on Australian service, back to Valparaiso route.
8.4.1889	Collided with the German vessel *Olympia* in the Straits of Magellan, beached and repaired.
15.4.1889	Refloated but then struck a rock and sank. The Kosmos Line vessel *Setos* rescued all 202 people on board.

Cotopaxi following collision in 1889.

PACIFIC STEAM NAVIGATION CO.

76. *Illimani* (1873–1879)
Sister of *Cotopaxi* (75)
4,022 grt, 2,579 n, 402.3 x 42.9 x 33.9 feet.
Iron, single-screw, compound inverted; 2 cyl; 600 hp; steam pressure 65 lb, by builder, 13 knots. Engine was slightly different for POTOSI (74).
Two decks.
Passengers: 100 first-class, 140 second-class and 320 third-class.
Delivered by John Elder & Company, Glasgow at a cost of £106,725.

16.12.1872	Launched.
26.3.1873	Maiden voyage Birkenhead–Valparaiso.
18.7.1879	While on the Australian service, she went aground on Mocha Island, off the coast of Yemen and sank.

77. *Britannia* (1873–1895)
4,129 grt, 2,480 n, 411.5 x 32.9 x 33.9 feet.
Iron single-screw, compound inverted; 2 cyl; 650 hp, steam pressure 65 lb, by builder, 12¾ knots.
Two decks.
Delivered by Laird Brothers, Birkenhead at a cost of £140,450.

27.5.1873	Launched.
2.8.1873	Maiden voyage
30.3.1885	Requisitioned as an auxiliary cruiser.
22.4.1885	Taken over at Valparaiso and sailed to Coquimbo for conversion. However, she was decommissioned and sent back to Liverpool.
4.9.1895	Grounded leaving Rio de Janeiro and sold for £1,000. Salvaged and repaired and sold to Camuyrano y Cia, Buenos Aires for £1,000.
1900	Purchased by Nogueira, Vives y Cia, Valparaiso.
1901	Broken up at Preston.

78. *Ayacucho* (1873–1890)
1,916 grt, 1,208 n, 311.9 x 38.2 x 21.1 feet.
Iron, single-screw, compound inverted; 2 cyl; 400 hp; steam pressure 65 lbs, by builder, 12 knots.
Two decks.
Delivered by T. Wingate & Company, Glasgow.

1873	Delivered for coastal services from Callao.
1890	Hulked.

79. *Lima* (II) (1873–1909)
Sister to *Ayacucho* (78)
1,804 grt, 1,132 n, 310.7 x 38.2 x 21.1 feet.
Iron, single-screw, compound inverted; 2 cyl; 400 hp; steam pressure 65 lbs, by builder, 12 knots.
Two decks.
Delivered by T. Wingate & Company, Glasgow.

1873	Built for services from Callao.
1880	Capt. Steadman towed a ship with a cargo of contraband to Peru

| 1909 | during the war between Chile and Peru and was dismissed. Lost off the coast of Chile. |

80. *Bolivia* (II) (1874–1895)
Sister to *Ayacucho* (78)
1,925 grt, 1,215 n, 310.7 x 38.2 x 21.1 feet.
Iron, single-screw, compound inverted; 2 cyl; 400 hp; steam pressure 65 lbs, by builder, 12 knots.
Two decks.
Delivered by T. Wingate & Company, Glasgow.

| 1874 | Delivered to operate on the coastal services. |
| 1895 | Hulked. |

81. *Oroya* (I) (1873–)
1,577 grt, 1,117 n, 270.11 x 35.6 x 22.6 feet.
Iron, paddle-steamer, compound direct acting, 2 cyl; 400 hp; by builder, 12 knots.
Two decks. Lengthened by 15 feet during construction.
Delivered by R. Napier & Company, Glasgow, at a cost of £65,000.

| 27.1.1873 | Delivered for Pacific coastal services. |
| 24.3.1879 | Sold to the Peruvian Government. |

82. *Islay* (1873–1883)
Sister of *Oroya* (81)
1,588 grt, 1,109 n, 271 x 35.6 x 22.6 feet.
Iron, paddle-steamer, compound direct acting, 2 cyl; 400 hp; by builder, 12 knots.
Two decks. Lengthened by 15 feet during construction.
Delivered by John Elder & Company, Glasgow.

27.4.1873	Delivered to company as their last paddle-steamer. For Pacific coastal services.
1881	On a voyage from Panama to Peru, during the Chile-Peru war she carried a cargo of rifles and was captured by Chilean naval vessels. When Capt. Petrice was released by the Chilean authorities he was sacked by the company.
1883	Hulked.

83. *Tacna* (1873–1874)
612 grt, 470 n, 219 x 26 x 13 feet.
Iron, single-screw compound direct acting; 2 cyl; by builder, 11 knots.
One deck and shelter deck.
Delivered by Laird Brothers, Birkenhead.

| 1873 | Delivered for the Pacific coastal services. |
| 7.3.1874 | On a voyage from Valparaiso to Port de Azucar she listed nine miles off Pichidaugue in a sudden squall of wind. An explosion occurred and the deck was blown out and she sank. Nineteen people lost their lives and Capt. Hyde was arrested by the Chilean authorities but was later released after protests by the British consul. |

84. *Amazonas* (1874–1886)
2,019 grt, 1,373 n, 301.8 x 38.11 x 20.5 feet.
Iron, single-screw, compound inverted; 2 cyl; 400 hp; steam pressure 65 lb, by Robert Napier, 11 knots.
Two decks and shade deck.
Delivered by J. Reid & Company, Glasgow.

6.1874	Delivered to Compania Sud Americana de Vapores, Valparaiso.
1874	Purchased by the PSNC.
1879	Delivered back to Chilean company for trooping services during the Chile-Peru war.

1881   Sold to Compania Sud Americana de Vapores.
1886   Deleted from Lloyds Register.

85. *Lontue* (1877–1888)
Sister to *Amazonas* (84)
1,648 grt, 1,121 n, 299 x 40 x 19.7 feet.
Iron, single-screw, compound inverted; 2 cyl; 400 hp; steam pressure 65 lb, by Blackwood & Gordon, Port Glasgow, 11 knots.
Two decks and shade deck.
Delivered by J. Reid & Company, Glasgow.

4.1873   Delivered to Compania Sud Americana de Vapores, Valparaiso.
1877   Purchased by PSNC
1879   Chartered to the Chilean Government and used as a supply vessel. It was stipulated in the charter agreement that she would not be used in any activity connected to the war with Peru.
1881   Resold to Compañia Sud Americana de Vapores.
1888   Re-purchased by PSNC, retaining the Chilean flag and later converted to a hulk.

86. *Lobo* (1874–)
106 grt, 89.7 x 18.4 x 8.9 feet.
Iron, single-screw water launch, compound.
Delivered by John Elder & Company, Glasgow at a cost of £4,950.

2.1874   Built for use as a water launch at Callao.

87. *Casma* (II) (1878–1899)
592 grt, 358 n, 180.5 x 30.1 x 14.9 feet.
Steel single-screw, compound inverted; 2 cyl; 95 hp, by builder, 10 knots.
Two decks, three masts, quarter deck 46 feet.
Passengers: 40.
Delivered by Laird Brothers, Birkenhead.

11.1878   PSNC's first steel ship, delivered for Pacific coastal services.
1899   Sold to J. J. McAuliffe & Company, Valparaiso, to be based at Coquimbo.
1900   Purchased by the government of Costa Rica.
1910   Broken up.

88. *Chala* (1879–1897)
Sister of *Casma* (87)
598 grt, 358 n, 180.5 x 30.1 x 14.9 feet.
Steel single-screw, compound inverted; 2 cyl; 95 hp, by builder, 10 knots.
Two decks, three masts, quarter deck 46 feet.
Passengers: 40.
Delivered by Laird Brothers, Birkenhead.

1879   Delivered for the Pacific coastal services.
1897   Hulked.

89. *Arauco* (1879–1899)
801 grt, 672 n, 200 x 29.2 x 15.6 feet.
Steel single-screw, compound; 2 cyl; 105 hp, by builder, 10 knots.
Three decks.
Delivered by Laird Brothers, Birkenhead.

4.1879   Delivered to company.
1899   Sold to J. J. McAuliffe & Company, Valparaiso, registered at Coquimbo, Chile, renamed Almirante Latorre.
1909   Deleted from Lloyds Register.

90. *Puchoco* (1879–1899)
Sister of *Arauco* (89)
804 grt, 673 n, 200 x 29.2 x 15.6 feet.
Steel single-screw, compound; 2 cyl; 105 hp, by builder, 10 knots.
Three decks.
Delivered by Laird Brothers, Birkenhead.
1879	Delivered to company.
1899	Sold to J. J. McAuliffe & Company, Valparaiso, renamed *Isidora*.
1900	Owned by Cia Esplotadora de Lota y Coronel, Valparaiso.
1906	Wrecked.

91. *Mendoza* (1879–1904)
2,160 grt, 1,357 n, 320 x 40.4 x 20.8 feet.
Steel single-screw, compound inverted; 2 cyl; 300 hp, by builder, 11 knots.
Two decks, the first British merchant ship to use electricity from a Gramme generator.
Delivered by Robert Napier & Sons, Glasgow.
1879	Delivered for the service from Valparaiso to Callao.
1904	Hulked.

92. *Pizarro* (I) (1879–1907)
Sister of *Mendoza* (91)
2,160 grt, 1,357 n, 320 x 40.4 x 20.8 feet.
Steel single-screw, compound inverted; 2 cyl; 300 hp, by builder, 11 knots.
Two decks.
One of the first British merchant ships to use electricity from a Gramme generator.
Delivered by Robert Napier & Sons, Glasgow.
1879	Delivered for the coastal services.
1907	Hulked.

93. *Puno* (1881–1904)
Sister of *Mendoza* (91)
2,398 grt, 1,504 n, 320 x 40.4 x 20.8 feet.
Steel single-screw, compound inverted; 2 cyl; 300 hp, by builder, 11 knots.
Two decks.
One of the first British merchant ships to use electricity from a Gramme generator.
Delivered by Robert Napier & Sons, Glasgow.
1881	Delivered for the coastal services.
1904	Hulked.

94. *Serena* (1881–1903)
Sister of *Mendoza* (91)
2,394 grt, 1,502 n, 320 x 40.4 x 20.8 feet.
Steel single-screw, compound inverted; 2 cyl; 300 hp, by builder, 11 knots.
Two decks.
One of the first British merchant ships to use electricity from a Gramme generator.
Delivered by Robert Napier & Sons, Glasgow.
1881   Delivered for the coastal services.
1903   Hulked.

95. *Ronachan* (1881–)
1,156 grt, sailing ship.
1881   The company purchased this vessel as a hulk from Rankin Gilmour to be stationed at Diego Garcia as a coaling storage hulk.

96. *Arran* (1881–)
962 grt, sailing ship.
1881   Bought with *Ronachan* (95) and also stationed at Diego Garcia.

97. *Arica* (II) (1881–)
1,771 grt, 1,310 n, 300 x 36.2 x 19.4 feet.
Steel single-screw, compound inverted; 2 cyl, 220 hp; by builder, 11 knots.
Two decks.
Delivered by Laird Brothers, Birkenhead.
1881   Delivered for the coastal services.
1913   Some records show she was hulked at Colon.
1921   Still shown on Lloyds Register.
1926   Not listed on Lloyds Register. Some records show she was sold to US interests.

98. *Ecuador* (1881–1905)
Sister of *Arica* (97)
1,768 grt, 1,310 n, 300 x 36.2 x 19.4 feet.
Steel single-screw, compound inverted; 2 cyl, 220 hp; by builder, 11 knots.
Two decks.
Delivered by Laird Brothers, Birkenhead.
1881   Delivered for the coastal services.
1905   Sank fourteen miles off Constitucion, Chile.

99. *Osorno* (1881–1899)
532 grt, 308 n, 176.2 x 27.1 x 13.9 feet.
Steel twin-screw, compound, 2 x 2 cyl; 90 hp, by builder 11 knots.
One deck, open topped bridge.
10.1881   Delivered for the Valparaiso–south Chilean ports service.
11.1899   Purchased by the Government of Nicaragua to be used as an armed transport vessel.

100. *Morro* (II) (1881–1902)
170 grt, 69 n, 125.9 x 23 x 8 feet.
Steel twin-screw, compound 2 x 2 cyl; 90 hp, by builder 11 knots.
One deck, schooner rigged.
Delivered by Scott & Company, Greenock.
8.1881   Delivered and replaced *Morro* (22) as the Panama tender.
1902   Sold to J. J. McAuliffe, Valparaiso.
1906   Renamed *Araucancita*.
1909   Renamed *Aramac*.

110 PACIFIC STEAM NAVIGATION CO.

1911   Purchased by Sociedad Lobitos Oilfield Ltd., Callao, a subsidiary of C. T. Bowring.

1922   Scrapped.

101. *Chiloe* (1882–1892)

2,309 grt, 1,326 n, 321 x 37.4 x 24.9 feet.
The last iron-hulled vessel constructed for the company.
Single-screw, compound inverted; 2 cyl; 400 hp, by builder, 11 knots.
Two decks.
Delivered by John Elder & Company, Glasgow.

1882   Delivered for the Pacific coast coastal services.

7.1892   Sank at Talcahuano on a voyage from Valparaiso to Puerto Montt.

102. *Manavi* (1885–1920)

1,041 grt, 615 n, 216 x 35.1 x 15 feet.
Steel single-screw, compound; 2 cyl, 90 hp; by builder, 10 knots.
Two decks and shade deck.
Passengers: 54.
Delivered by Robert Napier & Sons, Glasgow.

5.1885   Delivered for the Pacific coastal services.

1890   New boilers installed.

1920   Sold.

103. *Quito* (IV) (1888–1915)

Sister of *Manavi* (102)
1,089 grt, 815 n, 216 x 35.1 x 15 feet.
Steel single-screw, compound 2 cyl; 90 hp, by builder, 10 knots.
Two decks and shade deck.
Passengers: 54.

Manavi.

Delivered by Laird Brothers, Birkenhead.

1888   Delivered for Pacific coastal services.

1915   Sold to Etchegaray Onfray & Company, Valparaiso.

1925   Broken up.

104. *Oroya* (1887–1905)

6.057 grt, 3,359 n, 474 x 49.4 x 35.4 feet.
Steel, single-screw, triple expansion; 3 cyl; 1,200 hp, 7,000 ihp, by Naval Construction and Armament Company, Barrow, 12½ knots.
Four decks and double-bottom.

Passengers: 126 first-class, 154 second-class and 412 third-class.

The company's first straight-stemmed vessel and the largest ship built for them, to date.

Delivered by Barrow Shipbuilding Company, Barrow.

31.8.1886	Launched for the Australian service.
17.2.1887	Maiden voyage London–Suez Canal–Melbourne-Sydney.
4.3.1895	Aground and damaged in the Bay of Naples.
1905	Major overhaul where the funnels were heightened.
2.1906	Sold to the Royal Mail Line for their joint service to Australia.
1907	Renamed *Oro* for the delivery voyage to the shipbreakers in Genoa, Italy.

105. *Orizaba* (1886–1905)

Sister to *Oroya* (104)

6.077 grt, 3,359 n, 474 x 49.4 x 35.4 feet.

Steel, single-screw, triple expansion; 3 cyl; 1,200 hp, 7,000 ihp, by Naval Construction and Armament Company, Barrow, 12½ knots.

Four decks and double bottom.

Passengers; 126 first, 154 second and 412 third class.

Delivered by Barrow Shipbuilding Company, Barrow.

1886	Allocated to the Orient Line–managed Australia service.
30.9.1886	Maiden voyage Southampton–Suez Canal–Melbourne–Sydney.
17.2.1905	Aground off Garden Island, Sydney following bush fires ashore (Captain R. Archer) on a voyage from London to Sydney with 160 passengers. The wreck was later sold for £3,750 and the cargo for £500. At the Inquiry, Captain Archer was charged with having committed an error of judgement in attempting to take the vessel over Five Fathom Bank and was censured and ordered to pay half the costs of the Inquiry, although the court noted that the haze and strong current had contributed to the wrecking.
2011	The wreck is considered to be of historical interest as the vessel is an early reminder of ships involved in the shipment of mail and cargo from London to Australia during the last quarter of the nineteenth century. The wreck lies with its bow out to sea on a north-west by south-west axis, in a depth of water ranging from four to seven metres. The boilers are still intact as are the crank-shaft and other remains lying exposed on the reef top.

106. *Orotava* (1889–1906)

5,857 grt, 3,096 n, 430 x 49.3 x 34.2 feet.

Steel, single-screw, triple expansion; 3 cyl; 1,030 hp and 7,000 ihp, by Naval Construction & Armament Company, Barrow, 14½ knots.

Two decks.

Passengers: 126 first-class, 120 second-class and 400 third-class.

Delivered by Barrow Shipbuilding Company, Barrow.

1889	Delivered for Liverpool–Valparaiso route. Transferred to Orient Line management, for the Australian service after two voyages.
6.6.1890	First voyage London–Suez Canal–Melbourne–Sydney.
1896	While coaling at Tilbury she capsized. Four people lost their lives. She was raised and repaired.
2.1897	Returned to the Australian service.
1899–1903	She became Boer War Transport No. 91, in PSNC colours.
13.3.1903	Returned to the Australian service.
2.1906	Purchased by the Royal Mail Line.
5.3.1909	Last voyage on Australia route, transferred to West Indies service, with a capacity for 250 passengers.
10.1914	Requisitioned as an Armed Merchant Cruiser and allocated to 'B' Line of the 19th Cruiser Squadron.

11.1916 Returned to the Royal Mail Lines.

1919 Owned by the Shipping Controller, London (managed by Royal Mail Lines).

11. 1921 Scrapped.

107. *Oruba* (I) (1889–1906)
Sister to *Orotava* (106)
5,852 grt, 3,351 n, 430 x 49.3 x 34.2 feet.
Steel, single-screw, triple expansion; 3 cyl; 1,030 hp and 7,000 ihp, by Naval Construction & Armament Company, Barrow, 14½ knots.
Two decks.
Passengers: 126 first-class, 120 second-class and 400 third-class.
Delivered by Barrow Shipbuilding Company, Barrow.

1889 Delivered for the Liverpool–Valparaiso service.

1890 Transferred to the Orient Line service.

4.7.1890 First sailing to Australia.

2.1906 Royal Mail Line ownership on Australia service.

16.10.1908 Final sailing on Australian service, transferred to the Royal Mail Line route to Buenos Aires.

1914 Sold to the Admiralty and rebuilt as HMS *Orion*.

1915 Scuttled at Mudros Harbour as a breakwater during the Dardenelles campaign.

108. *Santiago* (IV) (1889–1907)
2,953 grt, 1,366 n, 350 x 45.2 x 22.6 feet.
Steel, single-screw, triple expansion; 3 cyl; 471 nhp, by Naval Armaments & Construction Company, Barrow, 12 knots.
Two decks.
Passengers; 130.
Delivered by Barrow Shipbuilding Company, Barrow.

1889 Delivered for the Valparaiso–Callao service.

18.6.1907 Sank near Corral.

109. *Arequipa* (II) (1889–1903)
Sister of *Santiago* (108)
2,953 grt, 1,387 n, 350x45.2 x 22.6 feet.
Steel, single-screw, triple expansion; 3 cyl; 471 nhp, by Naval Armaments & Construction Company, Barrow, 12 knots.
Two decks.
Passengers; 130.
Delivered by Barrow Shipbuilding Company, Barrow.

1889   Delivered for the Valparaiso–Callao service.
2.6.1903   Whilst loading cargo during a gale at Valparaiso buoys she keeled over and sank. There were 100 people on board and over 80 lost their lives.

110. *Assistance* (1891–1926)
214 grt, 60 n, 105 x 22.7 x 12 feet.
Steel, single-screw tug, compound; 2 cyl; stroke: 24 in; 63 rhp, by builder.
One deck.
Delivered by Gourlay Brothers & Company, Dundee.
1891   Based at Liverpool and then sent to Chile.
1926   Purchased by Oelckers Hermanos of Chile, renamed *Tautil*.
7.1929   Wrecked near Lota.

111. *Magellan* (II) (1893–1918)
3,590 grt, 2,320 n, 360.7 x 43.2 x 27.1 feet.
Steel, single-screw, triple expansion; 3 cyl; 302 nhp: 2,100 ihp, by builder, 12 knots.
Passengers: 12 second-class. Cargo: 234,000 cubic feet in four holds, nine derricks. Crew: 40. Coal: 1,235 tons.
Delivered by Harland & Wolff, Belfast.
1893   Delivered for the service to the West Coast of South America.
18.7.1918   Torpedoed and sank fifty-three miles north-east of Cape Serrat. One lost.

112. *Inca* (II) (1893–1923)
Sister of *Magellan* (111)
3,593 grt, 2,322 n, 350 x 45.2 x 22.6 feet.
Steel, single-screw, triple expansion; 3 cyl; 302 nhp: 2,100 ihp, by builder, 12 knots.
Passengers: 12 second-class. Cargo: 234,000 cubic feet in four holds, nine derricks. Crew: 40. Coal: 1,235 tons.
Delivered by Harland & Wolff, Belfast.
1893   Delivered for the UK to South America cargo service.
1923   Purchased by Soc. Anon y Comercial Braun y Blanchard, Punta Arenas, Argentina and renamed *Llanquihue*.
2.9.1928   Ran aground and wrecked in the Magellan Strait on a voyage from Valparaiso to Buenos Aires.
1929   Scrapped.

113. *Sarmiento* (I) (1893–1910)
Sister of *Magellan* (111)
3,603 grt, 2,332 n, 361 x 45.2 x 22.6 feet.
Steel, single-screw, triple expansion; 3 cyl; 302 nhp: 2,100 ihp, by builder, 12 knots.
Passengers: 12 second-class. Cargo: 234,000 cubic feet in four holds, nine derricks. Crew: 40. Coal: 1235 tons.
Delivered by Harland & Wolff, Belfast.
1893   Delivered for the UK to South America cargo service.
1910   Sold to Messageries Maritimes, Marseille and renamed *Normand* for their UK/French ports to the Black Sea service.
1923   Broken up in Italy.

114. *Antisana* (1893–1911)
Sister of *Magellan* (111)
3,584 grt, 2,317 n, 360.7 x 43.2 x 27.1 feet.
Steel, single-screw, triple expansion; 3 cyl; 302 nhp: 2,100 ihp, by builder, 12 knots.

Passengers: 12 second-class. Cargo: 234,000 cubic feet in four holds, nine derricks. Crew: 40. Coal: 1,235 tons.
Delivered by Harland & Wolff, Belfast.

1893	Delivered for the UK to South America cargo service.
1911	Sold to Messageries Maritimes and renamed *Basque* to operate alongside *Normand*.
18.2.1918	Torpedoed by UB 52 at 11.00 hours, at Marsa Sirocco. The second engineer, Achille Vidal died while attempting to fight the fire on board. He was awarded the Legion d'Honneur.
20.2.1918	Beached at Malta.
12.1920	Resumed service to Black Sea ports.
11.1923	Broken up in Italy.

115. *Orellana* (1893–1905)

4,821 grt, 3,095 n, 401 x 47.7 x 19.11 feet.
Steel, single-screw, triple expansion; 3 cyl; 483 nhp; by builder, 11 knots.
Three decks.
Passengers: 70 first-class and 675 emigrants.
Delivered by Harland & Wolff, Belfast.

7.12.1892	Launched.
12.4.1893	Maiden voyage, mainly cargo as emigrant service was seasonal.
1905	Purchased by Hamburg America Line, renamed *Allemania*.
1906	Sold to the Russian Government, renamed *Kowno*. Replaced vessels lost in the Russo-Japanese war.
1907	Owned by Hamburg America Line, becoming *Allemania* again.
4.1917	Taken over by the American Government, renamed *Owasco*, operating for the United States Shipping Board.
10.12.1917	Torpedoed by German submarine off Alicante, beached, and following a survey it was decided that she was beyond repair.
1918	Broken up in Spain.

116. *Orcana* (I) (1893–1905)

Sister to *Orellana* (115) 4,803 grt, 3,080 n, 401 x 47.7 x 19.11 feet.
Steel, single-screw, triple expansion; 3 cyl; 483 nhp; by builder, 11 knots.
Three decks.
Passengers: 70 first and 675 emigrants.
Delivered by Harland & Wolff, Belfast.

7.3.1893	Launched.
19.7.1893	Maiden voyage on same route as *Orellana* (115)
1899–1903	Used as a hospital ship during the Boer War as Transport No. 40.
1905	Purchased by the Hamburg America Line, renamed *Albingia*.
1906	Transferred to Russian Government, renamed *Grodno*.

1907	Renamed *Albingia*.
4.1917	Taken over by the American Government, renamed *Argonaut* and operated by the War Shipping Board.
5.6.1918	Attacked and sank by U-82 off Bishop Rock.

117. *Orissa* (1893–1918)

5,317 grt, 3,320 n, 421 x 48.9 x 33 feet.
Steel, twin-screw, triple expansion, 2 x 3 cyl; 568 nhp, two double ended boilers, by builder, 15 knots. Coal: 1,586 tonnes at 84 tonnes a day.
Three decks.
Passengers: 70 first-class, 104 second-class and 456 third-class. Crew: 120.
Delivered by Harland & Wolff, Belfast.

15.12.1892	Launched.
11.4.1893	Maiden voyage Liverpool-Valparaiso.
1899–1904	Transport No. 18 during the Boer War. Lord Kitchener, Sir John French and Sir Ian Hamilton travelled on her from Cape Town when the war ended. She had deck-houses fitted between the focastle and fore-mast and two pairs of vents, one to bridge height.
8.1906	Used as a refugee ship when an earthquake struck Valparaiso.
25.6.1918	Torpedoed and sank by UB-73, 21 miles south-west of Skerrymore Rock, on a voyage from Liverpool to Philadelphia, in ballast. Six people lost their lives.

118. *Oropesa* (I) (1895–1915)

Sister of *Orissa* (117)
5,303 grt, 3,308 n, 421 x 48.9 x 33 feet.
Steel, twin-screw, triple expansion, 2x3 cyl; 568 nhp, by builder, double ended boilers, 15 knots.
Coal: 1,586 tonnes at 84 tonnes a day.
Three decks.
Passengers: 70 first-class, 104 second-class and 456 third-class. Crew: 120.
Delivered by Harland & Wolff, Belfast.

29.11.1894	Launched.
28.2.1895	Maiden voyage Liverpool–Valparaiso, Capt Hayes.
11.1914	Requisitioned by the Admiralty becoming an Armed Merchant Cruiser of the 10th Cruiser Squadron. 6 x 6 in and 2 x 6 pounders. Capt. Percy Brown.
3.1915	Sank a U-boat off Skerryvore, Scotland.
12.1915	Transferred to the French Navy, renamed *Champagne*, retained her British crew.
15.10.1917	Torpedoed by U-96 and sank in the Irish Sea. Fifty-six lost their lives. In the Irish Sea south west of the Calf of Man, the lookout at the starboard side reported a periscope, and the

vessel was struck almost instantaneously by a torpedo in the engine room. The confidential books were locked in the steel safe by the decoding officers and all other confidential papers were destroyed. All steam was cut off and the main engines stopped, followed by another explosion on the port side in the forepart of the after welldeck. The order to abandon ship was given and the boats were lowered with difficulty due to the rough seas. Oliver Ward AB, RNVR, AB Ryan RNVR, LS Watkins RNR and LS Cox RNR all volunteered to remain by the foremost pair of guns. The four men remained at their post when the submarine came to the surface but Cox was the only one that survived the attack. Two of the lifeboats sailed to the Isle of Man and the others were towed there by fishing boats. Captain Brown said, 'The ship went down with a portion of her guns manned and ready to fire and traditions of the service were upheld. At the time of the attack we were going as fast as we could to keep up, lookouts were stationed all round the ship and were alert. We had no escorts'.

119. *Oravia* (1897–1912)
Sister of *Orissa* (117)
5,321 grt, 3,318 n, 421 x 48.9 x 33 feet.
Steel, twin-screw, triple expansion, 2 x 3 cyl; 568 nhp, by builder, double ended boilers, 15 knots.
Coal: 1,586 tonnes at 84 tonnes a day.
Three decks.
Passengers: 70 first-class, 104 second-class and 456 third-class. Crew: 120.
Delivered by Harland & Wolff, Belfast.

5.12.1896	Launched.
1.7.1897	Maiden voyage Liverpool–Valparaiso.
12.11.1912	On a voyage from Liverpool to Callao she went aground on Billy Rock, Port Stanley at the Falkland Islands and was abandoned on the 16 November.

120. *Chiriqui* (1896–1910)
643 grt, 343 n, 185 x 31.1 x 12.9 feet.
Steel, single-screw, compound inverted; 2 cyl; 90 rhp, by builder, 11 knots.
One deck, shade deck.

Above: *Oravia* aground at Port Stanley, Falkland Islands, in 1912.

Delivered by Wigham Richardson & Company, Newcastle.
1896   Delivered for West Coast coastal services.
28.9.1910   Sank following an explosion.

121. *Taboga* (1898–1909)
Sister of *Chiriqui* (120)
649 grt, 348 n, 185 x 31.1 x 12.9 feet.
Steel, single-screw, compound inverted; 2 cyl; 90 rhp, by builder, 11 knots.
One deck, shade deck.
Delivered by Wigham Richardson & Company, Newcastle.
1898   Delivered for the coastal services.
1901   Seized by the Government of Colombia and was released following an intervention by a British gun-boat.
1909   Purchased by Pinel Brothers, Panama.
5.1911   Wrecked.

122. *Perlita* (1896–)
49 grt, 8 n, 62 x 15.4 x 6.2 feet.
Steam launch, single-screw, compound; 2 cyl.
1896   Built to service vessels lying at the buoys at Valpariaso.

123. *Chile* (III) (1896–1923)
3,225 grt, 1,702 n, 350.4 x 43.1 x 19.5 feet.
Steel, twin-screw, triple expansion, 2 x 3 cyl; 324 nhp. By builder, 12½ knots.
Two decks, shade deck.
Passengers: 100 first-class, 50 second-class and 300 third-class.
Delivered by Caird & Company, Greenock.
1896   Delivered for the Valparaiso–Callao service.
1921   Transferred to the Valparaiso–Cristobal route.
1923   Purchased by Soc. Maritima y Comercial R. W. James y Cia, Valparaiso, renamed *Flora*
1934   Scrapped.

124. *Peru* (III) (1896–1923)
Sister of *Chile* (123)
3,225 grt, 1,702 n, 350.4 x 43.1 x 19.5 feet.
Steel, twin-screw, triple expansion, 2 x 3 cyl; 324 nhp. By builder, 12½ knots.
Two decks, shade deck.
Passengers: 100 first-class, 50 second-class and 300 third-class.
Delivered by Caird & Company, Greenock.
1896   Delivered for the Valparaiso–Callao route.
1921   Transferred to the Valparaiso–Cristobal service.
1923   Sold to Soc. Anon Gonzalez Soffia y Cia.
1928   Sold to Soc. Anon Maritima Chilena.
1944   Broken up.

125. *Corcovado* (II) (1896–1921)
4,568 grt, 2,950 n, 390 x 47.2 x 30 feet.
Steel, single-screw, triple expansion; 3 cyl; 2,300 ihp, by Wallsend Slipway Company, Newcastle,
10 ¾ knots.
Three decks.
Passengers: 12 second class. Crew: 51.
Delivered by Swan Hunter, Newcastle.
1896   Delivered for the cargo service to West coast of South America ports.
1921   Scrapped.

126. *Sorata* (II) (1896–1922)

Sister of *Corcovado* (125)

4,581 grt, 2,943 n, 390 x 47.2 x 30 feet.

Steel, single-screw, triple expansion; 3 cyl; 2,300 ihp, by Wallsend Slipway Company, Newcastle,

10 ¾ knots.

Three decks.

Passengers: 12 second-class. Crew: 51.

Delivered by Swan Hunter, Newcastle.

1896	Delivered for the cargo services to South America.
1914–18	Requisitioned by the Admiralty.
1922	Purchased by Schroder, Holken und Fischer of Hamburg and renamed *Otto Fischer*. Broken up that year.

127. *Ortona* (1899–1905)

7,945 grt, 4,115 n, 515 x 55.4 x 33.7 feet.

Steel, twin-screw, triple expansion, 2 x 3 cyl; 560 hp, steam pressure 190 lb, four double ended boilers, 16 furnaces, by Naval Construction & Armament Company, Barrow, 14 knots.

Two decks.

Passengers: 130 first-class, 162 second-class and 300 third-class.

24.11.1899	Maiden Voyage under joint Orient-PSNC service to Suez, Melbourne and Sydney.
6.1902	Transport No. 12, for trooping duty to South Africa, during the Boer War.
9.10.1903	On the Australian service.
25.8.1905	Left London for Australia and intercepted an eclipse path off the coast of Majorca. One hundred passengers were onboard to witness the eclipse, including Sir Oliver Lodge who was involved in the introduction of wireless telegraph.

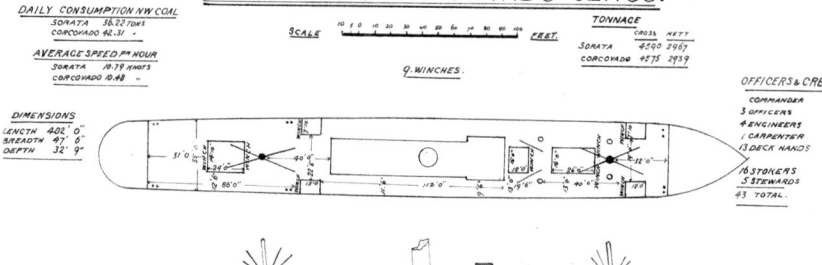

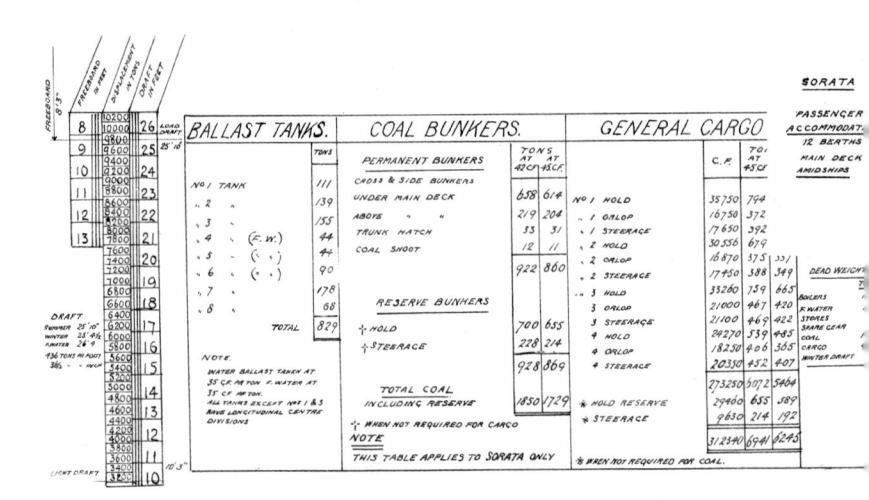

The eclipse passengers left the ship at Marseille, its next port of call.

2.1906	Purchased by the Royal Mail Line.
30.4.1909	Last Australian voyage.
1910	Converted for cruising and renamed *Arcadian*. Passengers: 320 one class.
1915	Converted to a troopship. At Gallipoli as Headquarters ship to Sir Ian Hamilton.
15.4.1917	On a voyage from Salonika to Alexandria she was torpedoed and sank. Out of 1,335 people on board, 279 lost their lives.

128. *Colombia* (II) (1899–1907)

3,335 grt, 1,764 n, 359.4 x 43.2 x 19.4 feet.
Steel, twin-screw, triple expansion 2 x 3 cyl; 324 hp, by builder, 12½ knots.
Similar type of engines fitted to *Chile* (123) and *Peru* (124).
Two decks and shade deck.
Delivered by Caird & Company, Greenock.

1899	Delivered for the service to the Pacific coast.
9.8.1907	Ran aground and wrecked at Saenze Point, off Lobos de Tierra, Peru on a voyage from Payta to Eten.

129. *Guatemala* (1899–1923)

Similar to *Colombia* (128)
3,227 grt, 1,757 n, 359.3 x 43.2 x 19.4 feet.
Steel, twin-screw, triple expansion 2 x 3 cyl; 324 hp, by builder, 12½ knots.
Similar type of engines fitted to *Chile* (123) and *Peru* (124).
Two decks and shade deck.
Delivered by Caird & Company, Greenock.

1899	Delivered for the Valparaiso–Arica–Mollendo–Callao service.
1921	Transferred to the Valparaiso–Cristobal service.
1923	Sold to James y Cia, Valparaiso, renamed *Fresia*.
1935	Owned by Soc. Anon. Maritima Chilena, Valparaiso.
1949	Scrapped.

130. *Talca* (II) (1900–1901)

1,081 grt, 789 n, 209.11 x 35.1 x 15.7 feet.
Steel, twin-screw, triple expansion; 2 x 3 cyl; by builder, 10 knots.
Two decks.

1900	Delivered for coastal services.
12.7.1901	Wrecked off Puchoco Point, Chile.

131. *Potosi* (II) (1900–1900)
5,300 grt, 3,310 n, 400.6 x 50 x 33.4 feet.
Steel, twin-screw, triple expansion; 2 x 3 cyl; 411 hp, by builder, 13 knots.
Three decks.
Passengers: 24 second-class and 338 third-class. Crew: 61.
Delivered by Wigham Richardson & Company, Newcastle.

1900	Designed and built for the Liverpool–Valparaiso route, but sold after completion to the Russian Volunteer Fleet and renamed *Kazan*.
1904	Captured by the Japanese, renamed *Kasato Matu*.
1918	Owned by Osaka Shosen K.K.
1930	Broken up in Japan.

132. *Galicia* (II) (1901–1917)
Sister of *Potosi* (131)
5,896 grt, 3,796 n, 400.6 x 50 x 33.4 feet.
Steel, twin-screw, triple expansion; 2 x 3 cyl; 411 hp, by builder, 13 knots.
Three decks.
Passengers: 24 second-class and 338 third-class. Crew: 61.
Delivered by Wigham Richardson & Company, Newcastle.

1901	Designed and built for the Liverpool–Valparaiso route. Completed without passenger accommodation.
31.7.1915	Mined in the English Channel and limped back to port.
12.5.1917	Mined off Teignmouth and sank.

133. *Perico* (1901–1924)
268 grt, 21 n, 125.6 x 23.1 x 9.5 feet.
Steel, twin-screw, compound; 2 x 2 cyl; 65 hp, by builder 9 knots.
One deck and shade deck.
Delivered by J. Jones & Sons, Birkenhead.

1901	Delivered as a tender at Panama, replacing *Morro* (100)
1924	Completed service.

134. *Panama* (III) (1902–1920)
5,981 grt, 3,507 n, 401.2 x 52.4 x 33.8 feet.
Steel, twin-screw, triple expansion; 2 x 3 cyl; 550 nhp, by builder, 13½ knots.
Coal: 1,304 tonnes at 78.33 per day.
Two decks, shade deck and promenade deck.
Passengers: 106 first-class, 104 second-class and 595 third-class. Crew: 123.
Delivered by Fairfield Ship Building & Engineering Company, Glasgow.

8.3.1902	Launched.
5.1902	Maiden voyage Liverpool–Valparaiso (later to coastal services).
1914–1918	Service as a hospital ship and was present at Gallipoli with accommodation for nineteen officers, 217 cots and 248 berths.
11.1918	Repatriated German prisoners of war.
1920	Became the Admiralty's permanent hospital ship *Maine*.
24.5.1922	Stationed at Malta.
1924	Stationed at Constantinople.
1.1927	Moved to China Station until November.
1935	Hotel ship for 500 guests at the Silver Jubilee of King George V.
1936	During the Abyssinian War she was based at Alexandria then based at Haifa during the Palestine troubles.
1937–38	Evacuated 6,574 refugees during the Spanish Civil War.
1939	Classed as the oldest hospital ship, given the No.1.
6.9.1941	Bombed at Alexandria, four lost their lives.
1945	At Piraeus.

22.10.1946	The British destroyers HMS *Saumarez* and HMS *Volage* struck Albanian mines and during the rescue operation in the Corfu Channel forty-five lives were lost, and *Maine* grounded severely.
21.2.1947	Paid off at Rosyth.
8.7.1948	Arrived at Barrow to be broken up.

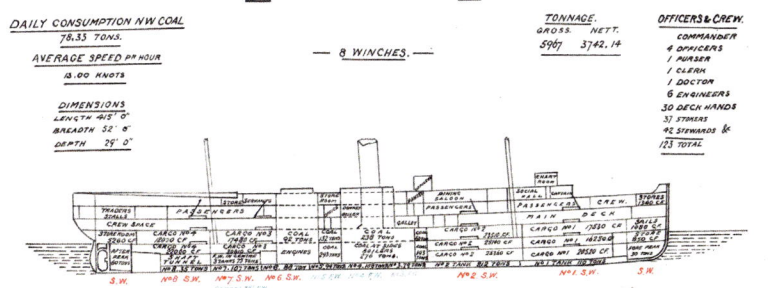

135. *Victoria* (1902–1923)
Similar to *Panama* (143)

5,967 grt, 3,742 n, 401.2 x 52.4 x 33.8 feet.
Steel, twin-screw, triple expansion; 2 x 3 cyl; 550 nhp, by builder, 13½ knots.
Coal: 1,304 tonnes at 78.33 per day.
Two decks, shade deck and promenade deck.
Passengers: 106 first-class, 104 second-class and 595 third-class. Crew: 123.
Delivered by Fairfield Ship Building & Engineering Company, Glasgow.

21.6.1902	Launched.
5.3.1903	Maiden voyage Liverpool–Valparaiso then on Callao service.
1914–18	Requisitioned by Admiralty.
1923	Broken up in Holland.

136. *Mexico* (1902–1922)
Similar to *Panama* (143)

5,549 grt, 2,994 n, 401.2 x 52.4 x 33.8 feet.
Steel, twin-screw, triple expansion; 2 x 3 cyl; 550 nhp, by builder, 13½ knots.
Coal: 1304 tonnes at 78.33 per day. Two decks, shade deck and promenade deck.
Passengers: 130 first-class, 104 second-class and 595 third-class. Crew: 123.

Delivered by Fairfield Ship Building & Engineering Company, Glasgow.

22.3.1902	Launched.
2.7.1902	Sailed on PSNC's first Norwegian cruise with 114 passengers on board.
30.7.1902	Maiden voyage Liverpool-Valparaiso.
23.3.1917	Whilst sailing through the English Channel she collided with a mine or torpedo. She steamed astern to the nearest port and cotton bales were used to stop the water entering the hull.
1922	Broken up.

137. *California* (1902–1917)
Similar to *Panama* (143)
5,547 grt, 2,991 n, 401.2 x 52.4 x 33.8 feet.
Steel, twin-screw, triple expansion; 2 x 3 cyl; 550 nhp, by builder, 13½ knots.
Coal: 1,304 tonnes at 78.33 per day. Two decks, shade deck and promenade deck.
Passengers: 130 first-class, 104 second-class and 595 third-class. Crew: 123.
Delivered by Fairfield Ship Building & Engineering Company, Glasgow.

21.6.1902	Launched on same day as *Victoria* (135).
2.10.1902	Maiden voyage Liverpool–Valparaiso–Callao and then placed on the Valparaiso–Callao service.
17.10.1917	Torpedoed and sank 145 miles NW off Cape Vilano by U-22, Capt. Hinrich Hermann Hashagen. She was on a voyage from Liverpool to Callao. Four people lost their lives.

138. *Rupanco* (1902–1914)
818 grt, 638 n, 182 x 32 x 17.6 feet.
Steel, twin-screw, compound; 2 x 2 cyl; 80 nhp; by Ross and Duncan, 9 knots.
Two decks.
Delivered by Howaldtswerke, Kiel.

1895	Built for Ferdinand Prehn, Keil.
1902	Purchased to replace *Talca* (130). Sailed to Valparaiso.
1914	Sank at Valparaiso.

139. *Gallito* (1902–1931)
130 grt, 69 n, 86 x 19 x 8.10 feet.
Steel, single-screw tug, compound; 2 cyl; 23 rhp; by Hutson & Son, Glasgow.
One deck.
Delivered by J. Shearer & Son, Glasgow.

1902	Built for towing duties in South American ports.
1931	Broken up.

140. *Orita* (I) (1903–1931)
9,266 grt, 5,824 n, 485.5 x 58 x 39.4 feet.
Steel, twin-screw, quadruple expansion, 2 x 4 cyl; 1,148 hp, steam pressure 215 lbs., three single ended boilers, twenty-seven furnaces, by builder, 14 knots. Coal: 1,493 tonnes at 94 tonnes a day.
Three decks.
Passengers: 169 first-class, 111 second-class and 528 third-class. Crew: 172.
Delivered by Harland & Wolff, Belfast.

15.11.1902	Launched as the largest vessel on the Valparaiso service.
8.4.1903	Maiden voyage Liverpool–Valparaiso–Callao.
10.2.1919	Sailed on the second of the company's sailings from Liverpool–Panama Canal–Callao–Valparaiso.
22.9.1927	Her final sailing, calling at Montevideo. Laid up.
1931	Sold
1932	Broken up at Morecambe.

PACIFIC STEAM NAVIGATION CO. 123

141. *Potosi* (III) (1905–1925)
4,375 grt, 3,155 n, 381.5 x 49 x 25.8 feet.
Steel, single-screw, triple expansion; 3 cyl; 429 hp: steam pressure 180 lbs, two single ended boilers, six furnaces, by G. Clark, Sunderland, 12 knots.
Four hatches. Cargo: 306,000 cubic feet.
Two decks and shelter deck.
Coal: 502 tonnes at 42 tonnes a day.
Passengers: 12 second-class and 397 third-class in dormitories.
Delivered by W. Pickersgill & Sons, Sunderland.

1905	Delivered as a cargo vessel.
1914	First British vessel to transit the Panama Canal.
1925	Sold to N. Kulukundis, Syra, Greece, renamed *Georgios M.*
1927	Owned by E. G. Culucundis and S. C. Costomeni, Syra, Greece. New boilers installed.
1929	Owned by S. G. Lyras and M. G. Lemos.
9.11.1931	On a voyage from Varna to Antwerp with a cargo of grain the cargo shifted in a gale. PLM 22 rescued five crew, but eighteen others lost their lives.

142. *Duendes* (1906–1927)
Similar to *Potosi* (141)
4,602 grt, 2,948 n, 381.5 x 49 x 25.8 feet.
Steel, single-screw, triple expansion; 3 cyl; 429 hp: steam pressure 180 lbs, two single ended boilers, six furnaces, by G. Clark, Sunderland, 12 knots.
Four hatches.
Two decks and shelter deck.
Passengers: 12 second and 397 third class in dormitories. Cargo: 306,000 cubic feet.
Coal: 502 tonnes at 42 tonnes a day.
Delivered by Sir James Laing & Sons, Sunderland.

1906	Delivered as a cargo ship.
1914–18	Requisitioned by the Admiralty as a munitions transport.
25.3.1916	Attacked by a German U-boat, seventy miles west of the Scillies, but was able to continue her voyage.
1927	Purchased by G. Lykiardopulo, Greece, renamed *Zachariosa*.
1932	Broken up.

143. *Esmeraldas* (1906–1917)
Similar to *Potosi* (141)
4,491 grt, 2,882 n, 381.5 x 49 x 25.8 feet.
Steel, single-screw, triple expansion; 3 cyl; 429 hp: steam pressure 180 lbs, two single ended boilers, six furnaces, by G. Clark, Sunderland, 12 knots.
Four hatches.
Coal: 502 tonnes at 42 tonnes a day.
Passengers: 12 second-class and 397 third-class in dormitories. Cargo: 306,000 cubic feet.
Two decks and shelter deck.
Delivered by Sir James Laing & Sons, Sunderland.

1906	Delivered as a cargo ship.
1916	Voyaged from Buenos Aires to Mombasa for the East African campaign.
10.3.1917	Sunk by the German Armed Merchant Cruiser, *Moewe* when on a voyage from to Baltimore to pick up a cargo of horses for the Brfitish Army in Europe. She was scuttled 420 miles west of Flores Island, Azores.

144. *Bogota* (II) (1906–1916)
Similar to *Potosi* (141)
4,603 grt, 2,949 n, 390 x 50 x 28.5 feet.
Steel, single-screw, triple expansion; 3 cyl; 429 hp: steam pressure 180 lbs,

two single ended boilers, six furnaces, by G. Clark, Sunderland, 12 knots.
Four hatches.
Two decks and shelter deck.
Passengers: 12 second-class and 397 third-class in dormitories. Cargo: 306,000 cubic feet.
Coal: 502 tonnes at 42 tonnes a day.
Delivered by Sir James Laing & Sons, Sunderland.

1906	Delivered as a cargo ship.
10.11.1916	Sunk by a torpedo in the North Atlantic when 120 miles SW of Ushant. She was torpedoed, without warning and sunk by U-50 when on a voyage from Coronel via Cristobal to London.

145. *Flamenco* (I) (1906–1916)
Similar to *Potosi* (141)
4,540 grt, 2,903 n, 381.5 x 49 x 25.8 feet.
Steel single-screw, triple expansion; 3 cyl; 429 hp: steam pressure 180 lbs, two single ended boilers, six furnaces, by G. Clark, Sunderland, 12 knots.
Four hatches.
Two decks and shelter deck.
Coal: 502 tonnes at 42 tonnes a day.
Passengers: 12 second-class and 397 third-class in dormitories. Cargo: 306,000 cu feet.
Delivered by Sir James Laing & Sons, Sunderland.

1906	Delivered as a cargo ship.
6.2.1916	Attacked by the German Armed Merchant Cruiser *Moewe*, 310 miles north-west of Pernambuco. She was on a voyage from Liverpool to Valparaiso with 4,000 tonnes of coal. Sank by depth charges and explosives, one person lost their life.

146. *Ortega* (I) (1906–1927)
7,970 grt, 4.519 n, 482 x 56.4 x 35.11 feet.
Steel, twin-screw, quadruple expansion; 2 x 4 cyl; 1,125 hp; steam pressure 215 lbs, three double and three single ended boilers, twenty-seven furnaces, by builder, 15½ knots.
Coal: 2,300 tonnes at 120 tonnes a day.
Three decks, fourteen derricks, thirteen winches.
Passengers: 160 first-class, 128 second-class and 300 third-class and 500 in 'tween deck dormitories. Crew: 177. Fitted with 'Bibby' tandem cabins.
Delivered by Harland & Wolff, Belfast.

22.3.1906	Launched.
19.7.1906	Maiden voyage Liverpool-Callao.
4.8.1914	She was at Montevideo when war was declared. Voyage to Callao, Capt. Douglas Kinnier.
16.9.1914	Sailed from Valparaiso and was followed by the German cruiser *Dresden*.
19.9.1914	When the German vessel ordered her to stop she entered the Nelson Strait and travelled 100 via the landward side of the

Queen Adelaide Archipelago and successfully navigated to the Smyth Channel and the Straits of Magellan. She was met by the Chilean warship *Admiral Lynch* which was looking for survivors.

1918	Transported American troops to France.
31.1.1919	First sailing to Valparaiso via the Panama Canal.
4.12.1924	Placed on the southern route to Chile.
3.3.1927	Last voyage Liverpool to Valparaiso.
1927	Sold for £19,500 and broken up at Briton Ferry.

147. *Oriana* (1906–1927)
Similar to *Ortega* (146)
8,086 grt, 4.532 n, 482 x 56.4 x 35.11 feet.
Steel, twin-screw, quadruple expansion; 2 x 4 cyl; 1,125 hp; steam pressure 215 lbs, three double and three single ended boilers, twenty-seven furnaces, by builder, 15½ knots.
Coal: 2,300 tonnes at 120 tonnes a day.
Three decks, fourteen derricks, thirteen winches.
Passengers: 160 first-class, 128 second-class and 300 third-class and 500 in 'tween deck dormitories. Crew: 177. Fitted with 'Bibby' tandem cabins.
Delivered by Barclay Curle & Company, Glasgow.

26.4.1906	Launched.
21.6.1906	Maiden voyage Liverpool-Callao on the southern route.
1915–19	Requisitioned by the Admiralty for trooping duties.
8.5.1918	On convoy she went aground in dense fog on Torcor Head by Rathlin Island. The destroyers, *Martial* and *Nicator* who were escorting the convoy also went aground. The Blue Funnel vessel *Aeneas* and the British India *Manora* were on the rocks. However, all were afloat within two weeks.
17.10.1919	Returned to the company's service.
11.1922	Transferred to the Panama Canal route.
1927	Broken up.

148. *Oronsa* (1906–1918)
Similar to *Ortega* (146)
7,989 grt, 4.516 n, 482 x 56.4 x 35.11 feet.
Steel, twin-screw, quadruple expansion; 2 x 4 cyl; 1,125 hp; steam pressure 215 lbs, three double and three single ended boilers, twenty-seven furnaces, by builder, 15½ knots. Coal: 2,300 tonnes at 120 tonnes a day.
Three decks, fourteen derricks, thirteen winches.
Passengers: 160 first-class, 128 second-class and 300 third-class and 500 in 'tween deck dormitories. Crew: 177. Fitted with 'Bibby' tandem cabins.
Delivered by Barclay Curle & Company, Glasgow.

26.5.1906	Launched.
13.9.1906	Maiden voyage (additional call added at Pernambuco)
28.4.1918	Torpedoed and sank off Bardsey Island by U-91 while in convoy (Captain Alfred von Glasenapp). Three lives lost. She was on a voyage from Talcahuano to New York and Liverpool.

149. *Callao* (II) (1905–1907)
4,206 grt, 2,691 n, 420.4 x 42.5 x 29.4 feet.
Iron, single-screw, 2 tandem compound inverted; 4 cyl; 500 hp; steam pressure 70 lb, by builder,
14 knots. Coal: 697 tonnes at 65 tonnes a day.
Three decks.
Passengers: 83 first-class, 44 second-class and 280 third-class. Crew: 104.
Delivered by Harland & Wolff, Belfast.

28.2.1885	Launched as *Gaelic* for the White Star Line.
18.7.1885	Maiden voyage Liverpool–New York, then to San Francisco

on charter to Occidental & Oriental Steamship Company of San Francisco.

10.11.1885	First sailing to Yokohama and Hong Kong.
13.12.1904	Final sailing from San Francisco.
1906	Purchased by the PSNC and renamed *Callao* for the Pacific coast route prior to the arrival of *Quillota* (154).
9.1907	Broken up at Briton Ferry.

150. *Huanchaco* (1907–1925)

4,524 grt, 2,840 n, 390.7 x 50.2 x 25.8 feet.
Steel, single-screw, triple expansion; 2 x 3 cyl; 463 hp; steam pressure 190 lb, three single ended boilers, twelve furnaces, by builder, 10 knots.
Coal: 1,077 tons.
Two decks and shelter deck.
Passengers: 18 second and 726 third class, in dormatories. Crew: 47.
Delivered by W. Beardmore & Company, Glasgow.

8.1907	Delivered to PSNC.
8.1914	Requisitioned by the Admiralty as a Government transport.
1919	Returned to the PSNC.
1925	Sold and renamed *Frank Sutton*.
1926	Owned by Aktiebolaget Bore, Abo, Finland, renamed *Bore VIII*.
1929	Broken up.

151. *Junin* (1907–1926)
Similar to *Huanchaco* (150)
4,536 grt, 2,846 n, 391.6 x 50.2 x 25.8 feet.
Steel, single-screw, triple expansion; 2 x 3 cyl; 463 hp; steam pressure 190 lb, three single ended boilers, twelve furnaces, by builder, 10 knots.
Coal: 1,077 tons.
Two decks and shelter deck.
Passengers: 18 second-class and 726 third-class in dormitories. Crew: 47.
Delivered by W. Beardmore & Company, Glasgow.

9.1907	Entered service.
1926	Sold to William Thomas Shipping Limited, Liverpool, Renamed *Cambrian Idylle*.
1929	Broken up.

152. *Kenuta* (I) (1907–1926)
4,953 grt, 3,134 n, 401.4 x 52.2 x 25.8 feet.
Steel, single-screw, triple expansion; 3 cyl; 485 hp. Steam pressure 180 lb; three single ended boilers, twelve furnaces, by builder, 10 knots.
Coal: 1,077 tons.
Two decks.
Twenty derricks, ten winches.

Passengers: 33 second-class and 250 third-class. Emigrant dormitories fitted fore and aft for 693 people. Crew: 57.

10.1907	Entered service.
1926	Sold to Pandelis Brothers, renamed *Vasilios Pandelis*.
1930	Managed by Constants (South Wales) Limited, Cardiff.
1933	Broken up in Italy.

153. *Lima* (III) (1907–1910)
Similar to *Kenuta* (152)
4,946 grt, 3,130 n, 401.4 x 52.2 x 25.8 feet.
Steel, single-screw, triple expansion; 3 cyl; 485 hp. Steam pressure 180 lb; three single ended boilers,
twelve furnaces, by builder, 10 knots.
Coal: 1,077 tons. Twenty derricks, ten winches.
Two decks.
Passengers: 33 second-class and 250 third-class. Emigrant dormitories fitted fore and aft for 693 people. Crew: 57.

12.1907	Entered service.
10.2.1910	Wrecked in the Straits of Magellan on Huamblin Island in a severe gale.; Capt. Percy Jacob. The Hathor Steam Ship Company vessel *Hatumet* rescued 188 passengers and seventeen crew. However, six crew lost their lives when a lifeboat overturned. The *Hatumet* (Captain J. Peters) took the 205 survivors to Ancud and the Chilean cruiser *Blanca Encalada* rescued the remaining eighty-eight people on board.

154. *Quillota* (1907–1923)
3,674 grt, 1,958 n, 361.5 x 46.2 x 22.2 feet.
Steel, twin-screw, triple expansion; 2 x 3 cyl; 550 hp, steam pressure 190 lb; four single ended boilers, twelve furnaces, by builder, 14 knots.
Two decks.
Passengers: 120 first-class, 100 second-class and 300 deck.
Delivered by W. Beardmore & Company, Glasgow.

2.1907	Delivered for the Valparaiso–Callao service.
1915	Chartered to the Royal Mail Line to replace *Berbice*, which was on war service.
1921	On the New York-Panama Canal–Guayaquil service.
1923	Purchased by Soc. Anon Maritima Chilena, renamed *Chile*. She was rebuilt with raised lifeboats and larger superstructure.
1928	Operated with *Peru* (124) on Chilean coastal services.
1931	Deleted from Lloyds Register.

155. *Quilpue* (1907–1922)
Similar to *Qauillota* (154)
3,669 grt, 1,959 n, 361.5 x 46.2 x 22.2 feet.
Steel, twin-screw, triple expansion; 2 x 3 cyl; 550 hp, steam pressure 190 lb; four single ended boilers, twelve furnaces, by builder, 14 knots.
Two decks.
Passengers: 120 first-class, 100 second-class and 300 deck.
Delivered by W. Beardmore & Company, Glasgow.

5.1907	Delivered for the Valparaiso–Callao route.
1915	On charter to the Royal Mail Line to replace *Balantia*, which was on war service.
12.6.1917	In combat with a U-boat, which later retreated.
1921	On the New York-Panama Canal–Guayaquil route.
1922	Purchased by the West Australian Steam Navigation Company; Bethell Gwyn & Company, managers, Liverpool, renamed *Gascoyne*.
1930	Broken up.

156. *Explorer* (1907–1914)
2,066 grt, 1,437 n, 300.4 x 34.8 x 25.2 feet.
Iron, single-screw, compound, 2 cyl; 9 knots.

1873	Built as *Crocus* for Hargreaves, Ferguson & Company.
1877	Renamed *Explorer* for T. & J. Harrison Limited, Liverpool.
1893–94	Galveston–Liverpool cotton trade
1907	Purchased by the PSNC as the last iron hulled ship to join the fleet. Retained the same name. Coal hulk at Panama and Valparaiso.

157. *Orcoma* (I) (1908–1933)
11,546 grt, 7,086 n, 511.7 x 62.2 x 29.1 feet.
Steel, twin-screw, quadruple expansion; 2 x 4 cyl; 7,100 ihp, steam pressure 210 lb, by builder, 14½ knots.
Coal: 2,847 tons.
Two decks and shelter deck, twenty-three derricks, twelve winches.
Passengers: 246 first-class, 202 second-class, 106 intermediate, 456 third-class. Crew: 247.
First vessel to exceed 10,000 in the company.
Delivered by W. Beardmore & Company, Glasgow.

2.4.1908	Launched.
27.8.1908	Maiden voyage Liverpool–West Coast of South America via the Magellan Straits.
1909	Operated the first Thomas Cook conducted tour of South America.
1914	Record crossing Liverpool–Callao of thirty-two days, twenty-two hours and forty minutes, via the Straits of Magellan.
10.1914	She missed the German victory at Coronel by a few hours.
3.1915	Requisitioned by the Admiralty as an Armed Merchant Cruiser on the Northern patrol with 10th Cruiser Squadron. 6 x 6 in and 2 x 6 pounder guns fitted.
7.11.1919	Returned to the company's service. To South America via New York and the Panama Canal.
1923	Converted to oil power and well deck plated over.
28.6.1933	Arrived at Blyth to be broken up by Hughes Bolckow, replaced by *Reina Del Paifico*.

158. *Ponderoso* (1911–1939)
285 grt, 115 n, 115.4 x 25.1 x 13.2 feet.
Steel, single-screw tug, triple expansion; 3 cyl; 103 nhp, steam pressure 160 lb; one single ended boiler, three furnaces, by Crabtree & Company, Great Yarmouth, 9 knots.
One deck.
Delivered by H. & C. Grayson, Liverpool.

1911	Stationed in South America.

1939	Sold to the stevedoring firm Kenricks in Vaparaiso. She was laid up at Valparaiso at the end of her working life and later towed to Talcahuano where she was laid up at a corner of the port. The vessel is still laid up at Talcahuano in 2011 and a preservation society has been set up (www.corpoderosa.cl).

159. *Andes* (I)
15,620 grt, 9,481 n, 570 x 67.3 x 43 feet.
Steel, triple-screw, triple expansion with one exhaust low pressure turbine connected to the centre shaft, 2 x 4 cyl; 14,000 ihp, by builder, 17 knots.
Three decks.
Passengers: 380 first-class, 250 second-class and 700 third-class.
Fitted with 2 x 4.7 in. guns aft.
Delivered by Harland & Wolff, Belfast.

8.5.1913	Launched, originally ordered for PSNC but transferred to the Royal Mail Line on the stocks.
29.9.1913	Maiden voyage for the PSNC Liverpool–Valparaiso but the on Southampton River Plate Royal Mail Line service.
4.1915	Requisitioned by the Admiralty as an Armed Merchant Cruiser, 8 x 6 in guns, 2 x 6 pounders plus depth charges fitted.
29.2.1916	Together with her sistership *Alcantara* she was in conflict with the German raider *Greif*. *Alcantara* and *Greif* were both sunk in the incident and *Andes* rescued the survivors, including 115 German sailors.
1917	Employed in Atlantic convoy duties and later repatriated submarine crews trapped by the Soviet Revolution at Murmansk.
1.1919	Sent to builders at Belfast for major overhaul.
10.1919	Resumed the Southampton–River Plate service.
1929	Converted to a cruise liner at Gladstone Dock, Liverpool. Painted white and renamed *Atlantis* to carry 450 first class passengers. Converted to oil fuel and a swimming pool was fitted.
1935	At the Silver Jubilee Naval Review at Spithead.
8.1939	Told to return to the United Kingdom, when at Danzig on a cruise.
25.8.1939	Arrived at Southampton and was converted into hospital ship No. 33, with 400 beds. She was joined by 130 medical staff and was initially based at Alexandria.
4.1940	Sent to Norwegian waters to assist in the Norwegian evacuation campaign and was bombed twice.
9.1940	Operating in the Indian Ocean for two years.
1942	Based at Diego Suarez and took part in Madagascar operations.
1943	Took part in repatriating Italian prisoners of war to Lisbon and Germans to Gothenburg.
1944–46	Hospital ship and repatriation duties steaming 280,000 miles and carried 35,000 wounded.
1948	On charter for four years to carry emigrants from the United Kingdom to Australia and New Zealand. Passengers: 900 third class.
1952	Laid up on the Clyde, sold and broken up at Faslane.

160. *Calbuco* (1914–1925)
55 grt, 27 n, 62.2 x 15.1 x 7.5 feet.
Single-screw tug, compound; 2 cyl; 14 rhp, steam pressure 130 lb, one single ended boiler, one furnace, by builder, 9 knots.
One deck.
Delivered by Lytham Ship Building & Engineering Company, Lytham, Lancashire.

161. *Ormeda/Orduna* (I) (1914–1951)

15,507 grt, 9,548 n, 570 x 67.4 x 43 feet.
Steel, triple screw, triple expansion exhausting to a direct acting turbine connected to the centre shaft; 2 x 4 cyl; 8,650 ihp; 1,362 nhp, steam pressure 215 lb, six double ended boilers, thirty-six furnaces, by builder, 15 knots. The turbines had no reverse gearing.
Coal: 2,272 tons. Cargo: 9,324 tons.
Four decks. Twenty-three derricks, nineteen winches.
Passengers 194 first, 217 second, 154 Intermediate and 564 third class.
Delivered by Harland & Wolff, Belfast.

2.10.1913	Launched as *Orduna*, originally intended to be *Ormeda*.
19.2.1914	Maiden voyage Liverpool–Valparaiso, black funnel.
10.1914	On charter to the Cunard Line for the Liverpool–New York service to replace vessels on war service. Funnel in Cunard colours.
1.11.1914	First sailing Liverpool–New York.
28.6.1915	Attacked by U-boat, twenty miles from the Smalls but escaped.
9.7.1915	Attacked by U-boat off Queenstown (Cobh) and was missed by a torpedo.
6.1918	Sank a German submarine by gunfire.
1.12.1918	Collided with the Elder Dempster vessel *Konakry*, off Galley Head and sank her.
31.12.1919	Returned to PSNC by Cunard at the end of the charter.
1.4.1920	First post war sailing to South America via Montevideo.
28.5.1921	On the Royal Mail Line's Hamburg–Southampton–New York route.
1922	Major refit at builders.
1.1.1923	On the South American service with ownership transferring to the Royal Mail Line.
1926	Converted to oil fuel.
1927	Returned to PSNC ownership.
7.4.1927	Liverpool–Valparaiso via the Panama Canal.
7.1940	Sailed from Liverpool to Lisbon, repatriating French nationals after the fall of France. She sailed on this voyage fully illuminated at night under an international safe conduct guarantee.
1941–46	Requisitioned as a troop carrier. After the fall of Madagascar she carried the Vichy French governor and his staff from Tamatave to Durban, and on the homeward voyage, she carried 500 French naval officers and ratings to Britain to join the Free French forces. She took part of the West African Division from Berbera to Durban and was later employed carrying American troops from Oran to Naples during the Italian campaign.
8.1945	Commodore ship of the Malaya invasion force following the surrender of Japanese forces and later carried 1,700 prisoners of war from Rangoon to Liverpool.
1946	Trooping duties to the East Indies, Indo-China and Japan.
10.1946	Carried the last British troops from French North Africa.
1950	Last trooping voyage from Singapore to Liverpool.
11.1950	Decommissioned and laid up.
1951	Broken up at Dalmuir.

162. *Orbita* (I) (1915–1950)

Similar to *Orduna* (161)
15,495 grt, 10,140 n, 570 x 67.4 x 43 feet.

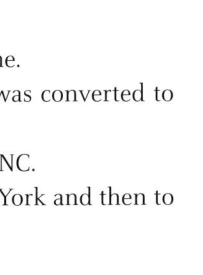

Steel, triple screw, triple expansion exhausting to a direct acting turbine connected to the centre shaft; 2x4 cyl; 8,650 ihp; 1,362 nhp, steam pressure 215 lb, six double ended boilers, thirty-six furnaces, by builder, 15 knots. The turbines had no reverse gearing.
Coal: 2,272 tons.
Four decks. Twenty-three derricks, nineteen winches.
Passengers 190 first, 221 second, 154 Intermediate and 476 third class.
Cargo: 9,324 tons.
Delivered by Harland & Wolff, Belfast.

7.7.1914	Launched.
1915	Requisitioned as an Auxiliary Cruiser, 6 x 6 in. guns fitted.
3.1919	Work to complete her was started.
26.9.1919	Maiden voyage Liverpool–Valparaiso via the Straits of Magellan.
30.4.1921	On charter to the Royal Mail Line for the Hamburg–Southampton–Cherbourg–New York service.
1.1.1923	Ownership transferred to the Royal Mail Line.
2.1923	Her first and second class accommodation was converted to Cabin class.
7.1926	Converted to oil fuel. Ownership back to PSNC.
10.9.1926	Last voyage Southampton–Cherbourg–New York and then to Liverpool.
4.11.1926	Liverpool–Panama Canal–Callao–Valparaiso.
1941	Requisitioned by Admiralty as a troopship.
1946	United Kingdom to Australia and New Zealand carrying immigrants. Her passengers were part of the first group of West Indian immigrants to Britain, after the *Empire Windrush*.
1950	Broken up by Thos. W. Ward at Newport.

163. *Jamaica* (1914–1918)

1,138 grt, 602 n, 220 x 34 x 14.11 feet.
Steel, single-screw, triple expansion; 3 cyl; 171 nhp; steam pressure 180 lb; two single ended boilers, four furnaces, by McColl & Pollock, Sunderland, 11 knots.
Two decks.
Delivered by W. Harkess & Son, Middlesbrough.

1908	Built for Imperial Direct West India Service, Elder Dempster & Company.
1914	Purchased by PSNC.
1915	Requisitioned by the Admiralty.
1918	Owned by the Royal Mail Line but continued on PSNC services.
1929	Purchased by Soc. Industrial del Aysen at Valparaiso, renamed *Coyhaique*.
1943	Broken up.

164. *Acajutla* (1915–1946)
1,170 grt, 654 n, 215.8 x 33.6 x 19.5 feet.
Steel, single-screw, triple expansion; 3 cyl; 174 hp; two single-ended boilers, by builder, 11 knots.
One teak deck.
Delivered by Swan Hunter & Wigham Richardson, Wallsend.

1911	Built for the Salvador Railway Company, London.
1915	Purchased with *Salvador* (165), for a fortnightly service through the Panama Canal.
1927	Rebuilt.
1946	Sold to Pandelis Line, Greece and renamed *Marathon*, operated by Neil and Pandelis, London for service in the Greek Islands.

165. *Salvador* (1915–1946)
Similar to *Acajutla* (164)
1,128 grt, 637 n, 215.8 x 33.6 x 19.5 feet.
Steel, single-screw, triple expansion; 3 cyl; 174 hp; two single-ended boilers, by builder, 11 knots.
One teak deck.
Delivered by Swan Hunter & Wigham Richardson, Wallsend.

1909	Built for the Salvador Railway Company, London.
1915	Purchased with *Acajutla* (164), for a fortnightly service through the Panama Canal.
1927	Rebuilt.
1946	Sold to Pandelis Line, Greece and renamed *Salamis*, operated by Neil and Pandelis, London for service in the Greek Islands. *Salvador* had made 779 transits of the Panama Canal, which was the greatest number of any merchant vessel. Consequently, the Panama Canal Company issued a certificate in honour of the ship. *Acajutla* also received a certificate.

166. *Cauca* (1915–1923)
1,448 grt, 890 n, 246 x 35.2 x 20 feet.
Steel, single-screw, triple expansion; 3 cyl; 193 nhp, by builder, 11 knots. One deck.
Delivered by Swan Hunter & Wigham Richardson, Wallsend.

1915	Delivered and based at Panama.
1923	Sold to Compagnie Indo-Chinoise de Navigation, Haiphong and renamed *Tonkin*.

167. *Lautaro* (1923–1947)
6,240 grt, 3,950 n, 399.1 x 52.2 x 33.10 feet.
Steel, twin-screw, oil; 4 stroke single acting; 12 cyl; 719 nhp, by Burmeister and Wain, Glasgow, 12 knots.
Two decks and awning deck.
Passengers: 12.
Delivered by Harland & Wolff, Glasgow.

12.1915	Built as *Bostonian* for the Leyland Line.
1916	Sold to Glen Line, renamed *Glengyle*.
10.6.1917	Attacked by a German submarine, which she fired upon and escaped.
1923	Purchased by PSNC and renamed *Lautaro*.
1947	Sold to the Jenny Steam Shipping Company, London and renamed *River Swift*.
1948	On fire at Rio de Janeiro, beyond economical repair.
1949	Broken up in South America.

168. *Orca* (1918–1923)
15,120 grt, 9,614 n, 574 x 67.4 x 43 feet.
Steel, triple-screw, triple expansion exhausting to a direct geared, forward drive only, turbine connected to the centre shaft; 4 cyl; 1,362 hp; steam pressure 215 lb; six double ended boilers with thirty-six furnaces, by builder, 15 knots. Engine identical to one installed on *Orduna* (161) and *Orbita* (162). She was originally designed as a cruiser sterned sister ship. Three decks with a fourth deck fore and aft of the machinery space. Boat deck 230 foot, ten bulkheads, six holds.
Passengers (from 1922) 190 first-class, 220 second-class and 480 third-class.
Delivered by Harland & Wolff, Belfast.

15.1.1918	Launched as a cargo vessel.
18.2.1921	Returned to builders to be refitted as a passenger ship.
12.1922	The refit was completed.
18.12.1922	First sailing Southampton–Hamburg–New York.
1.1.1923	Owned by the Royal Mail Line.
3.1.1923	Maiden voyage from Hamburg and Southampton to New York.
1.1927	Sold to the White Star Line, renamed *Calgaric*. 16,063 grt, 9,614n, Passengers: 290 first-class, 550 tourist, 330 third-class.
4.5.1927	First voyage Liverpool–Quebec–Montreal.
20.4.1929	First voyage on the London to Montreal route.
1931	Laid up at Milford Haven, making one cruise to the Baltic.
9.6.1933	Returned to the Liverpool–Montreal service.
9.9.1933	Laid up at Milford Haven.
1934	Transferred to the Cunard-White Star Line and sold for £31,000.
25.12.1934	Arrived at Inverkeithing to be broken up.

169. *Ballena* (1920–1932)
5,210 grt, 3,216 n, 400.1 x 52.4 x 26.5 feet.
Steel, single-screw, triple expansion; 3 cyl; 452 nhp; three boilers, by

North East Marine Engineering Company, Newcastle, 11 knots.
Coal: 490 tons.
Two decks.
Crew: 41.
Delivered by W. Dobson & Company, Newcastle.

7.11.1919	Launched as wartime standard 'B' type.
1920	Entered PSNC Service.
1932	Sold to Rethymnis & Kulukundis, Panama, renamed *Mount Ida*.
3.1937	Owned by Hamburg Sud Amerika Line, Hamburg becoming *Mendoza*.
8.12.1940	Collided off Flushing with *Adalia*, Hamburg Amerika Line.
22.3.1945	Sunk off Pillau by Russian bombers.

170. *Bogota* (III) (1919–1932)
Similar to *Ballena* (169)
5,167 grt, 3,127 n, 400.1 x 52.4 x 26.5 feet.
Steel, single-screw, triple expansion; 3 cyl; 452 nhp; three boilers, by North East Marine Engineering Company, Newcastle, 11 knots.
Coal: 490 tons.
Two decks.
Crew: 41.
Delivered by Cammell Laird & Company, Birkenhead.

18.3.1919	Launched as *War Lapwing*, renamed *Bogota* prior to delivery.
1932	Sold to Fratelli G. & F. Bozzo, Genoa and renamed *Madda*.
17.6.1937	Damaged in the Spanish Civil War.
6.1940	Followed by British warship, beached at Tenerife and refloated.
1945	Sold to Cia Nav. Sota y Aznar, Bilbao, renamed *Monte Nafarrate*.
1956	Owned by Angel Riva Suardiaz, Bilbao, becoming *Riva De Luna*.
1958	Renamed *Rivadeluna*.
1972	Owned by Naviera Rivadeluna.
1974	Broken up.

171. *Magellan* (III) (1920–1933)
6,553 grt, 4,055 n, 462.4 x 59.2 x 28 feet.
Steel, single-screw, quadruple expansion; 4 cyl; 723 nhp; 3,700 ihp, four single ended boilers, twelve furnaces, by builder, 12 knots.
Two decks and shelter deck.
Cargo: 635,000 cubic feet Coal: 1,310 tons.
Delivered by J. C. Tecklenborg, Geestemunde.

PACIFIC STEAM NAVIGATION CO. 135

1913	Built as *Alda* for the Roland Linie A. G., Bremen.
1919	Taken over by the British Government, managed by PSNC.
1920	Sold to PSNC, renamed *Magellan*.
1933	Broken up.

172. *Oropesa* (II) (1920–1941)

14,118 grt, 8,608 n, 530 x 66.4 x 41.2 feet.
Steel, twin-screw, six turbines, double reduction geared; 1,647 nhp, 7,500 ihp, six double ended boilers; by builder, 14½ knots.
Two decks and shelter deck.
Passengers; 141 first, 131 second and 360 third class. Cargo; 528,000 cubic feet.

Delivered by Cammell Laird, Birkenhead.

9.12.1919	Launched.
4.9.1920	Maiden voyage Liverpool-Rio de Janeiro-Buenos Aires.
14.5.1921	Chartered to the Royal Mail Line for the Hamburg–Southampton–New York service.
30.11.1922	Returned to PSNC for the Liverpool–Valparaiso service.
1924	Converted to oil fuel.
2.1927	Transferred to the Liverpool–Panama Canal–Valparaiso route.
1931	Conveyed the Prince of Wales and Prince George to South America.
10.1931	Laid up at Dartmouth for six years.
1937	Returned to service.
9.1939	Requisitioned by the Admiralty and used as a troopship.
16.1.1941	Attacked and torpedoed three times by U-96 off Ireland

(Captain Heinrich Lehmann-Willenbrock). She was on a voyage from Mombasa to the United Kingdom with copper, maize and general cargo and was commanded by Captain H. E. H. Croft. Sank with the loss of 113 lives.

173. *La Paz* (1920–1942)

6,548 grt, 4,052 n, 406 x 54.2 x 32.10 feet.
Steel, twin-screw, two-stroke, single-acting; 12 cyls; 810 hp; 3,200 bhp; by builder, 12 knots.
Two decks and sheltered deck.
Cargo: 462,000 cubic feet
Delivered by Harland & Wolff, Glasgow.

1920	Entered service.
1.5.1942	Attacked and torpedoed by the German submarine U-109 off Florida with a cargo of whisky. Beached and sold. Vessel later became the responsibility of the War Shipping Administration.
1945	Purchased by Construction Aggregates Corporation, Chicago.
1954	Deleted from Lloyds Register.

174. *Lobos* (1921–1952)

Sister of *La Paz* (173)
6,479 grt, 3,997 n, 406 x 54.2 x 32.10 feet.
Steel, twin-screw, two-stroke, single-acting; 12 cyls; 810 hp; 3,200 bhp; by builder, 12 knots.
Two decks and sheltered deck.
Cargo: 462,000.
Delivered by Harland & Wolff, Glasgow.

1921	Delivered and entered service.
1952	Broken up.

175. *Losada* (1921–1952)
Sister of *La Paz* (173)
6,520 grt, 4,021 n, 406 x 54.2 x 32.10 feet.
Steel, twin-screw, two-stroke, single acting; 12 cyls; 810 hp; 3,200 bhp; by builder, 12 knots.
Two decks and sheltered deck.
Cargo: 462,000.
Delivered by Harland & Wolff, Glasgow.

1921	Delivered and entered service.
1952	Broken up.

176. *Alvarado* (1922–1933)
2,464 grt, 1,448 n, 303.5 x 43 x 20.8 feet.
Steel, single-screw, triple expansion, 3 cyls; 265 nhp; two double ended boilers; six furnaces, by builder, 10½ knots.
Two decks.
Delivered by A. & J. Inglis, Glasgow.

10.1920	Delivered as *War Raisin* and bought by Mac Andrews & Company, renamed *Alvarado* for their Mediterranean services.
1922	Bought by PSNC.
1933	Sold to Cia Carbonifera Rio Grandense, Rio de Janeiro, renamed *Herval*.
1965	Broken up at Rio de Janeiro.

177. *Almagro* (1922–1933)
Sister of *Alvarado* (176)
2,464 grt, 1,438 n, 303.5 x 43 x 20.8 feet.
Steel, single-screw, triple expansion, 3 cyls; 265 nhp; two double ended boilers; six furnaces, by builder, 10½ knots.
Two decks.
Delivered by A. & J. Inglis, Glasgow.

23.4.1920	Launched, completed as *Almagro* for Mac Andrews & Company.
1922	Purchased by the PSNC for the New York–Valparaiso route.
1933	Sold to Cia Carbonifera Rio Grandense, Rio de Janeiro, renamed *Itaquy*.
1934	Renamed *Tuquy*, same owner.
1963	Renamed *Artico*.
1965	Purchased by Comissario Maritima Modesta Roma, Rio de Janeiro, becoming *Roma Um*.
2.1967	On a voyage from Manaus to Areia Branca she caught fire and was beached at Belem.
30.10.1967	Capsized and declared a total loss.

178. *Arana* (1922–1933)
Sister of *Alvarado* (176)
2,464 grt, 1,438 n, 303.5 x 43 x 20.8 feet.
Steel, single-screw, triple expansion, 3 cyls; 265 nhp; two double ended boilers; six furnaces, by builder, 10½ knots.
Two decks.

Delivered by A. & J. Inglis, Glasgow.

17.9.1919	Launched as *War Date*.
1.1920	Delivered as *Arana* for Mac Andrews & Company.
1922	Purchased by the PSNC for the New York–Valparaiso service.
1933	Sold to Cia Carbonifera Rio Grandense, Rio de Janeiro, renamed *Chuy*.
1943	Owned by Cia Commercio y Navegazione, Rio de Janeiro.
1958	Bought by Nav. Mercantil S. A., Rio de Janeiro.
5.1961	Broken up at Rio de Janeiro.

179. *Ebro* (1920–1935)
8,489 grt, 5,174 n, 450.4 x 57.9 x 30.7 feet.
Steel, twin-screw, quadruple expansion, 2 x 4 cyl; stroke: 45 in.; 1,055 nhp, steam pressure 215 lb, two double and two single ended boilers, twenty-four furnaces, by builder.
Two decks.
Passengers: 278 first and 328 third class. Crew: 320.
Delivered by Workman Clark & Company, Belfast.

8.9.1914	Launched for the Royal Mail Line.
28.4.1915	Maiden voyage to South America then requisitioned by the Admiralty and joined the 10th Cruiser Squadron.
1920	Purchased by PSNC for the New York–Panama Canal–Callao–Valparaiso route.
12.1930	Laid up on the River Dart.
2.1935	Sold to Jugoslavenska Lloyd, renamed *Princess Olga*.
1940	Purchased by Cia Colonial, Lisbon for a Lisbon–New York and South American service to Rio de Janeiro. Renamed *Serpa Pinto*.
14.8.1940	First voyage.
10.10.1945	Eleventh and final voyage Lisbon–Brazil.
1945–1953	Lisbon–New York–Baltimore or Philadelphia.
14.8.1953	Lisbon–Madeira–La Guiara–Curacao–Havana (twelve voyages).
9.7.1954	Lisbon–St Vincent–Rio de Janeiro–Santos (one voyage).
6.9.1955	Left Lisbon in tow for shipbreakers.
1955	Broken up in Belgium.

180. *Essequibo* (1920–1935)
Sister to *Ebro* (179)
8,489 grt, 5,174 n, 450.4 x 57.9 x 30.7 feet.
Steel, twin-screw, quadruple expansion, 2 x 4 cyl; stroke: 45 in; 1,055 nhp, steam pressure 215 lb, two double and two single ended boilers, twenty-four furnaces, by builder.
Two decks.
Passengers: 250 first and 250 third class. Crew: 320.
Delivered by Workman Clark & Company, Belfast.

181. *Orcana* (II) (1922–1924)

6,793 grt, 3,691 n, 454.10 x 55 x 30 feet.

Steel, twin-screw, triple expansion, 2 x 3 cyl; 1,218 nhp, steam pressure 200 lb, two double ended and one single ended boiler, twenty-one furnaces, by builder, 15 knots.

Three decks.

Passengers: 150 first-class and 170 third-class.

Delivered by Alex Stephen & Sons, Glasgow.

1903	Built as *Miltiades* for the Aberdeen Line.
6.7.1914	Launched for the Royal Mail Line.
18.11.1914	Maiden voyage, Capt. J. C. Chevet.
1915	Requisitioned as a hospital ship.
1917	Intercepted by U-54 at sea, boarded and allowed to continue on her voyage. The passengers cheered and U-54 sent the flag signal, 'God speed you' and *Essequibo* replied with 'Thank you', according to the submarines war log.
1920	Purchased by PSNC for the New York–Panama Canal–Callao–Valparaiso service.
1930	Laid up.
3.1935	Sold to Arcos Limited for Russian interests, renamed *Neva*.
1957	Deleted from Lloyds Register.

3.11.1903	Maiden voyage London–Cape Town–Melbourne–Sydney.
1913	Lengthened to 504.4 feet; 7,814 grt, 4,892 n, second funnel added (dummy). Passengers: 89 first and 158 third class.
1915	Requisitioned as a troopship.
4.6.1920	Returned to the Australian service.
20.11.1920	Last voyage from Australia. To the Royal Mail Line and renamed *Orcana*.
1922	Transferred to PSNC.
11.8.1922	On the 'Round South America' service, Liverpool–Montevideo–Valparaiso–Panama Canal–Liverpool. Withdrawn and laid up at Liverpool and then Dartmouth, after the first voyage.
1924	Taken to Holland under tow and broken up.

182. *Oruba* (II) (1921–1924)
Sister to *Orcana* (181)
6,795 grt, 3,695 n, 454.10 x 55 x 30 feet.
Steel, twin-screw, triple expansion, 2 x 3 cyl; 1,218 nhp, steam pressure 200 lb, two double ended and one single ended boiler, twenty-one furnaces, by builder, 15 knots.
Three decks.
Passengers: 150 first and 170 third class.
Delivered by Alex Stephen & Sons, Glasgow.

18.11.1903	Launched as *Marathon* for the Aberdeen Line.
27.1.1904	Maiden voyage London–Cape Town–Melbourne–Sydney.
1912	Lengthened as *Orcana* (181). 7,848 grt. Passengers: 90 first and 150 third class.
1915	Requisitioned as a troopship.
21.10.1920	Returned to the Australian service. Sold to the Royal Mail Line after one voyage, renamed *Oruba*.
1921	Transferred to PSNC.
26.5.1921	On the 'Round South America' service.
1922	Laid up at Liverpool, then Dartmouth.
1924	Broken up in Germany.

183. *Laguna* (1923–1952)
6,466 grt, 4,033 n, 420.6 x 54.2 x 33.4 feet.
Steel, twin-screw, oil; 4 stroke single acting; 12 cyl; 832 nhp, by builder, 12 knots.
Three decks.
Passengers: 12.
Delivered by Harland & Wolff, Glasgow.

| 1923 | Delivered for the UK–West Coast service via the Panama Canal. |
| 1952 | Broken up at Barrow in Furness. |

184. *Oroya* (III) (1924–1939)
12,257 grt, 7,380 n, 525.4 x 62.9 x 44.7 feet.
Steel, twin-screw, four turbines, single reduction geared; steam pressure 215 lb; four double ended boilers, twenty-four furnaces, by builder, 14 knots.
Two decks and shelter deck.
Passengers: 150 first, 123 second and 450 third class.
Delivered by Harland & Wolff, Belfast.

16.12.1920	Launched and then laid up.
1924	Maiden voyage Liverpool–Panama Canal–Valparaiso.
8.9.1931	Laid up at Dartmouth.
12.1938	Sold to shipbreakers.
1.2.1939	Left Dartmouth in tow of Smit tug *Rode See* for La Spezia to be broken up.

185. *Loreto* (1924–1951)
6,682 grt, 4,105 n, 406.2 x 54.2 x 32.11 feet.
Steel, twin-screw, oil; four-stroke single-acting; 12 cyl; by builder, 12 knots.
Two decks and shelter deck.
Delivered by Harland & Wolff, Glasgow.

7.1919	Built as *Glenade* for the Glen Line.
1924	Purchased by PSNC.
22.2.1941	Capt. Philip Hockey. In a convoy of six ships she sailed into a fog bank escaping from the *Scharnhorst* and *Gneisenau*, 400 miles off Newfoundland. The other five ships were attacked by the German vessels.
1951	Sold to Motor Lines Limited, Greenock, and renamed *Barbeta*.
11.1952	Broken up at Briton Ferry.

186. *Loriga* (1924–1951)
Sister of *Loreto* (185)
6,665 grt, 4,051 n, 406.2 x 54.2 x 32.11 feet.
Steel, twin-screw, oil; four-stroke single-acting; 12 cyl; by builder, 12 knots.
Two decks and shelter deck.
Delivered by Harland & Wolff, Glasgow.

1919	Built for Glen Line as *Glenariffe*.
1924	Purchased by PSNC, renamed *Loriga*.
1951	Sold to the Ocean Transportation Company, Panama and renamed *Oceanus Venus*.
1953	Broken up in Japan.

Loriga.

187. Lagarto (1924–1948)
5,075 grt, 3,208 n, 385.1 x 52.2 x 30.4 feet.
Steel, twin-screw, oil; four-stroke single acting; 12 cyl; 719 nhp, by builder, 12 knots.
Three decks.
Passengers: 12.

1915	Built for Glen Line as *Glenavy*.
13.6.1923	Purchased by PSNC.
23.6.1923	Renamed *Lagarto*, engines converted to airless injection.
1939–45	Remained on the South American services.
12.1947	Arrived at Liverpool with engine problems and laid up at Birkenhead.
1948	Broken up at Troon.

188. Temuco (1925–1942)
110 grt, 66 n, 86 x 19 x 9.9 feet.
Steel, single-screw tug, oil; two-stroke single acting; 2 cyl; machinery aft.
Delivered by Harland & Wolff, Glasgow.

1925	Delivered as a tug and water tender at Valparaiso.
1942	Sold to Chilean interests.

189. Champerico (1917–1934)
2,548 grt, 1,422 n, 290.1 x 41.8 x 17 feet.
Steel, single-screw, triple expansion; 3 cyl; 321 nhp; steam pressure 180 lb; three single ended boilers, nine furnaces, by builder, 12 knots.
Two decks.

Passengers: 100.

1911	Built for Yeoward Brothers, Liverpool as *Andorinha* for their Liverpool–Madeira–Canary Islands service.
1917	Purchased by the PSNC, renamed *Champerico* for the Peruvian and Central American coastal routes.
1934	Sold to Torres y Ward Cia, Valparaiso, renamed *Vina Del Mar*.
1937	Operated by Chilean State Railways.
1950	Transferred to Empresa Maritima del Estado de Chilena.
1966	Broken up.

190. *Reina Del Pacifico* (1931–1958)

17,702 grt, 10,720 n, 551.4 x 76.4 x 37.9 feet.
Steel, Quadruple screw, oil; four-stroke single-acting Buchi supercharged;
4 x 12 cyl; 2,844 nhp;
by builder, 18 knots.
Three decks, five holds.
Passengers: 280 first-class, 162 second-class and 446 third-class.

23.9.1930	Launched as PSNC's largest vessel. The first white hulled and first name that did not commence with an 'O'. Fore funnel a dummy.
27.3.1931	Three-day North Sea shake-down cruise.
9.4.1931	Maiden voyage Liverpool–La Rochelle–Vigo–Bermuda–Bahamas–Havana–Jamaica–Panama Canal–Guayaquil–Callao–Antofagasta–Valparaiso (25½ days).
19.1.1932	'Round South America' service, one voyage a year.
1936	Record passage to Valparaiso, twenty-five days.
9.11.1937	Britain's first Labour Prime Minister, James Ramsay MacDonald, died of heart failure while on board.
8.1939	Sent to Clyde from Liverpool to await orders.
3.9.1939	War declared.
7.9.1939	Left the Clyde in convoy of seventeen ships for the Far East.
12.1939	Undertook one voyage to Halifax prior to conversion to a troopship at Liverpool.
11.4.1940	Sailed from the Clyde to Harstad, Norway and to Bygden Fjord with *Empress of Australia*, *Batory* and *Monarch of Bermuda*, carrying men of the South Wales Borderers and Scots Guards, where depth charges were dropped by her escorts. Attacked by German bombers as the troops were disembarked.
5.1940	Evacuated troops from Norway.
5.1940	Service off West Africa.
24.7.1940	Sailed for Suez via Cape Town with RAF servicemen. Spitfires were taken on the aircraft carrier HMS *Argus*.
14.11.1940	Another voyage to Suez with the RAF.

1.1941	Took the 4th Indian Division from Suez to Port Sudan.
3.1941	Bombed at Avonmouth for three nights, moved to the Clyde, where she was also bombed.
22.3.1941	With troops on board she struck an object in the Bristol Channel and returned to Liverpool.
15.4 1941	Bomb exploded near her berth in Liverpool prior to her sailing to Cape Town with troops the following day. She also made a second voyage to South Africa and was then transferred to North Atlantic crossings from Halifax.
5.12.1941	Liverpool–Cape Town–Bombay–Colombo–Liverpool.
12.4.1942	Repeated the above voyage.
6.8.1942	Conveyed Canadian and American troops to Europe when a German U-boat captain claimed to have sunk her when she 'was torn to pieces and disappeared in a few seconds'. In drydock at Liverpool where lifeboats were replaced by landing craft.
13.9.1942	Sailed to the Clyde to undertake practice landing operations.
17.10.1942	At Loch Linne for a rehearsal for the North African landings.
21.10.1942	At Oran unloading troops as flagship to the Senior Naval Officer Landing.
7/8.11.1942	At Oran there were 102 ships assembled and her landing craft joined others in the assembly area. She later berthed at Oran.
24.11.1942	In the Clyde she took on troops for Algiers.
5.1.1943	Transported troops to Oran.
5.5.1943	At Suez to practice Sicily invasion.
29.6.1943	Embarked the 51st Highland Division.
10.7.1943	Landed troops at Avola Beach, Sicily. Sailed to Malta and then to Oran to evacuate 500 German prisoners of war and was attacked by German aircraft.
23.7.1943	Arrived back on the Clyde.
8.1943	Transported King Peter of Jugoslavia and others Liverpool–Suez. Then trooping voyages to Taranto and Port Augustus. Embarked the United States First Division Headquarters staff for Britain for their preparations for the Normandy landings.
15.11.1943	Trooping voyage Liverpool–Bombay. The convoy of twenty ships was attacked by over sixty planes. The Lamport & Holt vessel, *Delius* was the only casualty.
1.1944	Trooping voyage to East Africa and then in the Mediterranean.
12.1944	Liverpool–Iceland–New York and then trooping voyages in the Pacific.
1946	Sailed over 350,000 miles and carried 150,000 people as a repatriation ship.
1.1947	Sent to builders for major overhaul and refit.
10.9.1947	Trials commenced.
11.9.1947	Engine explosion killed twenty-eight people on board after a piston overheated and the engine blew up.
1948	Returned to Liverpool–Valparaiso service.
8.7.1957	Aground on Devil's Flat, Bermuda. Refloated later.
11.1957	Lost a propeller at Havana and a new one was sent out on *Salinas* (195).
27.4.1958	Her final voyage. Broken up by John Cashmore at Newport.

191. *Talca* (III) (1947–1953)
7,219 grt, 4,454 n, 422.9 x 57 x 34.9 feet.
Steel, single-screw, triple expansion; 3 cyl; 450 nhp; steam pressure 225 lb, two watertube boilers, by General Machinery Corporation, Hamilton, Ontario, 14 knots. Electric welded.
Two decks.

Delivered by Bethlehem Fairfield Shipyard Inc., Baltimore, Maryland.

1943	Laid down as *Orville P. Taylor*, completed as *Samothrace* operated by the Royal Mail Line.
1947	Transferred to the PSNC, renamed *Talca*.
1953	Sold to Cia Naveira Aris S.A., Puerto Limon, Costa Rica, renamed *Popi*.
1961	Owned by the Atlas Maritime Finance Corporation, Beirut, Lebanon, becoming *Lydia*.
7.1967	Broken up at Whampoa, China.

192. *Samanco* (1943–1956)

6,413 grt, 3,759 n, 466.4 x 62.9 x 34.9 feet.

Steel, single-screw, oil; two-stroke direct acting; 8 cyl; 1,643 nhp; by builder, 15 knots.

One deck and shelter deck.

Delivered by Harland & Wolff, Belfast.

8.1943	Delivered to company.
17.10.1951	In collision with the *George Uhler* of the Prudential Steam Shipping Company, off Dungeness.
1956	Sold to Deutsche Dampschiff 'Hansa', becoming *Reichenfels*.
1962	Broken up in Spain.

193. *Sarmiento* (II) (1943–1969)

Sister of *Samanco* (192)

6,393 grt, 3,743 n, 466.4 x 62.9 x 34.9 feet.

Steel, single-screw, oil; two-stroke direct acting; 8 cyl; 1,643 nhp; by builder, 15 knots.

One deck and shelter deck.

Delivered by Harland & Wolff, Belfast.

10.1943	Delivered.
1969	Sold to Monomachos Cia Nav. S.A., Piraeus, renamed *Monomachos*.
1970	Owned by the Eagle Ocean Shipping Company, Famagusta, Cyprus and renamed *Gladiator*.
28.2.1971	Sailed from Havana for Shanghai and broken up in China.

194. *Salamanca* (1948–1967)

6,704 grt, 3,923 n, 467 x 62 x 30 feet.

Steel, single-screw, oil; two cycle double acting; 8 cyl; 1,933 nhp, by builder, 13 knots.

One deck.

Passengers: 12.

1948	Entered service on the UK–Bermuda–Bahamas–Cuba–Colombia–Panama–Colombia (Pacific coast)–Ecuador–Peru–Chile service.
1967	Sold to El Chaco Cia Nav. S.A., Piraeus, becoming *Kronos*.
17.10.1972	Left Singapore for Shanghai to be broken up in China.

195. *Salinas* (1947–1968)

Sister of *Samanco* (192)

6,705 grt, 3,923 n, 466.4 x 62.9 x 34.9 feet.

Steel, single-screw, oil; two-stroke direct acting; 8 cyl; 1,643 nhp; by builder, 15 knots.

One deck and shelter deck.

Delivered by Harland & Wolff, Belfast.

1947	Delivered to company.
1956	Used as a store ship during the Suez conflict.
1968	Sold to Polyfimos Cia Nav., Greece, renamed *Polyfimos*.
6.12.1972	Left Singapore for Shanghai to be broken up in China.

196. *Salaverry* (1946–1967)
Sister of *Samanco* (192)
6,647 grt, 3,879 n, 466.4 x 62.9 x 34.9 feet.
Steel, single-screw, oil; two-stroke direct acting; 8 cyl; 1,643 nhp; by builder, 15 knots.
One deck and shelter deck.
Delivered by Harland & Wolff, Belfast.

8.1946	Delivered.
12.1964	On a voyage from South America to Liverpool a cargo of fishmeal overheated and she was forced to call at Horta, on the island of Fayal in the Azores, for part of the cargo to be discharged.
22.10.1965	In collision with the Norwegian tanker *Jamunda*, in the Queens Channel near the Mersey Bar. She was holed below the bridge. *Jamunda* was inward bound and later berthed at the Queen Elizabeth Dock at Eastham.
23.10.1965	Towed to Gladstone Dock, Liverpool by three tugs. She was on a voyage to San Juan, Puerto Rico and other South American ports. She was later dry-docked and repaired.
1967	Sold to Detabi Cia Nav Pireaus, Greece, renamed *Pelias*.
12.12.1972	On a voyage from Macceio to Saigon she sank 250 miles south of Durban. A leak caused the engine room to flood. No casualties.

197. *Santander*. (1946–1967)
Sister of *Samanco* (192)
6,648 grt, 3,879 n, 466.4 x 62.9 x 34.9 feet.
Steel, single-screw, oil; two-stroke direct acting; 8 cyl; 1,643 nhp; by builder, 15 knots.
One deck and shelter deck.
Delivered by Harland & Wolff, Belfast.

5.1946	Delivered.
1967	Sold to Navmachos Steam Shipping Company, Famagusta, Cyprus, renamed *Navmachos*.
9.12.1971	Broken up in Spain.

198. *Reina Del Mar* (1956–1973)
20,750 grt, 8,260 n, 600.8 x 78.4 x 44 feet.
Steel, twin-screw, two double reduction geared Parson's turbines; 18,700 shp at 112 rpm, by builder, 18 knots.
Three decks, Denny Brown stabilisers, five holds.
Passengers: 207 first-class, 216 cabin-class and 343 tourist-class. Crew: 327.

7.6.1955	Launched.
3.5.1956	Maiden voyage Liverpool–Panama Canal–Valparaiso.
1963	Chartered to the Travel Savings Association.
16.1.1963	First call at Port Everglades, Florida. Captain Idris Jones, DSC, RD, RNR, was given the Freedom of the Port.

10.3.1964	Arrived at builders to be converted to a cruise liner. 21,501 grt. Passengers: 1,047 in one class.
10.6.1964	Managed by the Union Castle Line and first cruise Southampton-New York.
11.1964	Painted in Union Castle Line colours.
1967	Tonnage became; 20,750 grt.
1969	Owned by the Royal Mail Line.
9.1973	Purchased by the Union Castle Line.
30.7.1975	Arrived at Kaohsiung, Taiwan to be broken up.

199. *Kenuta* (II) (1950–1971)
8,494 grt, 4,501 n, 512.7 x 66.4 x 29.7 feet.
Steel, single-screw, three double reduction turbines; 10,340 shp; by Parson's Marine Turbine Company, 16 knots.
One deck and shelter deck.
Passengers: 12. Cargo; 630,000 cubic feet.
Delivered by the Greenock Dockyard Company, Greenock.

8.1950	Completed. She had been laid down for the Clan Line and was purchased on the stocks with *Flamenco* (200).
1971	Towed to Antwerp by the tug *Mumbles* to be broken up.

200. *Flamenco* (II) (1950–1966)
Sister to *Kenuta* (199)
8,491 grt, 4,504 n, 512.7 x 66.4 x 29.7 feet.
Steel, single-screw, three double reduction turbines; 10,340 shp; by Parson's Marine Turbine Company, 16 knots.
One deck and shelter deck.
Passengers: 12. Cargo; 630,000 cubic feet
Delivered by the Greenock Dockyard Company, Greenock.

12.1950	Delivered to company.
1966	Sold to Cia de Nav. Abeto S.A., renamed *Pacific Abeto*.
1982	Broken up at Chittagong.

Flamenco.

201. *Potosi* (IV) (1955–1972)
Sister to *Kenuta* (199)
8,564 grt, 4,556 n, 512.7 x 66.4 x 29.7 feet.
Steel, single-screw, three double reduction turbines; 10,340 shp; by Parson's Marine Turbine Company, 16 knots.
One deck and shelter deck.
Passengers: 12. Cargo; 630,000 cubic feet.
Delivered by the Greenock Dockyard Company, Greenock.

23.2.1955	Launched.
1972	Sold to Granvias Oceanicos Armadora S.A., Piraeus, renamed *Kavo Pieratis*.
10.1976	Broken up by W. H. Arnott & Company at Dalmuir.

202. *Pizarro* (II) (1955–1972)
Sister to *Kenuta* (199)
8,564 grt, 4,556 n, 512.7 x 66.4 x 29.7 feet.
Steel, single-screw, three double reduction turbines; 10,340 shp; by Parson's Marine Turbine Company, 16 knots.
One deck and shelter deck.
Passengers: 12. Cargo; 630,000 cubic feet.
Delivered by the Greenock Dockyard Company, Greenock.

14.10.1955	Maiden voyage to South America.
1972	Sold to Navieros Progresivos S.A., Piraeus, becoming *Kavo Maleas*.
11.1974	Broken up at Kaohsiung.

203. *Cotopaxi* (II) (1954–1972)
8,559 grt, 4,552 n, 512.6 x 66.4 x 27.11 feet.
Steel, single-screw, double reduction geared turbine; 9,400 shp; two Babcock & Wilcox boilers, steam pressure 510 lb, by builder, 16 knots.

One deck and shelter deck.
Passengers: 12. Cargo: 630,909 cubic feet.
Delivered by Wm. Denny & Company, Dumbarton.

4.1954	Delivered.
1972	Sold to Transportes Mundiales Armadora S.A., Piraeus, renamed *Kavo Longos*.
11.1975	Broken up in China.

204. *Cuzco* (II) (1951–1965)

8,038 grt, 4,588 n, 501 x 64.2 x 28.1 feet.

Steel, single-screw, three double reduction steam turbines; 8,800 shp, by Parson's Marine Turbine Company, 15½ knots.
Two decks and shelter deck.
Passengers: 12. Cargo: 754,249 cubic feet.
Delivered by the Blyth Dry Docks & Shipbuilding Company, Blyth.

1951	Laid down as *Thurland Castle*, for James Chambers & Company, Liverpool. Sister *Penrith Castle*. Purchased by PSNC and named *Cuzco*.
1965	Sold to Ben Line and renamed *Benattow*.
25.9.1977	Arrived at Kaohsiung to be broken up.

205. *Eleuthera* (1959–1971)

5,407 grt, 2,760 n, 386.2 x 54.3 x 25.10 feet.
Steel, single-screw, two-stroke single acting; 4 cyl; 4,500 bhp, by Harland & Wolff, Glasgow, 13½ knots.
Cargo: 354,000 cubic feet.
Delivered by Hall Russell & Company, Aberdeen.

5.1959	Delivered.
1970	Laid up in the River Fal, advertised for sale.
1971	Purchased by Seahunter Shipping Company, Famagusta, Cyprus, renamed *Mimi-M*.
1974	Sold to Valient Bay Shipping Company, Piraeus, renamed *Maria*.
1.11.1984	Arrived at Gadani Beach to be broken up.

206. *Somers Isle* (1959–1970)

Sister of *Eleuthera* (205)
5,684 grt, 2,995 n, 386.2 x 54.3 x 25.10 feet.
Steel, single-screw, two-stroke single acting; 4 cyl; 4,500 bhp, by Harland & Wolff, Glasgow, 13½ knots.
Cargo: 354,000 cubic feet.
Delivered by Harland & Wolff, Belfast.

1959	Delivered for the Bermuda-Caribbean ports-Panama services.
1970	Laid up in the River Fal, advertised for sale.
1970	Purchased by the Sealord Shipping Company, Famagusta, renamed *Eldina*.

1975	Sold to Commencement Compania Naviera S.A., Famagusta, Cyprus becoming *Commencement*.
1982	Renamed *Caribbean*.
1983	Renamed *Melpol*, owned by Commencement Maritime Enterprises, Jersey.
8.12.1983	On a voyage from Lisbon to Bremen, *Melpol* sent a call for assistance as she was on fire in a force eight gale, forty miles from St. Catherines Point. The RFA *Engadine* sent two Royal Navy Sea King helicopters of 737 Squadron. The crew of *Melpol* were winched from the deck and transferred to *Europic*. Twenty-eight crewmen were rescued and another lost in the fire. The Sea King crews received the Queens Commendations for the rescue as did RFA *Engadine*'s fire fighters and salvage teams.
1984	Laid up and scrapped.

207. *Cienfuegos/Chandeleur* (1959–1971)
Sister to *Eleuthera* (205)
5,224 grt, 2,760 n, 386.2 x 54.3 x 25.10 feet.
Steel, single-screw, two-stroke single acting; 4 cyl; 4,500 bhp, by Harland & Wolff, Glasgow, 13½ knots.
Cargo: 354,000 cubic feet.
Delivered by Hall Russell & Company, Aberdeen.

11.1959	Delivered as *Cienfuegos*.
1968	Renamed *Chandeleur*, chartered to the Royal Mail Liine.
1970	Laid up on the River Fal, advertised for sale.
1971	Sold to the Seacomber Shipping Company, Famagusta, Cyprus and renamed *Emma-M*.
1974	Purchased by the Green Bay Shipping Company, Piraeus, renamed *Lela*.
1981	Owned by the West Asia Shipping Company, Singapore, becoming *Jetpur Viceroy*.
2.11.1982	Sold to breakers at Chittagong.
1983	Broken up.

208. *Oroya* (IV) (1968–1972)
6,311 grt, 3,281 n, 475 x 64.4 x 27.1 feet.
Steel, single-screw, oil, two-stroke single acting; 9 cyl; by builder.
Cargo: 596,825 cubic feet. Grain: 11,000 cubic feet, refrigerated.
Delivered by Bremer Vulkan, Vegesack.

1956	Delivered to Shaw Savill & Albion as *Arabic*.
1968	Transferred to the PSNC, renamed *Oroya*.
1970	Operating for Furness Withy as *Pacific Ranger*.
1971	Renamed *Oroya*.

Oroya (IV) and *Potosi* (IV) at Liverpool.

| 1972 | Sold to the Hong Kong Ocean Shipping Company Panama, renamed *Lamma Island*. |
| 5.1983 | Broken up at Inchon, Korea. |

209. *Orita* (II) (1968–1972)
Sister of *Oroya* (208)
6,311 grt, 3,281 n, 475 x 64.4 x 27.1 feet.
Steel, single-screw, oil, two-stroke single acting; 9 cyl; by builder.
Cargo: 596,825 cubic feet. Grain: 11,000 cubic feet, refrigerated.
Delivered by Bremer Vulkan, Vegesack.

1957	Delivered to Shaw Savill & Albion as *Afric*.
1968	Transferred to the PSNC, renamed *Orita*.
1972	Sold to the Hong Kong Islands Shipping Company, Panama, renamed *Hong Kong Island*.
5.1983	Broken up at Inchon, Korea.

210. *Oropesa* (III) (1968–1972)
Sister of *Oroya* (208)
6,553 grt, 3,281 n, 475 x 64.4 x 27.1 feet.
Steel, single-screw, oil, two-stroke single acting; 9 cyl; by builder.
Cargo: 596,825 cubic feet. Grain: 11,000 cubic feet, refrigerated.
Delivered by Bremer Vulkan, Hamburg.

4.1957	Delivered to Shaw Savill & Albion as *Aramaic*.
1968	Transferred to the PSNC and renamed *Oropesa*.
1970	Operated by Furness Withy as *Pacific Exporter*.
1970	Became *Oropesa* again.
1972	Sold to the Hong Kong Atlantic Shipping Company, Panama, renamed *Lantao Island*.
1982	Broken up at Kaohsiung.

211. *William Wheelwright* (1960–1976)
31,320 grt, 16,872 n, 753.6 x 98.5 x 52.6 feet.
Steel, single-screw, two steam turbines, double reduction geared; 16,000 shp, steam pressure 703 lb; two water tube boilers 900°F, by builder, 16 knots.
Cargo: 2,097,502 cubic feet (59,359 cubic metres), oil in twenty-six tanks with seventeen bulkheads.
Delivered by Harland & Wolff, Belfast.

7.1960	Owned by Pacific Maritime Services Limited.
26.12.1975	Aground in ballast off Sinoe, south of Monrovia.
29.12.1975	Refloated and towed to Lisbon, found to be beyond economic repair. Transferred to PSNC ownership.
10.1976	Towed to Santander to be broken up by Recuperaciones Submarines S.A.

212. *Coloso* (1961–1976)
293 grt, 176 n, 101 x 26.1 x 12.8 feet.
Steel, single-screw tug, oil, two-stroke double acting with single reduction reversing gear; 8 cyl; 970 bhp, by Ruston & Hornsby, Lincoln, 11 knots.
Delivered by A. Hall & Company, Aberdeen.

1961	Delivered for duties at Antofagasta. Registered as owned by Servicios Maritimos S.A., Antofagasta and flew the Chilean flag.
1976	Sold to Ultramar Agencia Maritima, Valparaiso, renamed *Ultramar* IV.

213. *George Peacock* (1961–1969)
19,153 grt, 11,307 n, 643.3 x 80.11 x 45.6 feet.
Steel, single-screw, oil two-stroke single acting; 7 cyl; 11,600 bhp, by builder, 15 ¾ knots.
Cargo: 1,346,454 cubic feet (38,105 cubic metres) in twenty-seven tanks.
Delivered by Harland & Wolff, Belfast.

7.1961	Owned by Pacific Maritime Services Limited.
1969	Sold to V. J. Vardinoyannis, Piraeus, renamed *Georgios* V.
1981	Purchased by Varnicos (Varnima Corporation).
24.11.1992	Arrived at Gadani Beach to be broken up.

214. *Orcoma* (II) (1966–1979)
10,300 grt, 3,984 n, 14,614 dwt., 508.9 x 70.2 x 27.11 feet.
Steel, single-screw, oil; two single acting B&W type; 8 cyl; Harland & Wolff auxiliary boilers, steam pressure 110 lbs, by builder, 18 knots.
Two decks Refig; 15,520 cubic metres.
Delivered by Harland & Wolff, Belfast.

1966	Built for Nile Steamship Company (Furness Withy subsidiary). Chartered to PSNC for twenty years.
1970	British Exhibition ship.
1971	Returned to South American services.
10.1979	Sold to P. T. Samudera, Indonesia, renamed *Ek Daya Samudera*.
31.3.1984	Arrived at Kaohsiung to be broken up by Tai Yuan Steel & Iron Company.

215. *Orbita* (II) (1973–1980)
8,396 grt, 4,302 n, 529.8 x 73.4 x 44 feet.
Steel, single-screw, oil two-stroke single acting; 8 cyl; type 8K74EF; 13,720 bhp, Burmeister & Wain by J. G. Kincaid & Company. Unmanned engine room, 18 knots.
Two decks Cargo: 858,869 cu ft (24,306 cu m) grain, 300x20 ft containers.
Delivered by Cammell Laird & Company, Birkenhead.

1973	Built for PSNC which was now part of the Royal Mail Division of Furness Withy.

Orbita (II) in experimental livery at Liverpool.

1980	Sold to Cia Sud Americana de Vapores, Valparaiso, becoming *Andalien*.
1980	Sold to Wallem & Company, Hong Kong, renamed *Morning Sun*.
1980	Returned to Cia Sud Americana de Vapores, becoming *Rubens*.
1993	Seabell Shipping Company Limited (Bogazzi Servizi Navali S.r.l.) renamed *Antwerp Express*.
3.4.1999	Arrived at Alang to be broken up.

216. *Orduna* (II) (1973–1980)

Sister of *Orbita* (215)
8,396 grt, 4,302 n, 529.8 x 73.4 x 44 feet.
Steel, single-screw, oil two-stroke single acting; 8 cyl; type 8K74EF; 13,720 bhp, Burmeister & Wain by J. G. Kincaird & Company. Unmanned engine room.
Two decks.
Cargo: 858,869 cubic feet (24,306 cubic metres) grain, 300 x 20 foot containers.
Delivered by Cammell Laird & Company, Birkenhead.

3.1973	Delivered for the South American services.
1980	Owned by the Royal Mail Line, PSNC managers.
30.9.1982	Renamed *Beacon Grange*, Furness Withy Shipping.
1984	Sold to Cenargo Limited to carry building materials to the Falkland Islands for the new runway being constructed, renamed *Merchant Pioneer*.
1993	Purchased by Jennyship S.A., Panama, Managers; The Great Circle Shipping Agency Limited, Panama becoming *Jennifer*.
16.9.1997	Arrived at Chittagong to be broken up.

217. *Ortega* (II)/*Andes* (II) (1973–1980)

Sister of *Orbita* (215)
8,396 grt, 4,302 n, 529.8 x 73.4 x 44 feet.
Steel, single-screw, oil two-stroke single acting; 8 cyl; type 8K74EF; 13,720 bhp, Burmeister & Wain by J. G. Kincaird & Company. Unmanned engine room.
Two decks.
Cargo: 858,869 cubic feet (24,306 cubic metres) grain, 300 x 20 foot containers.
Delivered by Cammell Laird & Company, Birkenhead.

7.1973	Delivered.
4.1980	Owned by Royal Mail Line, renamed *Andes*.
8.1982	Sold to the Blue Haven Company Limited, Hong Kong and renamed *Oceanhaven*.
1987	Owned by Pacific International Lines (Pte) Limited and renamed *Kota Akbar*.
1996	Sold to Internet Investments S.A., Panama, renamed *George B*.
11.9.1998	Arrived Alang to be broken up.

218. *Oroya* (V) (1978–1985)

9.015 grt, 5,529 n, 535.3 x 75.4 x 44 feet.
Steel, single-screw, oil two-stroke single acting; 6 cyl; 12,000 bhp, Sulzer type by Scotts Engineering Company, Greenock, 16 ¼ knots. Two decks.
Delivered by Lithgows Limited, Port Glasgow.

4.1978	Delivered, Ardgowan Shipping as owner, Furness Withy Shipping as managers.
1985	Shaw Savill & Albion as owners.
1986	Renamed *Yinka Folawiyo*, Nigerian Green Lines.
1989	Sold to Cenargo, renamed *Merchant Premier*, managed by V Ships (UK) Limited.
1999	Owned by John McRink & Company Limited of Hong Kong,

Lady Aryette.

2001   Broken up in India.

219. Oropesa (IV) (1978–1982)
Sister of *Oroya* (218)

9,015 grt, 5,529 n, 535.3 x 75.4 x 44 feet.

Steel, single-screw, oil two-stroke single acting; 6 cyl; 12,000 bhp, Sulzer type by Scott's Engineering Company, Greenock, 16 ¼ knots.

Two decks.

Delivered by Lithgow's Limited, Port Glasgow.

4.1978   Entered service, owned by Blackhall Shipping Company.
1982   On Shaw Savill & Albion service from Liverpool.
1984   Sold with *Orduna* (216) to Cenargo Limited for a service to the Falkland Islands, renamed *Merchant Principal*.

1999   Owned by John McRink & Company Limited of Hong Kong, *Lady Danielle*.
27.2.2001   Arrived at Alang to be broken up.

220. Andes (III) (1984–1994)

32,150 grt, 18,016 n, 37,900 dwt., 662.7 x 105.6 x 61.6 feet.

Steel, single-screw, oil. 5 cyl B&W type 5L90 GBE, 19,300 bhp, by builder, 18½ knots.

Two decks, bow thruster.

Crew: 24.

2,145 TEUs Holds; 2, 3, 4, and 6 equipped for bulk copper with TEUs over. No 1 hold; dangerous cargoes. Hold No. 5; refrigerated; 254 TEUs for bananas. All holds were strengthened for fork-lift trucks. 1 x 40 tonne O&K gantry crane railed to all forward holds.

16.11.1983   Launched for Furness Withy, on PSNC management.
1984   Operated as one of seven ships on the Eurosal (Europe South America Line) service. *Andes* was the Furness Withy contribution to the service. The seven ships replaced twenty-eight freight vessels.
1994   Renamed *Cgm Magellan* by Furness Withy (Shipping) Limited, Hong Kong.
1997   Renamed *Cap Blanco* by Andes Shipping Company, Cayman Islands.
23.2.2009   Arrived at Alang to be broken up.
28.2.2009   Beached.

CHARTERED VESSELS

221. *Albemarle* (1955–57)
3,364 grt, 1,574 n, 364.9 x 51.2 x 18.7 feet.
Steel, single-screw, oil two-stroke single acting; 4 cyl; 3,300 bhp, by Hawthorne Leslie & Company, Newcastle, 14 knots.
One deck and shelter deck.
Passengers: 12.

1950	Built as *Afric* for the Prince Line and allocated to Shaw Savill & Albion service.
1955	Transferred/chartered to PSNC, renamed *Albermarle* for a new service between Bermuda–Caribbean ports–Panama. The route was successful and led to the building of *Cienfuegos* (207), *Eleuthera* (205) and *Somers Isle* (206).
1957	Returned to Prince Line, renamed *Scottish Prince*.
1968	Sold to Klimnos Shipping Company, Cyprus, renamed *Grigorios*.
1972	Owned by Milos Steam Ship Company, Cyprus, becoming *Milos*.
1975	Renamed *Nestor II*.
23.12.1977	Arrived at Gadani Beach to be broken up.

222. *Walsingham* (1955–57)
Sister of *Albemarle* (220)
3,343 grt, 1,519 n, 364.9 x 51.2 x 18.7 feet.
Steel, single-screw, oil two-stroke single acting; 4 cyl; 3,300 bhp, by D. Rowan & Company, Glasgow, 14 knots.
One deck and shelter deck.
Passengers: 12.

1950	Built as *Sycamore* for Johnson Warren Lines.
1955	Chartered to PSNC with sister, renamed *Walsingham*.
1957	Back to Johnson Warren service as *Sycamore*.
1966	Transferred to Prince Line, becoming *Merchant Prince*.
1968	Sold to Kaldelion Shipping Company, Limassol, renamed *Elias L*.
1975	Owned by Melteco Navigation Limited, Limassol, renamed *Meltemi*.
1978	Sold to Green Spirit Incorporated, Limassol, becoming *Temi*.
10.5.1979	Arrived at Gadani Beach to be broken up.

SAILING SHIPS

223. *Elizabeth* (1840–)
445 grt, wood.
1832   At Bristol for Miles & Company, for service in Jamaica.
1840   Purchased by the PSNC for the carriage of coal to Valparaiso and then to be used as a coal hulk. Crew refused to sail her around Cape Horn.
2.1840   Sold.

224. *Portsea* (1840–)
451 grt, wood.
1808   At Calcutta for the London-Calcutta route.
2.1840   Purchased by the PSNC to replace *Elizabeth* (223). Converted to a coal hulk at Valparaiso, topmasts and yards removed.

225. *Cecilia* (1841–)
325 grt, sailing barque.
1815   At Dunbar for Alexander & Company, Glasgow for the Glasgow–Australia service.
1841   Purchased by the PSNC to use as a coal hulk at Valparaiso, topmasts and yards removed. Carried a cargo of coal on her delivery voyage.

226. *Jasper* (1841–)
1841   Carried a cargo of coal on her delivery voyage to Valparaiso, then used as a coal hulk.

Fire drill on board the *Orbita*.

FLEET LIST INDEX

Ship name	Order of entry into service
Acajutla (1915–1946)	164
Acongagua (1872–1895)	57
Albemarle (1955–57)	221
Almagro (1922–1933)	177
Alvarado (1922–1933)	176
Amazonas (1874–1886)	84
Andes (I) (1913–)	159
Andes (III) (1984–1994)	220
Anne (1859–1864)	19
Antisana (1893–1911)	114
Arana (1922–1933)	178
Araucania (1869–1897)	43
Arauco (1879–1899)	89
Arequipa (1870–1887)	50
Arequipa (II) (1889–1903)	109
Arica (I) (1867–1869)	36
Arica (II) (1881–)	97
Arran (1881–)	96
Assistance (1891–1926)	110
Atacama (1870–1877)	46
Atlas (1867–1890)	39
Ayacucho (1873–1890)	78
Baja (1872–)	71
Ballena (1920–1932)	169
Bogota (I) (1852–1878)	9
Bogota (II) (1906–1916)	144
Bogota (III) (1919–1932)	170
Bolivia (I) (1849–1879)	3
Bolivia (II) (1874–1895)	80
Britannia (1873–1895)	77
Calbuco (1914–1925)	160
Caldera (1870–1879)	40
California (1902–1917)	137
Callao (I) (1858–1880)	16
Callao (II) (1905–1907)	149
Casma (II) (1878–1899)	87
Cauca (1915–1923)	166
Cecilia (1841–)	225
Chala (1879–1897)	88
Champerico (1917–1934)	189
Chile (I) (1840–1852)	1
Chile (II)(1863–1883)	25
Chile (III) (1896–1923)	123
Chiloe (1882–1892)	101
Chimborazo (1871–1895)	53
Chiriqui (1896–1910)	120
Cienfuegos/Chandeleur (1959–1971)	207
Cloda (1857–1865)	17

Colombia (I) (1873–1890)	64	*George Peacock* (1961–1969)	213
Colombia (II) (1899–1907)	128	*Guatemala* (1899–1923)	129
Colon (1866–1872)	35	*Guayaquil* (1860–1870)	21
Coloso (1961–1976)	212	*Huacho* (1870–1914)	51
Coquimbo (1870–1901)	47	*Huanchaco* (1907–1925)	150
Corcovado (I) (1872–1875)	61	*Iberia* (1873–1903)	72
Corcovado (II) (1896–1921)	125	*Illimani* (1873–1879)	76
Cordillera (1869–1882)	44	*Ilo* (1872–1882)	66
Cotopaxi (I) (1873–1889)	75	*Inca* (I) (1856–1874)	14
Cotopaxi (II) (1954–1972)	203	*Inca* (II) (1893–1923)	112
Cuzco (I) (1871–1878)	54	*Iquique* (1871–1877)	52
Cuzco (II) (1951–1965)	204	*Islay* (1873–1883)	82
Duendes (1906–1927)	142	*Jamaica* (1914–1918)	163
Ebro (1920–1935)	179	*Jasper* (1841–)	226
Ecuador (1881–1905)	98	*John Elder* (1869–1892)	45
Ecuador (I) (1845–1850)	4	*Junin* (1907–1926)	151
Ecuador (II) (1863–)	29	*Kenuta* (I) (1907–1926)	152
Eleuthera (1959–1971)	205	*Kenuta* (II) (1950–1971)	199
Elizabeth (1840–)	223	*La Paz* (1920–1942)	173
Esmeraldas (1906–1917)	143	*La Perlita* (1853–)	10
Essequibo (1920–1935)	180	*Lagarto* (1924–1948)	187
Eten (1871–1877)	49	*Laguna* (1923–1952)	183
Explorer (1907–1914)	156	*Lautaro* (1923–1947)	167
Favotita (1865–1871)	34	*Liguria* (1874–1903)	73
Flamenco (I) (1906–1916)	145	*Lima* (I) (1851–1863)	7
Flamenco (II) (1950–1966)	200	*Lima* (II) (1873–1909)	79
Galicia (I) (1873–1898)	69	*Lima* (III) (1907–1910)	153
Galicia (II) (1901–1917)	132	*Limena* (1865–1874)	32
Gallito (1902–1931)	139	*Lobo* (1874–)	86
Garonne (1871–1897)	55	*Lobos* (1921–1952)	174

Lontue (1877–1888)	85
Loreto (1924–1951)	185
Loriga (1924–1951)	186
Losada (1921–1952)	175
Lusitania (1871–1878)	56
Magellan (I) (1868–1893)	41
Magellan (II) (1893–1918)	111
Magellan (III) (1920–1933)	171
Manavi (1885–1920)	102
Mendoza (1879–1904)	91
Mexico (1902–1922)	136
Morro (I) (1860–1881)	22
Morro (II) (1881–1902)	100
New Granada (I) (1846–1851)	5
Oravia (1897–1912)	119
Orbita (I) (1915–1950)	162
Orbita (II) (1973–1980)	215
Orca (1918–1923)	168
Orcana (I) (1893–1905)	116
Orcana (II) (1922–1924)	181
Orcoma (I) (1908–1933)	157
Orcoma (II) (1966–1979)	214
Orduna (II) (1973–1980)	216
Orellana (1893–1905)	115
Oriana (1906–1927)	147
Orissa (1893–1918)	117
Orita (I) (1903–1931)	140
Orita (II) (1968–1972)	209
Orizaba (1886–1905)	105
Ormeda/Orduna (I) (1914–1951)	161
Oronsa (1906–1918)	148
Oropesa (I) (1895–1915)	118
Oropesa (II) (1920–1941)	172
Oropesa (III) (1968–1972)	210
Oropesa (IV) (1978–1982)	219
Orotava (1889–1906)	106
Oroya (1887–1905)	104
Oroya (I) (1873–)	81
Oroya (III) (1924–1939)	184
Oroya (IV) (1968–1972)	208
Oroya (V) (1978–1985)	218
Ortega (I) (1906–1927)	146
Ortega (II)/*Andes* (II) (1973–1980)	217
Ortona (1899–1905)	127
Oruba (I) (1889–1906)	107
Oruba (II) (1921–1924)	182
Osorno (1881–1899)	99
Osprey (1852)	11
Pacific (1865–1870)	30
Panama (I) (1856–)	13
Panama (II) (1866–1870)	33
Panama (III) (1902–1920)	134
Patagonia (1869–1894)	42
Payta (1864–1878)	28
Perico (1901–1924)	133
Perlita (1896–)	122
Peru (I) (1840–1852)	2
Peru (II) (1861–1881)	24
Peru (III) (1896–1923)	124
Peruano (1861–1874)	23

PACIFIC STEAM NAVIGATION CO.

Pizarro (I) (1879–1907)	92
Pizarro (II) (1955–1972)	202
Ponderoso (1911–1939)	158
Portsea (1840–)	224
Potosi (I) (1873–1897)	74
Potosi (II) (1900–1900)	131
Potosi (III) (1905–1925)	141
Potosi (IV) (1955–1972)	201
Prince of Wales (1858–1859)	18
Puchoco (1879–1899)	90
Puno (1881–1904)	93
Puno (I) (1873–1875)	62
Quillota (1907–1923)	154
Quilpue (1907–1922)	155
Quito (1867–1882)	37
Quito (I) (1852–1853)	8
Quito (II) (1863–1865)	27
Quito (IV) (1888–1915)	103
Reina Del Mar (1956–1973)	198
Reina Del Pacifico (1931–1958)	190
Rimac (1872–1877)	65
Ronachan (1881–)	95
Rupanco (1902–1914)	138
Salamanca (1948–1967)	194
Salaverry (1946–1967)	196
Salinas (1947–1968)	195
Salvador (1915–1946)	165
Samanco (1943–1956)	192
San Carlos (1860–1874)	20
Santa Rosa (1872–1890)	63
Santander. (1946–1967)	197
Santiago (I) (1851–1857)	6
Santiago (II)(1865–1869)	31
Santiago (III) (1871–1882)	58
Santiago (IV) (1889–1907)	108
Sarmiento (I) (1893–1910)	113
Sarmiento (II) (1943–1969)	193
Serena (1881–1903)	94
Somers Isle (1959–1970)	206
Sorata (I) (1872–1895)	60
Sorata (II) (1896–1922)	126
Supe (1867–1882)	38
Taboga (1898–1909)	121
Taboguilla (1871–1893)	59
Tacna (1873–1874)	83
Tacora (1872–)	68
Talca (I) (1862–1880)	26
Talca (II) (1900–1901)	130
Talca (III) (1947–1953)	191
Temuco (1925–1942)	188
Truxillo (1872–1882)	67
Valdivia (I) (1853–1857)	12
Valdivia (II) (1870–1882)	48
Valparaiso (I) (1856–1871)	15
Valparaiso (II)(1873–1887)	70
Victoria (1902–1923)	135
Walsingham (1955–57)	222
William Wheelwright (1960–1976)	211